The Story of
the French Foreign Legion

by the same author

*

THE SINAI CAMPAIGN, 1956

THE
STORY OF
THE FRENCH
FOREIGN LEGION

by

EDGAR
O'BALLANCE

FABER AND FABER
24 Russell Square
London

First published in mcmlxi
by Faber and Faber Limited
24 Russell Square, London W.C.1
Printed in Great Britain
by Ebenezer Baylis and Son, Limited
The Trinity Press, Worcester, and London
All rights reserved

Contents

PREFACE   *page* 15

1. THE OLD LEGION   21

2. THE CONQUEST OF ALGERIA (1837–70)   42

3. NINETEENTH-CENTURY WARS IN EUROPE   61

4. OTHER NINETEENTH-CENTURY CAMPAIGNS   74

5. AFRICA (1871–1914)   98

6. THE WORLD WARS   145

7. BETWEEN THE WORLD WARS (1918–39)   172

8. INDO-CHINA (1945–54)   183

9. ALGERIA (1954–60)   203

10. A FEW FACTS ABOUT THE LEGION   213

    APPENDIX 'A'
    PRINCIPAUX FAITS D'ARMES DE LA LÉGION   255

    APPENDIX 'B'
    MADAGASCAR 1947 AND SUEZ 1956   259

    INDEX   261

Illustrations

PHOTOGRAPHS

In Southern Oran Province. The Legion patrol leader checks the
route *facing page* 64

An aerial view of the famous Legion Depot at Sidi Bel Abbes 65

Guarding the southern approaches against F.L.N. infiltration 80

A Legion patrol halts for refreshment 80

A sudden patrol encounter 81

A Legion Section stalk on to an F.L.N. position 128

Legionnaires taking part in a 'sweep' near the Tunisian barrage 129

A vehicle of one of the Saharienne companies in a little difficulty 144

A Legion desert fort from the air 144

Legionnaires of the 13th Demi-Brigade co-operating with a helicopter against the F.L.N. in the Aures Mountains 145

Legionnaires of the 13th Demi-Brigade moving forward to
attack an F.L.N. position 145

Legionnaires of the 13th Demi-Brigade patrolling in the Aures
Mountains 192

Patrolling Legion Cavalry near the Tunisian barrage 193

A Legion mortar section on the alert 208

A Saharienne company on parade 209

The Colour Party of the 4th R.E.I. 209

UNIFORMS

Legionnaire of the 2nd Regiment in full marching order. *page* 48
1846

ILLUSTRATIONS

A Legionnaire. Tonkin. About 1884   *page* 89
Legion Mounted Infantry. About 1924   218
A 'Saharienne'   227

MAPS

Algeria   *page* 30
Spain 1835–38   35
Mexico 1863–66   75
Indo-China 1883–95   86
Dahomey 1892   105
Morocco   119
Madagascar   133
Indo-China   185
Dien Bien Phu   197
Algeria 1958   207

Acknowledgments

My sincere thanks are due to Monsieur le Chef de Bataillon Hallo, of the 1e Régiment Etrangère, who, as chief of the *Service du Moral et des Oeuvres de la Légion Etrangère*, unreservedly placed all the Legion records at my disposal, and so made my pleasant task of research into its history an easy one.

During the time I spent at Sidi Bel Abbes the members of the Historical Section were extremely helpful. My thanks go to them for answering the long lists of questions I presented to them, and for reading and commenting upon my original MS.

Also, my thanks are due to Monsieur le Capitaine Rodier, the Chef du Service d'Information, for the help he has given me, and for obtaining permission to reproduce the photographs, illustrations and maps which are included in this book.

I would like to record my appreciation of my old friend, Monsieur le Lieutenant-Colonel Jacques Brule, of the 2me Régiment Etrangère, for showing me something of the Legion in action, and for the interest and kindness shown to me by all Legion officers I came into contact with, both French and foreign.

The plaque unexpectedly presented to me by the company commander and his officers, and signed by them, at the remote outpost of Bou Alam, a 'Beau Geste' type fort set in hostile territory, still hangs in a place of honour at my home.

Abbreviations

R.E.I. =Régiment Etrangère d'Infantérie.
R.E.C. =Régiment Etrangère de Cavalerie.
B.E.P. =Bataillon Etrangère Parachutiste.
C.S.P.L. =Compagnie Saharienne Port de la Légion.

Preface

This is a regimental history with a difference. It is the story of a world-famous corps of mercenary soldiers—perhaps the last and best known of a long line of gallant free-lance bands of fighting men—which gives glimpses through a cross section of French military history, French nineteenth century colonial expansion, and some French triumphs and disasters of more recent date, a few of which are little known to the average English-speaking reader. It is the story of the French Foreign Legion.

Few have not heard of it, and its fame has been spread in fiction, on the screen and by television, as well as by deeds in action on the field of battle. The mere mention of its name conjures up visions of romantic young men joining to 'forget', or of 'Beau Geste' type forts in the desert manned by desperate sun-tanned adventurers continually holding out against hordes of screaming Arabs, or of exhausting, inhuman marches through the burning sands under a blazing sun by columns of heavily burdened legionnaires tormented by thirst, thoughts of torture and fear of sudden death. Most accounts err heavily on the dramatic or romantic side: few are accurate or reliable, some are highly fictional.

'What actually is the French Foreign Legion, and what exactly has it done?' is a question often asked, but one to which few can give a full and truthful answer. I have been privileged recently to see the Legion in action, at work and play, on ceremonial parades and in training. In addition, what is more important still, the records and staff of the Historical Section at Sidi Bel Abbes were placed at my complete disposal.

Therefore this account may do much to answer this question. It is designed mainly, but not wholly, for the military student, and the story is unfolded against the background of a period of military history that may be familiar.

Today, the French Foreign Legion is unique in that it is a mercenary corps in which all the other ranks are foreigners, as are also about one third of the officers. In these days, when whole populations are mobilized in the event of national emergencies, there is little place for such bodies, which were a regular feature of the military scene centuries ago. The Legion is the last survivor of a long and glittering line of mercenary troops fighting for a country other than their own. It is a relic of the Middle Ages, of the days when Europe swarmed with 'Grand Companies' led by swashbuckling captains who sold their swords to the highest bidder.

From earliest times, rulers, whenever they were able to afford it, were glad to employ mercenary soldiers, preferably foreign ones, to fight their battles for them. They are mentioned in the Bible and other ancient histories, and they had their place in the Roman Army. In Mediaeval Europe the mercenary soldier was commonplace, and few countries, England not excepted, scorned to make use of him whenever they could.

Perhaps over a long period and during her many wars France employed mercenaries as much, if not more, than most other countries. Foreign soldiers in particular came to be associated with the French kings' bodyguard, a practice which began in the ninth century, developed, and remained a tradition until 1830.

It may be something of a surprise to many to know that the traditional fore-runners of the present day Legion were the Scots, and that for centuries Scottish soldiers had, in France, a fighting reputation second to none. It is recorded that as early as the year 886 the King of France had a Scottish bodyguard, and this became a practice, although it does not seem to have had a continuous and exclusive existence as such. On occasions detachments of several nationalities formed part of the French Royal Household troops, but Scotsmen were seldom absent for long. In the year 1400, for example, the Scottish contingent was reported to be about 7,000 strong and included 75 archers.

Charles VII (1429–1461) formed a personal bodyguard exclusively of Scottish soldiers, and the traditional answer of members of this bodyguard, when answering roll call, came to be 'Hay Hamir', a corruption of 'I am here'.

During the fifteenth and sixteenth centuries bands of Scottish mercenaries were periodically employed by the French kings, and for a short time there was even a body of Scottish gendarmerie, but few precise details of these forces have come down to us. Gradually, the 'regiment' took the place of the 'band', and one of the first Scottish ones was formed in 1589, being composed of about 1,000 infantrymen. Others followed, but mostly whole units were brought over to France, and they came and went according to the need for them.

For a good many years Scottish mercenaries held pride of place in French military life, but they began to be rivalled by the Irish, especially from the beginning of the eighteenth century. The Irish mercenary had, of course, frequently appeared upon the French scene much earlier, but by 1714 there were seven Irish regiments in the pay of France. During the ensuing years this number fluctuated, but generally there were seldom less than three Irish units employed at a time in that country.

English mercenary soldiers were by no means left out of the picture, and over a period of time a number of English regiments were in the service of France. There was one in the sixteenth century, but little is known about it. There were certainly two in 1646, oddly enough known as the 'Stewart Regiment' and the 'Bavarian Regiment', but it seems that in spite of the titles the personnel were English. Later in the same century another four were used by the French.

Although the number of Scottish, Irish and English, especially the last, declined as the use of other foreign troops increased, their traditions lingered on, and there were invariably British units of one kind or another in the French service.

However, as the reputation of the Swiss fighting men rose they came to be widely employed by the French, and they gradually displaced the Scottish personnel of the royal bodyguard, rendering loyal service, often in adversity. Over 700 Swiss Royal Guards, for example, were massacred at the Tuileries in Paris, defending Louis XVI from the mobs of the revolution. The Swiss Royal Guards were granted the motto *Honneur et Fidélité*, and their name became synonymous with faithful service throughout France.

Other nationalities too were freely used as mercenaries and at various times there were German, Polish, Spanish, Dutch, Balkan and Italian soldiers in the French service, sometimes in large numbers. In 1791, all the regiments of foreigners disappeared in the wave of the revolution, at which time Swiss, Irish, Germans, Poles and Swedes predominated.

The new French Revolutionary Government was not above making use of any soldiers it could get, foreign or otherwise, and the next year (1792) the title 'Foreign Legion' (*Légion Etrangère*) was used for the first time to designate a number of formations raised from the disbanded royal bodyguard and other foreign mercenary troops who had previously been in the pay of the King. The former Swiss Guards were bought over almost to a man, the Poles came next and the others followed.

Under Napoleon foreign troops were again extensively used, both as conscripts and volunteers, and there was a high proportion of them in the Grand Army of 1812. After that year, with the reduction of his army, fewer remained. It should not be overlooked that a small unit of foreign mercenary soldiers accompanied Napoleon in his exile to Elba.

During the 'Hundred Days', eight foreign regiments were raised, under the title of the 'Royal Foreign Legion', but none were ready in time to take part in the battle of Waterloo. There were, however, detachments of foreign troops on that battlefield, one of which was a unit of Bavarian Jews, which fought under Napoleon.

At the Restoration, the king employed only Swiss troops in his bodyguard, and three Swiss units were formed for this purpose. One other foreign regiment was in the service of France, and that was the 'Legion of Hohenlohe', (so called after its leader) which had formerly been a unit of the 'Royal Foreign Legion'. It later became known as the 'Regiment of Hohenlohe', and fought briefly in Greece. The only other foreign unit remaining in France was composed of Spanish and Portuguese, being jointly maintained by the three countries concerned.

In 1830 when King Louis Philippe was under pressure to rule democratically, he was obliged to disband all the foreign units in his pay. The Swiss bodyguard in particular was eyed with suspicion by a large section of French opinion. A general reaction had set in against the employment of foreign soldiers on the soil of France. From these disbanded Swiss mercenaries and others the French Foreign Legion was raised in Algeria.

Since its creation it has had a wide and varied experience. Apart from service in many countries and a part in many battles whose names have become well known, the Legion has fought in countless actions in wild, inaccessible places whose names are not only difficult to pronounce, but often completely unknown. It has been used frequently as mounted infantry, being mounted on camels and mules, as well as M.T.

The Legion took part in the battle which gave rise to the International Red Cross movement, in which incidentally the military-balloon was also used for the first time in war; it has set fire to live Arabs in grottos, it has fought women soldiers and has taken part in the bitter fighting in the streets of Paris against the Communes, when some 70,000 people were killed.

In the field of constructional work, especially in road-making and building, its record is unrivalled, and it has left its lasting mark in many countries.

It has been said that the Legion has been both a great destroyer and a great builder.

Its name has always carried some mysterious magic and elusive glamour: few have not heard of the French Foreign Legion, and few are not inspired and pause unconsciously when it is mentioned.

In this story I have not included every single place where the Legion has ever fought, nor mentioned every single action in which it took part—there are so many, and a long catalogue would only weary. I have selected those which are the most interesting or important.

As regard the spelling of place names, I have no doubt that some will disagree with my interpretation of many of them. Where a name is well known in Britain I have used the conventional British spelling, otherwise the French, or I have had to choose among a variety of spellings. The latter course has had to be adopted particularly in the case of names in Africa and Indo-China.

EDGAR O'BALLANCE

1

The Old Legion

The French Foreign Legion (*Légion Etrangère*) was founded by a Royal Ordinance, written on a small piece of official French War Office notepaper dated March 9th, 1831, and signed by the then reigning monarch of France, Louis-Philippe. He had been on the throne for barely eight months when he authorized this measure, which was as much a product of necessity as of careful planning, although there may be divided views on this.

The reasons for forming the French Foreign Legion were probably twofold. In the first place the men of the disbanded royal bodyguard and the Regiment of Hohenlohe, suddenly turned loose on to the streets of a capital seething with unrest, unemployed and perhaps disgruntled at their abrupt dismissal, were a potentially dangerous element. They were trained to the use of arms, and should they become tools of the politically ambitious or discontented they would present a distinct menace to the new régime, not yet too firmly established and sure of itself.

For some time Paris had been swarming with countless other discharged foreign soldiers who had served in the French army at various times under the Empire and the Republic, many of whom were in needy circumstances and open to suggestion, whilst others were openly looking for trouble and always ready to take part in any disturbance. It was clearly both expedient and desirable to remove these dangers as far away from the capital as possible.

Next, the Algerian adventure had begun, and it appeared that this might prove expensive in lives. The more Frenchmen killed in North Africa, the less popular the government at home would be, so if foreign cannon fodder was available so much the better. The Algerian landing had been viewed with mixed feelings in a politically divided France, but there does not seem to have been any marked indication on the part of the politicians that they were unanimous that the occupation should be abruptly terminated; most were wary and many apprehensive as to how the Algerian business would turn out.

The formation of a foreign legion seemed therefore to be an ideal method of killing these two birds with one stone. Once the conditions were made clear there does not seem to have been any serious opposition.

Marshal Soult was reputed to be the man behind the scheme both for removing and using the unemployed foreign ex-soldiers. He could not have failed to recognize, once they were formed into disciplined units, how useful they would be, both for garrison duty and for active operations in Algeria, nor the fact that if their casualties were heavy or their conditions not of the best, there would be no embarrassing reaction for agitation in France on their behalf.

The Royal Ordinance decreed that there should be a legion formed of foreigners for service outside France, which was to be called the 'Foreign Legion' (*Légion Etrangère*), and it was to be part of the French army and under the control of the War Minister. It laid down that as far as possible companies should be composed of men of the same nationality or who spoke a common language. Algeria was not specifically mentioned but as it was the only scrap of foreign territory of any size possessed by France at that moment, there was no doubt as to the meaning of the phrase 'outside France'.

In the anxiety to get dubious, restless characters out of the country no questions were asked as to nationality, previous record or history, and no proof of identity was required. The name and particulars given by the recruit were accepted at face value and many gave *noms de guerre*, for understandable reasons. Thus the practice began, and the tradition started of 'asking no questions'. This tradition of guaranteeing anonymity began to develop quickly, although it was not until later that it was carried to the extreme of denying all knowledge of any individuals who were in its ranks and of refusing point blank to answer questions or to allow any outside contact with the legionnaires.

This step, expedient though it was, was unusual and a departure from the normal procedure in France where recruits had to produce identification papers.

During the spring of 1831, recruiting started and a large number of unemployed mercenaries roaming the capital were scooped up into this new body. Once the decision was made no time was lost, and a recruiting depot was established at Langres in France under Major Sicco, who can perhaps be regarded as the first officer of the French Foreign Legion. He had served under Napoleon and had been wounded in the fighting in Moscow during the French advance into Russia.

By all contemporary accounts he had a wild, turbulent collection on his hands. Not only had ex-soldiers flocked or been sent to Langres, but it must have seemed that all the undesirables in France, both French and foreign, had also been sent there by the local authorities in the faint hope that the Legion would accept them and carry them out of the country.

It had been thought necessary to issue hastily a special decree on March 18th, ten days after the original ordinance, forbidding Frenchmen to enlist, but they still could, and did, simply by declaring themselves either to be Swiss or Belgian.

By the beginning of July the framework of the first battalions had taken shape, and a Swiss officer, Colonel Stoffel, was appointed to command. In small batches, they were shipped over to Algeria as fast as possible.

During the remainder of that year (1831) detachments of the newly formed corps were hurriedly landed at Algiers, and the military authorities were not only unimpressed, but frankly disgusted and sceptical of their military value. Although at Langres the men had been sorted out into companies and even battalions, this was very much on paper only and did not always work out in practice, as in the absence of firm control, ex-soldiers, civilians, friends, strangers and enemies were jostled together, or sorted themselves out into congenial groups regardless of the nominal rolls.

French officers were far too few, and the keynote of the whole recruiting procedure in the first instance does not seem to have been one of efficiency, but haste—haste to get the men overseas. In many cases the men either elected their own officers, or persons who claimed to have been officers formerly were given companies and detachments to look after. Many of the latter had extremely dubious claims, but there was no time to disprove them. Many were incapable of exercising command. The language question made control more difficult and at times almost impossible, as a multiplicity of tongues was spoken. The French officers were frequently unable to make their orders understood. Drink added to the confusion, causing insubordination, quarrels and brawls.

This pattern of chaos and disorder seems to have been the rule rather than the exception: the chief exception being the elements of the Swiss

Guards and the Regiment of Hohenlohe. These had many of their former officers still with them and they remained in intact groups, thus keeping some semblance of discipline. The remainder, in contrast, were at times little better than an excited mob.

Mixed in amongst the wild variety of ex-soldiers and would-be soldiers, were a number who were obviously physically unfitted for military life, and others who had been induced to join under the pretext that they were being shipped out to Algeria as settlers and that matters would be sorted out when they landed.

There are several contemporary accounts of these detachments arriving from France, and all are similar. They describe motley groups of men being disembarked from the ships to the shore, often in a disorderly manner. Many still wore remnants of a gaudy variety of military uniforms; some were too old, some were too young, many were unfit, and frequently many were drunk. These scenes were a trial to the military authorities and strong detachments of military police had to be on hand to deal with the drunken and insubordinate. Many a legionnaire of those early days spent his first few days in Africa in a cell.

The screening, the first effective one, took place on the dockside, and those obviously unfitted for military service were separated from the others and taken off to a settlers' organization. Those who appeared to be fit and acceptable at first sight were marched off to one of the several army camps in the vicinity.

Colonel Stoffel, an experienced officer of ability, and French officers who had been sent to help him, energetically tackled this wild tangle, and by the end of the year had reduced it to a semblance of order. He asked for more French officers and also a number of French *sous-officiers*, to train this new formation and to enforce discipline. However, there seems to have been some reluctance on the part of both the French officers and *sous-officiers* to join the Legion, and inducements, such as accelerated promotion and extra pay, had to be offered.

The foreign officers, self-appointed or otherwise, were vetted and numbers of them weeded out. A few of the best were retained, but in those early days the Legion had for the most part a high proportion of regular French officers seconded to it. Suitable foreign officers continued to be accepted for service with the Legion.

The first five battalions were formed, or rather reorganized, in Algeria, on the principle of grouping together units of men of the same nationality as far as possible. The rule that companies must be composed of men of the same nationality was strictly adhered to. Foreign officers were put in units with their countrymen as a general rule, but there were exceptions to this.

Although by the end of the year five battalions were functioning passably well, there were minor reorganizations the next year, and later, when recruiting became better organized, another two battalions were formed, making a total of seven in all. These were composed of companies of men of the same nationality, as follows:

1st — Former Swiss Guards and Hohenlohe Regiment.
2nd — Swiss and Germans.
3rd — Swiss and Germans.
4th — Spanish.
5th — Mixed, but mainly Italians and Sardinians.
6th — Belgian and Dutch.
7th — Polish.

There seems to have been a surplus of Polish companies, and most of the battalions had one or more attached to them.

After a little while the Spanish battalion was shipped off to Oran, farther along the coast to the west, and later the Belgian and Dutch battalion was shipped in the opposite direction to Bone, to form part of the French garrison there. The remainder of the Legion were in camps and bivouacs in and around Algiers.

Discipline was a problem. As can be imagined, many of the legionnaires—but by no means all—were hard cases and had to be handled firmly: accordingly punishments were severe, the cells were often full and forms of field punishment were resorted to. In the early years there were incidents of drunkenness, insubordination, damage and faction fights. On occasions the French officers and *sous-officiers* were beaten up. Ample, cheap strong drink was the root cause of much of this trouble. As a result the Legion gained a reputation for being a brawling, indisciplined corps, and many were dubious as to what sort of show it would put up in action. Indeed, for a while it appears that the authorities hesitated to commit the Legion to battle.

The fact that the various nationalities were together in companies was not a satisfactory arrangement and did not work very well as it tended to foster quarrels and disputes, both between the companies and within them. The nationals themselves were often bitterly divided politically and throwing them together aggravated their differences.

Another aspect which caused some worry, was the high desertion rate. The native Algerians offered rewards to tempt Europeans to desert and go over and fight for them against the French. There were at times several small European units of soldiers fighting against France, formed largely from such deserters from the Legion. So it can be seen that the French military authorities had reason to view the Legion doubtfully and to wonder whether it would be a completely reliable instrument when it came to the test.

Once the initial confusion was sorted out, and it was tacitly agreed that the Legion would be allowed to carry on—or rather no positive move was made to suppress it—attention was turned to further recruiting and the setting up of a system to ensure a sufficient flow of volunteers for the future. After the weeding out it was found that only about half the establishment, which had been provisionally fixed at 6,000, was filled.

Several countries in Europe were in a state of political unrest and became a source of supply. In 1832 three other recruiting depots were set up in France near the frontiers, one to recruit men from Central Europe, one to recruit men from Spain, and the other to recruit men coming from Italy. The following year yet another was established, and as a result a flow of recruits, all volunteers, began to be fed into the Legion. It is true that practically all had a compelling reason for leaving their own country, but these measures brought the strength to just over the 5,000 mark, and kept it in that region.

Training was carried out, and the battalions were brought up to a reasonable pitch of efficiency. In spite of this there was hesitation over sending them into action, and for months, when not training, they were employed on constructional work. The legionnaires built their own camps and some others, constructed many roads and causeways in and around Algiers, and sank a number of wells. Artisans were found in the ranks and these tasks were well done. In spite of the adverse circumstances that attended its birth the Legion began to settle down.

Algeria, where it had been so unceremoniously dumped, was a tempestuous country in which the French had but a tiny, and not too secure, foothold. Algeria was the cradle of the Legion, it made the Legion, and it is true to say that the Legion in turn did much to make Algeria. The conquest of that country is largely the history of the Legion: the two are almost inseparable.

Therefore it is felt that a brief account of that country, and such

26

beginnings of the French occupation as had taken place before the
Legion became active, is both necessary and helpful as a background
against which to unfold the first part of the story of the French Foreign
Legion.

Algeria did not receive that name until about 1839, when the occupied
territory around the seaport of Algiers was so called by the French.
However, although French North Africa was only conquered and
brought under control by stages, it will be more convenient if, when I
refer to Algeria, Morocco or Tunis, it is taken that I mean the present-
day territory encompassed by those three countries as shown on a
modern atlas.

Geographically, Algeria is divided into at least two distinct sectors,
the northern and the southern, the southern consisting of large stretches
of desert country. The northern section is more complex and two large
mountain ranges cut laterally across it. To the north is the Mediterranean Sea, on the coastline of which there are a number of small
harbours and landing-places, but all are rather open to the north winds.
Southward from the sea there is a narrow but fertile coastal plain, which
extends in a varying width to the first mountain range, which is known
as the Lesser, or Maritime, Atlas.

Southwards again there is an expanse of terrain consisting of fertile
valleys, areas of flat land and ridges of small hills, which extends to the
main backbone of the Atlas Mountains, at the southern foothills of
which begins the Sahara Desert proper, arid and waterless, with only
infrequent oases.

With the spread of militant Mohammedanism, the Arabs flooded in
from the east, seizing many parts of the country, causing the Berbers,
the inhabitants, to retire to their mountains. From this period there
remained in Algeria both Berbers, mainly in the mountainous districts,
and Arabs, but the country was almost at once plunged into a state of
anarchy. For centuries it was wild and turbulent, sometimes a kingdom,
but more often than not just a heaving mass of warring tribes, each a
law unto itself.

The seaport of Algiers became a fortified pirates' nest, and their
activities caused the northern part of Algeria to become known as the
Barbary Coast. The word 'barbarian' is derived from Berber. These
brave but ruthless Muslim pirates preyed upon merchant shipping,
occasionally provoking Christian nations to send punitive expeditions
against them.

Eventually some Turkish janissaries were sent, and Algeria nominally became part of the Ottoman Empire. But this overlordship was never more than a fiction, and only succeeded in attracting Muslim adventurers, and piratical activities became more extensive and daring. European nations were periodically stung into taking action, and in 1683, for instance, a French fleet set fire to Algiers. There were other similar expeditions, but all were of a punitive nature and were not followed up, so the pirates were able to re-establish themselves and begin all over again when the Europeans sailed away.

The Barbary pirates not only seized booty, but took slaves as well, either for their own use or to sell in the interior. Estimates vary widely as to the actual number of Christians there were in slavery, but that there were indeed Christian slaves there can be no doubt. Some say that there were seldom fewer than 30,000, whilst other sources indicate that 80,000 may have been nearer the mark.

By the beginning of the nineteenth century, the extreme northern part of Algeria was divided into Beyliks, which all nominally owed allegiance to Constantinople. The Beys (one was a Dey in fact) all had bodies of janissaries to support them, and the tribes and towns in their areas were kept in some sort of submission by the age-old policy of playing one off against the other. In short, the rulers of Algeria rode a turbulent sea only with the support of a few thousand regular soldiers.

The Dey and the Beys themselves were invariably foreign adventurers who had seized the territory by force or intrigue, or owed their position to the janissaries, who in some cases had taken on the powers of a Praetorian Guard.

The Dey had his seat in Algiers, and the other Beyliks were those of Oran, Titteri and Constantine. The Deylik of Algiers included the inland town of Miliana; the Beylik of Oran, the inland towns of Tlemcen and Mascara; while Constantine, itself an inland town, included the ports of Bone and Bougie. Titteri could be thought of as the immediate hinterland of Algiers, centring around the town of Medea.

Both Dey and Beys changed frequently, sometimes with amazing rapidity, as one adventurer ousted the other. The countryside between the towns was usually in a state of near anarchy, and often it was only by local arrangement, threats or bribes, that the garrison of some towns could be provisioned.

That was the picture of Algeria in the early 1800s.

France began to take an interest in Algeria, and her statesmen were

beginning to look southwards into Africa. Technically, the quarrel with
the Dey is alleged to have stemmed from an incident in April 1827 when
the French Consul was struck by the Dey. An apology was not forthcoming, and Algiers was blockaded by the French navy. This was not
really effective, and the Algerians sneered at the French efforts, which
provoked them into taking more serious action.

The French mustered an expeditionary force, which took Algiers in
June 1830. At once they began to probe inland, and a small expedition
was sent to Blida, about thirty miles from Algiers. It was badly mauled,
and other attempts to penetrate the interior were not always successful.
A small detachment was sent by sea to Bone, where the French had a
trading post, but it was recalled after a short time.

However, in May 1831, the inhabitants of Bone, who were hard
pressed by the Bey of Constantine, asked for French help, which was
again sent. After helping to hold the town for a time the janissaries
turned on the French and ungratefully evicted them.

To the west a small garrison was established at Oran, but it shared
the town with a detachment of wary janissaries. As it was realized that
Oran was a key point, being adjacent to independent Morocco, the
French garrison was gradually increased over the months.

In all, the French had perhaps 35,000 troops in the country, most of
whom were in or around the port of Algiers, facing an active, armed,
hostile population that may have numbered anything between two and
four millions—no one knows exactly—which figure is thought to com-
prise the inhabitants of 'northern' Algeria.

The story of the Legion now starts properly, and as the elements of
this new corps arrived from France they were put into camps. For the
first months of its existence, the Legion formed no part of the several
columns that traversed the immediate countryside, 'showing the flag',
nor did they take part in the several actions that were fought.

The authorities seemed to have been uncertain of the Legion, and it
was put to work instead of being sent out to fight. Eventually, the 4th
Battalion was sent off to reinforce the garrison at Oran. Although the
Spaniards had the reputation of being first-class fighting men, they were
notorious for their indiscipline in the slacker periods, so one feels that
selection for this far-away job was not left entirely to chance.

Attacks and nuisance raids were of nightly occurrence, so a strong
chain of entrenched positions, along which blockhouses were built, was
constructed a short distance from Algiers. The legionnaires were put to

work on it, and it was in the course of clearing an area for this purpose
that the first action took place in which the French Foreign Legion
fought. The first blood went to the 3rd Battalion, when some of its
Swiss and German companies were sent out to move some Arabs from
a prominent building, known as Maison Carrée.

The attack was launched on April 27th, 1832, in a businesslike
manner and the Arabs were ejected from the building and the area
around it after a short, stiff fight. Having done this the legionnaires were
ordered to stay where they were, which they did. A little while later

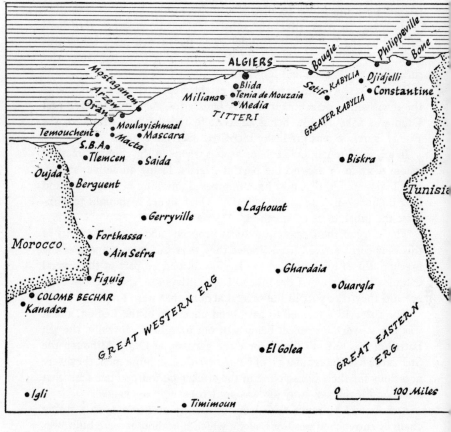

Algeria

30

they successfully repulsed a fierce counter-attack. Maison Carrée then remained a Legion outpost.

A series of small night attacks were made on it, otherwise nothing of note happened to the Legion until the next month, when a detachment of 1 officer and 26 legionnaires was caught in the open near Maison Carrée by a large body of Arab horsemen. The legionnaires stood firm and fought back, but all were killed before they could be rescued. About 70 Arabs were killed before the legionnaires were overwhelmed.

For the remainder of the year the Legion units continued to be employed on constructing the defensive belt, but a new Governor-General regarded them in a slightly different light from his predecessors, perhaps because of the action at Maison Carrée. As a result, the Legion took its place in the fighting line and began to be employed on sorties. In October, for instance, several companies of the Legion accompanied a column which was detailed to penetrate to the inland town of Kola, and blow up its walls and defences.

A company of the Legion also accompanied a column which penetrated to Blida on a similar mission.

Towards the end of the previous year, 1831, there rose in the interior a native leader who united the tribes and persuaded them to march against the French. His name was Abdul El Kader. He was the son of a marabout, that is a local holy man, who lived in Mascara, who being too old to take the field himself against the French sent his son instead, whilst he stayed at home using his influence to stir up the tribes in his support. Kader was young, still in his twenties, clever and brave, ambitious and unscrupulous: he also had an attractive personality and was a good orator. He developed into an able leader and the legionnaires came to know his cunning at first hand.

The tribes rallied to him from around Mascara, and he was able, in May 1832, to advance without difficulty right to the doorstep of Oran, where his men were defeated and scattered. Undaunted, he made another attempt later in the year and he again reached the outskirts of Oran. In November, he was again defeated and his forces dispersed near a place called Sidi Chabal, in which battle the Spanish battalion of the Legion played a big part.

By the spring of 1832 Bone was firmly in French hands, and the garrison was built up. Amongst the reinforcements sent was the 5th Battalion of the Legion, consisting mainly of Italian companies. During the summer the town was attacked and the legionnaires played a part in repulsing the attackers. Several other small actions in which the Legion took part were fought during the autumn in and around Bone.

Colonel Stoffel had worked wonders during its first twelve months of its existence and transformed the Legion into a fighting force. Firm measures had been necessary but he had succeeded, and to him must go the initial credit for forging such a good weapon out of such unpromising material. Perhaps to Colonel Stoffel should go the credit for the fact that there still was a Legion at all, as in those early months there were many who thought that its existence was undesirable.

In June 1832, Stoffel handed over the Legion to a regular French officer, Colonel Combe, who brought with him the first Regimental Colour. Combe did not remain long but handed over to Colonel Bernelle, who was a good organizer and a strict disciplinarian. He continued to improve the efficiency of the Legion.

There were several actions during the course of 1833, around Algiers, Oran and Bone, in which the legionnaires figured creditably, and of these the capture of Arzew is perhaps the most notable. It was decided to occupy Arzew, a small port not far from Oran, and in June a force, which contained the 4th Battalion and some companies of Italians from the 5th Battalion, set out from there.

In the skirmishing *en route* the Spanish legionnaires were in their element, as many of them were veterans of the Spanish wars, being expert at guerrilla warfare and good at using ground and cover. For the first time the Arabs were beaten at their own game. Arzew was taken on June 5th, with little loss, the Italian legionnaires playing a prominent role in its capture. Kader retreated before them.

In August, a French force, containing some Legion units, moved and occupied the nearby port of Mostagenem, and once in occupation had to withstand an assault by Kader's followers. There was a clash, and the Arabs were dispersed. Following this success, the French made a counter-attack, in which the Spanish companies took part. It was also a success and a number of prisoners were rescued, but in its retirement this force was severely harassed.

For the rest of the year the Spanish and Italian companies of the Legion at Oran were in almost constant action against Kader, whose men continued to press the French hard. In this fighting the Spanish did extremely well, winning praise from the French commanders, as it was a type of warfare they knew little about. The French were learning fast, but the hard way, and were still thinking in terms of European warfare, with the result that they had few successes to their credit in Algeria as a whole at this stage, the main exceptions being the Legion actions around Oran.

A new Governor-General, General Voirol, appeared, who adopted a less stern policy and concentrated upon consolidating the French position. He undertook few offensive operations, none of any importance. However, he was probably the first real friend the Legion had amongst the French generals, and he was the first to openly praise the legionnaires and to speak of the Legion as 'having a hopeful future', a sentiment not yet fully shared. Nevertheless, the proved fighting ability of the legionnaires had made them all think a little.

The year 1834 was quieter, partly owing to the new policy and partly owing to the fact that Kader was fully occupied in putting his own house in order. The French decided to see if it was possible to work with him, and a treaty was made whereby Kader was recognized as the Emir of Mascara and given a free hand with all the tribes in the interior of western Algeria, on the condition he acknowledged the supremacy of France.

Kader established his capital at Mascara and spent the whole year bringing the local tribes under his thumb. For him it was a year of consolidation and success, he took the towns of Miliana and Medea from the Bey of Titteri, and began to plan an expedition to Constantine. He engaged European technicians and set up his own arsenals. There were in fact several Europeans working for him, and a British colonel was his military adviser for a time.

On the other hand, 1834 was spent by the Legion mainly in constructional works, with only the occasional sortie to break the monotony. The legionnaires at Oran were probably the most active, although those at Bone were also frequently in action.

The French passive policy continued, and caused Kader to become confident, so instead of attacking Constantine, he decided he was strong enough to eject the French. He had only accepted the treaty to obtain a respite for his own ends, and early in 1835 he moved to take Tlemcen, which was held for France by some janissaries. Not being able to take that town, he bypassed it, advancing northwards.

A composite force was assembled to go out and meet him, in which the Legion was represented by several companies of Spanish, Italian and Polish legionnaires. It moved out of Oran, but its progress southwards was slow as it was accompanied by a large baggage train of cumbersome carts.

The advanced guard consisted of three Polish companies, which indicated that the reputation of the Legion was improving. On reaching the foothills at a gap known as Moulay Ishmael, on June 26th, the advance guard was attacked by Kader's men. The legionnaires tried to fight their way forward but the route through the gap was solidly barred. At this moment Kader hurled some of his men on to the remainder of the strung out French column, but the Italian companies of the Legion were rushed to block this move and they managed to hold the Arabs where they were. To the front the Polish companies stood firm, like a wedge in the gap, plugging the opening and preventing Kader's hordes from flooding through. Their blood literally ran down the track in streams.

A bugler sounded the 'Retreat', and confusion ensued. The commander decided to withdraw to the open plain behind, and during this move the legionnaires formed the rearguard, holding back the Arabs and enabling the unwieldy carts to turn round and get clear.

A day was spent in regrouping and collecting the wounded, and next day the French force slowly began to make its way back. Armed Arabs pressed hard on all sides, and when it got near the Macta salt marsh, on June 28th, it was ambushed. The advanced guard consisted of the Italian companies of the Legion and they stood and drove back several attacks, but eventually the sheer weight of numbers told and the Arabs broke through to attack the baggage train, which they started to loot. Panic set in and the drivers cut their traces and galloped off, abandoning their carts: the wounded in them were all massacred.

The companies of the Legion remained intact to form the rearguard screen, under cover of which some of the French guns, which had been taken, were rescued, and the main body of the attackers contained to some extent. During the night, still screened by the legionnaires, the remnants limped back to Oran.

Moulay Ishmael and Macta were disasters, both in fact and prestige, as they gave Kader confidence and caused French morale to sag. However, they put the Legion on the map, as the conduct of the legionnaires throughout had been superb. They proved that they could fight as well as brawl.

Meanwhile, the Carlist War had broken out in Spain over the succession to the Spanish throne, and France decided to send a contingent to

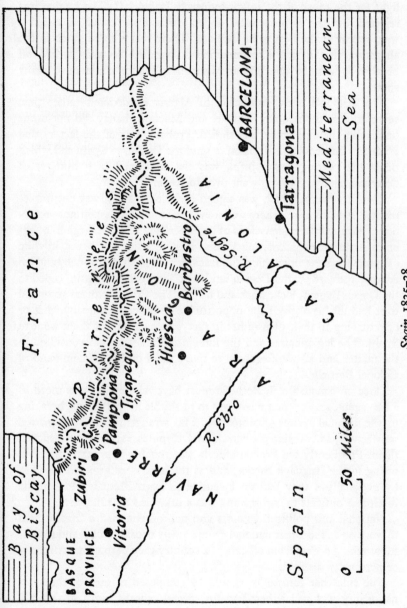

Spain 1835-38

fight for the cause of the infant monarch, Isabella II. The Legion was selected, but the circumstances under which it was ceded, as ceded it was, appear at the best to be dubious. There seems to be much in the allegation that it was unceremoniously bundled up and packed off because it was the one military formation France could most easily spare.

The Legion's early reputation in Algeria condemned rather than saved it, and the Moulay Ishmael and Macta gallantry did not occur until after the agreement was signed. Probably one of the factors that tended to influence this decision to send the Legion to Spain and which made the parting less painful, was the continued high number of deserters, many of whom went over to Kader.

The agreement, which was signed in January 1835, was not implemented straight away: there was some hesitation and last-minute reluctance. Meanwhile, unconscious of its impending fate, the Legion fought on in Algeria with increasing success and efficiency. However, in spite of some apparent opposition the transfer was pushed through, and on August 19th, 1835, the Legion landed at Tarragona, in Spain, ceded to the Queen Regent, lock, stock and barrel. The French officers seconded to it had all been given the opportunity of either accompanying it or of returning to their own units: in fact, just over half of them went to Spain. The legionnaires and the foreign officers were not consulted in the matter and all were ordered to move there under the command of Colonel Bernelle.

Once on Spanish soil, Bernelle must have felt that he was more of a free agent, and his first move was to re-shuffle his battalions, breaking up the national groups of companies. This arrangement had not proved satisfactory, as it fostered quarrels and disputes rather than douched them. Frequently the French officers were unable to speak to the men owing to the language barrier, and as the men were grouped together by nationalities they had no incentive to learn French, which made discipline difficult to enforce and was a drawback to efficiency.

National and political agitators and malcontents had a fruitful field to work on as the larger national groups easily became sullen and resentful at taking orders from officers of a country they perhaps traditionally or personally disliked.

The rule that companies should be composed of men of the same nationality was still adhered to for several months, until in fact the Legion strength became so low that it was impossible to follow it: the battalions themselves were 'mixed' in that they each contained companies of Swiss, Germans, Poles, Italians and so on. In the first instance, there were six of these 'mixed' battalions, but this number decreased as time went on. This experiment of Colonel Bernelle's worked quite well.

On landing at Tarragona, the Legion was enthusiastically received as it marched through the streets. Its bearing, marching and discipline impressed several observers, which shows that it had come a long way since its birth. The Legion was not allowed to linger in Tarragona and was quickly moved to the scene of operations.

The supporters of the Queen Regent, known as 'Christinos', were based on Madrid and abounded in the southern provinces, whilst the followers of Don Carlos, known as 'Carlists', were generally in the north, especially in the north-east. Their main stronghold was situated in the area of rough country to the north and east of the Rivers Ebro and Sagre, where the inhabitants were sympathetic to his cause.

The plan was roughly—very roughly indeed, as planning was not a strong point with the Spanish command—that the Christinos should advance northwards and squeeze the Carlists against the wall of the Pyrenees and crush them. A general move northwards was made, but few Spanish units were ready or able to march, and the Legion found itself in the van and almost alone at times, scattered on a wide front.

From August to December, it operated in the area of Catalonia, where it was split up and distributed out in company detachments, engaged either in guerrilla warfare or patrol work. The recent experience of Algerian fighting proved to be invaluable, and the legionnaires did extremely well in those early days of the Spanish hostilities.

Unlike the Legion, the Spanish army could not claim that things were going well, and gradually, during these months, the initiative seemed to pass from it to the Carlists. The main body of the Christinos advanced casually northwards, having some small successes at first, but soon ran into trouble, suffering a jarring defeat near a place called Estella, on the road to Pamplona, which caused it to recoil.

As a result the policy changed and, instead of being loosely strung out over a large expanse of countryside, the Christino army began to concentrate. This suited Bernelle admirably, as he had been impatient and disliked having his command broken up into tiny fragments. All the Legion companies came under his firm hand again.

The Christinos concentrated and moved out to attack the enemy in

January 1836, but were hampered by the bad weather and the extreme cold. This assault went badly, and a hopeless impasse followed. For three days and nights the Christinos remained where they were on the ground, the Legion included, blanketless and freezing. The Legion, which had only taken a minor part in this abortive attack, then moved back through the snow and ice to Vittoria.

The attitude of the inhabitants was unfriendly as the Legion was now in country sympathetic to the Carlist cause. As the Legion marched through Vittoria it was jeered—a new experience. After a little while the legionnaires moved off towards Pamplona, where for the remainder of the winter they held a sector against the Carlists.

On April 26th, 1836, the Legion took part in an action at a place called Tirapegui, when three Carlist battalions attacked the position held by the Legion 4th Battalion. Colonel Bernelle was there at the time and he sent forward two companies to hold the assault, whilst more reinforcements came up. The 5th Battalion arrived, thus making an over-all total of about 1,000 legionnaires in the position. On the other side the Carlists were reinforced too, and had about 5,000 men in all. Three times they assaulted the main position unsuccessfully, and then the Legion disengaged and withdrew.

For the remainder of the summer the legionnaires took part in sporadic fighting in the Pyrenean valleys of north-east Spain.

Another battle was fought on August 1st. The Legion was on the right wing of the Spanish army which came up against a Carlist fortified line near a village called Zubiri. Two Legion battalions assaulted and in the fighting the Polish companies especially distinguished themselves. The enemy were driven from their positions, and retreated leaving some 1,500 men on the field, either dead or as prisoners. Bernelle had formed a squadron of mounted Polish lancers, who did very well in this fight.

After Zubiri, there was more skirmishing, patrol work and guerrilla activity during the autumn, before the Legion settled down in winter quarters, when it was given the task of holding a sector near Pamplona.

Colonel Bernelle became involved in disputes with French ministers, and after some months was relieved of his command. Major Lebeau commanded for a short time, and then, in November 1836, Colonel Conrad arrived to take over.

By this time the strength had begun to shrink. The Legion had been about 5,000 strong when it first landed in Spain, but the wastage was heavy. Only two detachments of reinforcements, about 3,000 men in all, arrived, which meant that the aggregated strength of the Legion during its stay in Spain could never have amounted to more than about 8,000. Casualties, sickness and desertion made inroads into this, and the strength had so dwindled by January 1837 that it had to be reorganized into three battalions only.

The legionnaires were beginning to fall into a precarious state, being neglected and unpaid, badly fed and inadequately clothed. Spain had clearly hoped that France would at least assist materially, but France accepted less and less responsibility for the whole business. The Legion was thrown on the mercy of the inefficient, creaking Spanish commissariat, already almost totally submerged under the unaccustomed number of Spanish soldiers it had to cater for. Rations for the Legion were poor and often insufficient, powder was sparse and clothing replacements non-existent. This poor treatment began to have effect and morale began to suffer—the desertion rate was stepped up.

The Spanish military authorities showed less and less interest as the weeks went by. The Legion had to get along by resorting to the time-honoured method of living on the country, which did not endear it to the inhabitants. The severe winter especially hit the legionnaires hard as they had insufficient clothing or bedding, and many died of cold. The sickness rate shot up alarmingly. The officers, who were mainly French, showed great devotion to the men under their command, and worked with enthusiasm and vigour under these depressing conditions.

Active hostilities were resumed again in March 1837, and the depleted Legion marched out from its winter quarters, under Conrad, on to the plains of Aragon. There was some guerrilla activity and then, rather unexpectedly, on June 2nd, the Spanish force of which the Legion was a part was violently attacked by the Carlists near the village of Barbastro. In this fighting, four Legion companies and a Spanish unit, all under Conrad, became isolated and had to fight for their lives.

By an odd coincidence, the Carlist formation opposing the Legion was also a volunteer legion of mixed foreigners. There were a number of units of foreign volunteers fighting on both sides. The two foreign legions recognized each other before the action was joined, and the Carlist legion immediately opened fire at short range on the French Foreign Legion, as it had the advantage of surprise. The men, recognizing many of their countrymen in the opposing ranks, jeered at them and abuse flowed freely. Political hatreds were fanned into flame, and after the initial volleys, as was the practice in those days, the Carlists charged in with the bayonet.

The French Legion stood firm and met the charge squarely. Confused and bitter fighting then raged in and among the olive groves near Barbastro village. No quarter was given as men slaughtered their own countrymen without compunction, and in their blind hatred neither side would willingly give way. Eventually something had to give: it could not last, human beings could not stand the pace. The two foreign legions were locked together in what proved to be their death struggle.

During the heat of the fighting, the French Legion wavered at one stage and, seeing this, Colonel Conrad dashed into the thickest of the battle to rally his men. He was struck by a musket ball and died almost at once, sword in hand. He was the first of many Legion commanding officers to be killed in battle at the head of his troops.

After some hours of this deadly combat, the fighting stopped through sheer exhaustion and lack of fighters. The two legions literally fought each other to a standstill, and neither was fit to fight again in Spain. They had battered themselves to pieces, and neither recovered sufficiently to be committed into battle again. In theory, the Carlists won the day as they remained in their positions, and the decimated remnants of the French Legion left the disastrous battlefield.

Barbastro was for all practical purposes the finish of the French Foreign Legion in Spain. The survivors, unpaid and neglected, were quartered around Pamplona. An ever-increasing number of deserters filtered over the Pyrenees into France. The French officers, who loyally remained with it, felt this humiliating position keenly and made earnest representations to France to have this sad state of affairs ended.

On December 6th, 1838, the French Foreign Legion was formally disbanded, and the survivors returned to France the following month. The French officers with it had served the Legion well and faithfully, and had refused to abandon it in its hour of need.

In Spain, the Legion had started off well, and although neglected had always fought with bravery and determination. It did not deserve the fate that was so unceremoniously accorded to it. The official casualties during the three years in Spain tell a story in themselves of bravery in adversity: 23 officers were killed and 109 were wounded. Of the legionnaires, 3,600 were either killed in battle or died of wounds or sickness, thus leaving a silent figure of about 4,000 unaccounted for. Presumably this was the total number of deserters.

Only about 500 legionnaires remained on the strength when the Legion was disbanded. Of this number, nearly 400, having volunteered to remain in the French service, were sent to Algeria to join the new French Foreign Legion which had been formed.

So sadly closed one of the most depressing episodes of Legion history.

2

The Conquest of Algeria (1837-70)

Another Royal Ordinance, of December 1835, authorized the recruiting of what amounted to another foreign legion. When the old Legion had been sent to Spain, recruiting carried on normally for a time and some reinforcements were sent to it. Then there was a lull in recruiting, whether by design or accident is not clear, but a small unit was built up and trained in France when there was no longer any interest in the Carlist War. This developed into a battalion of about 800 men, under the command of Major Bedeau.

In December 1836 it was shipped over to Algeria. The French Foreign Legion—this time the 'New' Legion—was back again on African soil where it was to play a full part in winning Algeria for France. No flags were put out on its arrival.

In Algeria, French pride had been touched to the quick by the defeats of Moulay Ishmael and Macta, causing determined measures to be set afoot to avenge them, although at this period the French Government still wavered hesitantly over whether to evacuate Algeria or to adopt a policy of conquest and occupation. During the spring of 1836 expeditions had been sent out against Kader in western Algeria, and also against the Bey of Constantine in eastern Algeria, which met with limited and varied success. The mountain massifs in the east of Kabylia, the centre of Berber power, were rightly considered to be the key to that part of Algeria, and in particular the fortress town of Constantine was prominent as a bastion on the northern edge. The Bey of Constantine had withdrawn into his own territory after the French victory at Algiers in 1830, where he remained, aloof and menacing. He still claimed Bone, but was unable to take possession of it because of the French garrison. The French made a disastrous attempt to reduce Constantine in 1836.

A new Governor-General arrived and at once began to make preparations for another attempt. The defeat had been reflected in the attitude of the Kabylies and the Arabs, who had become bolder in their raids. Reinforcements poured into Algeria. In order to be able to concentrate the bulk of the troops against Constantine, it was decided to try and come to some agreement with Kader, so as not to have to fight on two fronts at the same time.

In the province of Oran, Kader was busily asserting his authority, and had collected a number of regular soldiers to help him to do this. His Arab warriors were extremely difficult to control especially once they were in action, and although they formed the basis of his support, he began to form units of regular mercenaries. At Macta, he had one such unit over which he never completely lost control, and this made an impression on him. He had a number of Europeans fighting for him, many deserters from the Legion, and small units of them were attached to some of his mercenary native battalions.

After some desultory fighting, an agreement, known as the Treaty of Tafna, was concluded between the French and Kader, which although regarded as unsatisfactory gave some breathing space to allow the French troops to concentrate on eastern Algeria.

This time, almost as soon as it landed, the new Legion battalion was used on operations in and around Algiers. It took part in an expedition into the Isser Valley, and accompanied several of the columns that went out into the countryside.

Recruiting in France revived again and the strength swelled so much that in July 1837 it was decided to form another battalion, and the Legion again officially became a 'regiment'. A colonel was appointed to command. This time a better type of French officer began to be attracted to serve with it.

No agreement could be reached with the Bey of Constantine, who would not listen to moderate terms, so the expedition began to form up at Bone. What is important is that this time the Legion was asked to send a small battalion to take part in it. This was done and it was commanded by Major Bedeau, who had retained command of the original battalion.

In October, a large French force, containing the Legion battalion, moved out of Bone, and after a harassing six days of marching, arrived before the towering fortress town of Constantine. It was a walled town and the fortifications had been strengthened since the previous year's unsuccessful bombardment. There was a garrison of 'regular' janissaries with about sixty artillery pieces of different sorts and sizes. As the French approached the rains came, and drenched to the skin they stood looking up at the fortified citadel.

The morale of the defenders was high after the previous French defeat, and at once an eager sortie was made from the town. This was repulsed by the French force.

Siege batteries were established with some difficulty on the rocky slopes, and for four days the French pounded the walls in an effort to make a crack in the side on which the town could be the most easily assaulted. Eventually a breach appeared and all fire power was concentrated upon widening it.

Whilst this was happening, the men were engaged in repulsing periodic sallies from the garrison, and also from the Kabylies, who appeared from the hills on the flanks and the rear. The Legion was occupied in this manner on October 11th, when the Kabylies made a bigger attack during which the legionnaires suffered several casualties, including a captain killed, before the enemy was driven off.

Two breaches were made in the walls and it was decided to launch an attack on October 13th. Ammunition and supplies were running short. Three assaulting parties were formed, each about 700 strong, and in the centre one was a detachment of legionnaires, at least 100 strong. Reports vary as to the precise number—there may have been many more. The centre assaulting party was led by Colonel Combe, who had briefly commanded the Old Legion in 1832.

When the French troops were forming up for this assault it was noticed by one eye-witness that the men of the Legion 'fell in' on parade some distance apart from the others. Whether this was because the Legion was not yet fully accepted by the French troops or whether it was because the legionnaires were already beginning to develop a superiority complex is not apparent; perhaps a little of both.

The assault was launched during the afternoon, the storming parties aiming at getting through the two breaches. The centre column, containing the legionnaires, charged through the widest gap, and when trying to enlarge it with the aid of powder bags, part of the masonry fell on a number of legionnaires, injuring them.

Once through the wall, the legionnaires, who were leading the way, hit up against a building—used as the barracks for the janissaries—which barred the way. Here there was some fierce fighting before the defenders were driven out. The 'first' assaulting column got through

44

the other gap, and once inside the town moved towards the main gate.

Next, the legionnaires had to cross a wide street, and then go through some smaller ones, in the course of which they suffered casualties through sniping and rocks being thrown down on them. They were halted by a brick wall, but fortune was with them as it was part of a magazine, which at this moment blew up—how is not quite clear. Again, legionnaires were hurt by falling bricks.

Colonel Combe led his party through the debris and stormed a barricade in the street beyond. There was a brief scuffle with bayonets and swords in which Combe was mortally wounded. He stood there urging his men through the barricade and the legionnaires charged over it to assault a second similar barricade, formed of French transport wagons which had been abandoned the previous year. In this initial break-through, when the attackers paused for a moment, a Legion sergeant-major dashed forward and seized a Kabylie flag. His men followed spontaneously scattering the enemy group. Having seen his men charge forward successfully, Colonel Combe struggled back alone to die in his tent outside the walls.

By this time, the 'first' assaulting column had taken the main gate and opened it, allowing the 'third' column waiting outside to swarm through to add its weight to the struggle. Fighting street by street, the French forced their way to the centre of the town, and in a short space of time were the masters of Constantine. The resistance had been fierce and desperate, and accordingly casualties were high. Many of the defenders jumped or were pushed over the walls to crash down in the deep ravines below. By nightfall the French were in complete possession and the Legion battalion was one of the units left to garrison the town.

During the initial assault the legionnaires were divided into two bodies, one commanded by Bedeau, who did not mean to be left out of it, and the other by a young officer named Captain St. Arnaud, later to become a Marshal of France.

After this battle, one of the two Legion battalions remained at Bone, half of which was stationed at Constantine for the time being, and the other was at Algiers, where, as recruits came in, another battalion, the 3rd, was formed. Later, in October 1839, yet another battalion was formed at Pau, in France: the 4th, composed almost entirely of fugitives from Spain. The Regiment of the Foreign Legion now had four battalions: it was growing again.

The French concentrated on strengthening defences, building forts and improving roads, but this had little more success than the former policy of marching about 'showing the flag'. The posts were easily cut off and surrounded. Some were overrun.

The Bey of Constantine remained at large in the remote depths of Kabylia, keeping the pot boiling; and a number of expeditions were sent out from Bone, in which the Legion battalion took part.

To the west, Kader was busy building up a small 'regular' army, which at its peak was estimated to have consisted of some 5,000 infantry, 1,000 cavalry and 150 trained gunners, in which there was a proportion of Legion deserters. His battery of gunners was commanded by a Hungarian Legion deserter.

The treaty had only been a matter of convenience and as soon as he was ready, in November 1838, Kader advanced northwards into what was now regarded as French territory, besieging a number of posts which were only relieved with difficulty. For a few days it was critical, but when it was seen that it was not going to be an easy walk-over, the tribes dispersed. The next year Kader's 'regulars' suffered heavy loss at French hands.

In 1840, the French were ready to hit back, and in late April a contingent, which included two battalions of the Legion, moved out in the direction of Medea, meeting slight resistance as it advanced until it was finally halted at the pass of Tenia de Mouzaia, where previous battles had been fought, which was blocked by the Arabs, who were supported by a small unit of Europeans, mainly deserters from the Legion.

On May 12th, this pass was assaulted and a Legion battalion led the way. There was a short but bloody battle as legionnaire fought ex-legionnaire: the pass was carried and the troops hurried through it to enter Medea. On its return, this French force was ambushed at this spot and had to fight its way clear. The legionnaires again distinguished themselves.

At the beginning of June, another large French force set out to take Miliana, containing the same two Legion battalions. Once again there was a stiff fight to get through the Tenia de Mouzaia, and the Legion led the way. Meliana was taken with little opposition. It was then decided to leave a garrison on a nearby hill, which had been taken from the Arabs. It consisted predominantly of the two Legion units.

When the main body of the French force withdrew, Miliana was immediately besieged by the natives, and for four months the defenders fought off almost daily attacks. In addition—not to mention the heat—fever and dysentery struck the garrison, decimating the ranks. Meliana was not relieved until October, by which time there were only 288 legionnaires surviving, a third of whom were in the field hospital.

The survivors returned to the coast, and when the two battalions had been made up to strength they were sent to a place in the foothills, named Fondouk. Again, bad luck dogged the Legion and it was swept by fever which carried off the commanding officer and over 200 men within a few days.

In the eastern part of the country a number of small expeditions were sent out, and one of the most noteworthy was that conducted by the Legion battalion stationed at Bone, when it was sent to reduce a rocky stronghold, known as Djidjelli. The Polish companies led the assault in fine style, and after a fierce action the position was overrun. The battalion commander was killed in the assault. After taking the stronghold, the legionnaires were surrounded and had to fight their way clear again. This battalion later took part with distinction in several actions against the Kabylies in and around Bougie.

In 1840, the French at last adopted a policy of total conquest and permanent occupation: until this moment they had been undecided and their occupation was confined mainly to the coast. It had only been with reluctance that expeditions inland had been agreed to. Now matters changed.

General Bugeard, who had already seen some Algerian fighting, and who came to be regarded as one of the more successful generals in North Africa, took over. The garrison in Algeria was increased. Bugeard reduced the number of defended posts and introduced 'flying columns'. Wheeled transport was practically eliminated and mules were introduced instead. The equipment carried by the men was drastically lightened so that they could march faster and further. He introduced guerrilla tactics, and brought into use small mountain guns, which were carried by mules, thus enabling him to penetrate quickly into the interior to catch Kader's men by surprise.

General Bugeard established the tradition of the 'razzia', the swift, ruthless surprise punishment raid on offending villages when crops were burnt, cattle seized and prisoners taken. Those who resisted were sometimes killed. The razzia was usually carried out at night.

By using these tactics, French influence was extended and Kader driven farther southwards, so that by the end of 1842 western Algeria was practically cleared. Kader retired over the border into Morocco to lick his wounds and recoup.

In the spring of 1841, the Legion was formed into two regiments. The 1st Regiment was made up of the first three battalions, which were already in the provinces of Oran and Algiers. This kept the Colour

Legionnaire of the 2nd Regiment in full marching order. 1846

which had been presented the previous year in recognition of the fighting at Constantine and Djidjelli. For the next fifteen years the 1st Regiment operated in the western parts of Algeria.

The new 2nd Regiment consisted, in the first place, of the 4th and 5th Battalions (the latter only recently established), to which was added another, the 6th, a little later. This regiment operated in eastern Algeria, and moved from Bone to Setif, which became its base.

The 1st Regiment was commanded by a foreign officer, but after a year he was succeeded by a Frenchman, who did not stay more than a few months. He was followed by Colonel Mouret, in 1843, an able officer, under whom the 1st Regiment developed into a fine fighting formation. The 2nd Regiment had a long succession of colonels, whose tenures of command varied from three months to as many years. One of these was MacMahon, later to become a Marshal of France, who commanded for almost a year.

During 1843, Kader returned to Algeria, rallied several tribes under his banner, and resumed harassing French forts. However, Bugeard's flying columns had considerable success, and Kader did not stand up well against them. His followers were scattered and his 'regulars' reduced in strength. Brought to battle in November, the remnants of the 'regulars' gallantly formed square, but it was broken up by a French attack. Again, Kader retired to recoup.

To supply the numerous flying columns, Bugeard set up small provisioning depots at suitable points, and these became known as 'Biscuitvilles', from the type of ration that was to achieve fame in other wars and other armies too. These were scattered all over northern Algeria.

In 1843, the 3rd Battalion of the Legion was ordered to establish one about sixty miles south of Oran, in a shallow plain, just short of the foothills. This unit, of the 1st Regiment, searched about and found that the most suitable and convenient place was between a small piece of high ground, little more than a mound, on which was situated the tomb of a marabout, and the River Mekera. The marabout's name had been Sidi Bel Abbes, 'Lord, the Happy One'. The last time I was in Sidi Bel Abbes his tomb was the site of the Legion's mule lines.

This biscuitville was established and at first the troops were simply in tents in a sort of entrenched camp. For a time all was quiet except for casual marauders, but at the end of December the following year the local tribes began to cluster. Then a series of attacks were made on the camp. Notably, one night assault was mounted in January 1845, and the whole camp was encircled. The Arabs were beaten off, and the next morning the legionnaires found over 40 enemy dead outside their defences. These were buried at the foot of a large tree, now known as the 'Poplar of Kader', in the present Public Gardens.

After this series of attacks the Legion battalions (there were now two in occupation, the 1st and the 3rd) were ordered to construct a

D

strongly fortified camp with permanent buildings. An engineer officer, Captain Prudhon, was in charge of the constructional work, and he planned the layout of what developed into a small town. At first all these erections were sheltered merely by a thick mud wall, sufficient to protect those inside from small arms fire. The legionnaires got to work, and masons, carpenters, craftsmen and draughtsmen were produced from the ranks. One Legion company is said to have produced five qualified architects. Within the next few years the tall barrack blocks, which are still in use today, and many other buildings were put up.

Unconsciously, the legionnaires were adopting the traditions of the ancient legions of Rome, of building as well as fighting. Ten miles to the north of Sidi Bel Abbes in the hills are the remains of a Roman garrison, Fort Tessala. There are indistinct remains of another Roman station about twenty miles to the south as well. The nineteenth-century legionnaires were working and fighting in the footsteps of the Roman legionnaires of centuries ago.

The Sultan of Morocco, who so far had maintained an attitude of neutrality towards the French in Algeria, became openly sympathetic towards Kader, who had previously repeatedly sought shelter unofficially in his territory, and began to give him both material and moral aid. Bugeard's tactics were successful, and although in 1844 Kader raised the tribes, he was soon pressed back into Morocco. The Moorish frontier tribes, hostile and frequently raiding into Algeria, now abetted the Sultan, who in fact had little control over them at the best of times.

These factors caused the French to advance over the border and occupy the Moroccan town of Oujda. Bugeard wanted to continue and march on through to Fez, the capital of Morocco, but his government would not allow him to do this, and French troops withdrew back into Algeria.

This was taken as a sign of weakness, and the raids were intensified from Morocco. In August, the Sultan advanced from Fez towards Algeria, with his regular force and a horde of armed irregulars. He had a small regular army amounting to about 10,000 infantry and 6,000 cavalry. He arrived and camped on the west bank of the River Isly, which roughly marked the frontier between the two countries.

Bugeard mustered a force of about 8,000 men, which included the 1st Regiment of the Legion complete, and marched to meet him. The

French crossed the river at night and hit the Moorish camp on three sides at daybreak on the 13th. After some hard fighting the legionnaires broke through the side of the camp allocated to them and wrought havoc amongst the Moorish soldiers. French troops broke through on the other two sides and the morning was spent in confused fighting, in which the Legion was well to the fore throughout. By noon the enemy broke and began to retire in confusion. As the Sultan withdrew, the local border tribes turned against him, and it was only with difficulty that he and the main body of his troops regained the capital. Over 800 dead Moors were left on the field of battle. The Legion lost one captain killed, and 24 men wounded.

An agreement was made between the French and the Sultan, of which only one detail is of any importance. The French exacted the right to pursue raiders who came into Algeria back across the border into Morocco. This right was frequently used in the ensuing years and caused a lot of trouble and misunderstanding.

Kader remained full of energy and cunning, and spent the next three years raiding French posts, only in his turn to be harried off his feet by the flying columns, which busily buzzed all over the countryside. He had many escapes, and bore a charmed life. The Legion crossed swords with him with zest: he was their favourite enemy.

The Legion was kept busy, marching and fighting. In one operation it marched to the relief of a French force which was encircled at a place called Temouchent. The legionnaires broke through and routed the besieging Arabs.

We now come to an incident which has been magnified out of all proportion and which has been held against the Legion for years, especially by those who allege that it is brutal and sadistic: the burning of Arabs alive in caves.

In April 1845, the 2nd and 3rd Battalions of the 1st Regiment formed part of a column commanded by General St. Arnaud (who as a captain had led a Legion detachment at the taking of Constantine), when a band of Arab rebels it had been pursuing took refuge in some mountain grottoes. The legionnaires could not get at them, and the Arabs would not surrender. The legionnaire who took the message asking them to do so was seized and killed. It was decided to smoke them out and fires were lit for this purpose. The Arabs still refused to come out and were asphyxiated. The Legion was accused of sadistically and deliberately burning about 600 natives alive. About that number of Arabs died, and perhaps a few were burnt in the incident, but it should be remembered that the Legion was only carrying out orders, and that the object was to try and smoke the rebels out.

In December 1847, there was fighting in the area of the River Isly, in which several companies of the 1st Regiment took part, and Kader was again driven into Morocco. By this time he was wearing out his welcome and the local tribes were turning against him. The French, aware of this, set a watch along the border, and several Legion companies were dispersed along it.

This time it was the end for Kader. Inside Morocco he had a brief but unsuccessful struggle with the Moors, during which the last remnants of his followers were scattered. The French watched and waited for him, but eluding them he slipped over the frontier farther to the south, and headed towards the Sahara, only to be caught at an outpost on December 22nd. His adventurous career had come to an end. The wily Arab leader, who had been a thorn in the side of the French for so many years, and had become a respected foe of the Legion, was sent out of the country to die in exile. When he had gone the tribes simmered down.

In eastern Algeria the Kabylie warriors gave the French no rest and continually raided down from the mountains. The Bey of Constantine was still at large urging them on, so it was decided both to hunt for him and to extend French influence to the edge of the Sahara. Southward probing began.

A *bataillon de marche* of the Legion, consisting of the *compagnies d'élite* of the 2nd Regiment, was formed for this purpose, and in February 1844, under Colonel MacMahon, went southwards through mountains to enter Biskra, the key to the south, which has since achieved literary fame as the 'Garden of Allah'.

The next month, this same Legion *bataillon de marche*, again under MacMahon, in its probing hit up against a Kabylie stronghold, known as M'Chounech, held by about 3,000 tribesmen. It was a natural defensive position on a rocky ridge. Two French Line battalions assaulted and failed, having to retire. Again they tried, and again they failed.

MacMahon called upon the Legion battalion and spoke to the men. The legionnaires then crossed a ravine under fire and swarmed up the steep side of the ridge to overrun the position. In twenty minutes the fighting was over and the panting legionnaires sat on the top of M'Chounech. The two sons of the king of France were present at this action and had watched this feat of arms by the Legion, and as a result the 2nd Regiment was awarded a Regimental Colour. The other Legion Colour was held by the 1st Regiment at Sidi Bel Abbes.

This type of operation in the mountains continued during 1845 and for the two following years. The legionnaires distinguished themselves on numerous occasions in this expansion southwards. All the units of the Legion, of both the 1st and the 2nd Regiments, were now efficient and hard-hitting. The men knew the country, had adapted themselves to it and were beating the Arabs and Kabylies at their own game. The Greater Atlas range was penetrated, and the legionnaires poked their noses through it into the Sahara proper.

Foreign sounding Arab and Berber names, difficult to pronounce, convey little to a reader, and the story would become a confused mass of detail if all the many actions fought by the legionnaires were solemnly listed in full. It is sufficient to say that there were few places the legionnaires did not visit and few fights in which they were not represented. The Legion became synonymous with Algeria, and although perhaps the gaudily clad Zouaves, now manned by Frenchmen and not natives, stole most of the limelight, the blue-coated legionnaires provided the core and backbone, when steadiness and endurance were required as well as dash and courage.

After the defeat of Kader the 1st Regiment fought only a few spasmodic actions and did a little tax-gathering, being mainly employed on constructing roads, building camps and boring wells. Particularly did it work on the new roads branching out in all directions from its headquarters, Sidi Bel Abbes. Its *compagnies d'élite* were in almost continual action penetrating southwards. For example, in May 1847, they fought an action to clear the way into Ain Sefra, on the edge of the Sahara.

The legionnaires of the 2nd Regiment continued to pound away at Greater Kabylia, not too successfully, but at the same time the French did not relax their efforts to penetrate through to the Sahara Desert in as many places as possible, and several actions were fought.

However, one of these, in which the legionnaires played an outstanding part worthy of mention, was against the oasis of Zaatcha, near Biskra. Revolt suddenly flared up there and in July 1849 a French column, which included two battalions of the Legion, was ordered to move against Zaatcha.

Zaatcha was in fact a large group of oases almost merged together and at first sight had the appearance of a forest of palms. Closer examination showed that hidden under the trees was a criss-cross of irrigation canals, and liberally dotted about were strongly built houses, each in a walled garden, resembling tiny fortresses. Thick mud walls had been built as protection for part of the oasis, and a seven-foot-wide canal protected much of another section of it.

The rebels were organized by a leader named Bou Ziane, and he collected nearly 2,000 fighting men. The French assaulted on July 16th, but were repulsed. Their small guns made little impression on the thick walls, and also the unexpected obstacles in the form of irrigation canals were a hindrance. The French force withdrew a little way and began what was actually a partial siege. The legionnaires scoured the countryside around and had two or three successful encounters with groups of rebels coming in to join Bou Ziane.

In October, heavier guns, engineers and more men were brought up, and the French began sapping operations. Palm trees were cut down and spaces cleared so that the guns could be brought into action against the walls and the houses.

The ground prepared, on the 20th the French attacked in two columns, in which the Legion naturally took part. But although two breaches had been made in the main surrounding wall the attackers were unable to get through in strength and so had to retire. During the night Bou Ziane led a sortie and succeeded in destroying several French guns. Meanwhile, Arabs and Kabylies poured in, and several of these reinforcement bodies were successfully attacked, this task frequently being given to the Legion.

By the 26th, all was ready and another assault on Zaatcha was mounted. There were three assaulting columns, each preceded by a detachment of engineers with powder bags to blow gaps in the walls and the houses, and followed by a small mountain gun. The legionnaires led one of these columns, all of which broke through and began to converge on the centre of Zaatcha. It was desperate fighting and the advance was slow as each house encountered was fiercely defended. The womenfolk fought alongside the men, and no quarter was given.

The methodical approach of the attackers and the liberal use of powder bags won the day, and step by painful step the centre of the oasis was reached. The guns could not be used in such limited visibility. Finally the centre was reached. Bou Ziane surrendered to the Zouaves, who killed him, after which organized resistance fell apart.

With the reduction of the Zaatcha group of oases, French occupation and influence was complete in that area. From this long, trying period of hardship, skirmishing and sickness, the Legion had come out well. The two Legion battalions of the 2nd Regiment had been present throughout this siege, and although numbers had been sadly reduced during the course of it they took a full share of the fighting.

In both east and west Algeria the next three years were spent in consolidating the gains made and confirming the occupation in the northern part of the country. There were a number of small punitive and tax-collecting expeditions, in which detachments of the Legion took part, and this was really their main activity. Greater Kabylia still remained inviolate, but for the time being the French left it alone.

In 1851, a number of Kabylie tribes rose and attacked the French, causing an expedition to be mounted against them. The *compagnies d'élite* of the 2nd Regiment were again formed into a *bataillon de marche*, and with another battalion of that Legion regiment, went into action against them. The legionnaires took part in several skirmishes in these operations, but particularly distinguished themselves in May of that year by clearing defiles held by the Kabylies on two separate occasions. Slowly the rebels were pressed backwards by MacMahon, who was in charge of these operations, and by the end of the summer they had been scattered and many of them driven over the border into Tunisia.

The next year, two battalions of the 1st Regiment took the field in western Algeria to punish an unruly tribe, known as the Beni Snassen, near the border of Morocco. In 1853, another fairly large expedition, in which the Legion was included, was mounted and which penetrated the fringes of Greater Kabylia, but it had little success.

In April and May of that year, a detachment of some 200 legionnaires, mounted on camels, took part in operations in the direction of Ouargla, in the northern Sahara. By this time the French were the acknowledged masters of the whole of the northern part of Algeria, except the massifs of Greater Kabylia. The story of this conquest is the story of the Legion.

Algeria proved to be a school for French generals, most of whom either served with, commanded or had detachments of the Legion under them at one time or another. All were familiar with it and its capabilities. Such future generals included Plessier, Canrobert, St. Arnaud and MacMahon. The Legion itself, battle-tried and confident, was happily consolidating. The 2nd Regiment was established at Setif, and generally speaking it had less time to devote to constructional work than its sister regiment at Sidi Bel Abbes, as it was more frequently used on operations and in the pacifying columns that constantly threaded their way through the maze of mountains on the fringe of the Sahara, as well as containing Greater Kabylia.

In 1848, Algeria legally became part of metropolitan France, and the area then effectively occupied was divided up into the three departments of Oran, Algiers and Constantine. New colonists were recruited, many from the unemployed of France, and with others, shipped over to Algeria, causing a class of *Colons* to develop whose interests were closely bound up with the country.

On the outbreak of the Crimean Campaign the French garrison in Algeria was reduced, as large numbers of experienced soldiers went off to fight the Russians. Three battalions went from each of the two Legion regiments (each of which then had four), leaving one each behind in Algeria, one at Sidi Bel Abbes and the other at Setif. The Arabs and Berbers took advantage of this fact and there were several revolts and insurrections.

It will perhaps be convenient at this stage to begin referring to Arabs, Berbers and Kabylies collectively as Arabs or Muslims, as the distinction between them no longer has any importance in this story.

Both Legion battalions took part in operations against the rebels. There was an expedition in 1854, in which the battalion of the 2nd Regiment took part, but it only had moderate success. The main stronghold of Greater Kabylia was still not penetrated. The next year, 1855, was quieter altogether, although both Legion battalions were constantly out on column.

However, in 1856, the Arabs in the Kabylia area rose and caused trouble, so as soon as the troops began to return from the Crimea it was decided to send a large expedition against them. The Arabs in the Kabylia area were not in a constant state of revolt, but had a fierce, warlike, excitable nature, which was easily roused, and marabouts had little difficulty in persuading them periodically to rise and attack either the French or rival tribes. Since 1838 there had been fourteen separate French expeditions against the Kabylia massifs, and none had been really successful, as only the fringes had yet been penetrated.

During this year, a force of some 15,000 was assembled, which included two of the battalions of the 2nd Regiment which had just returned from the Crimea. This was not really successful as only a small portion of the rebel area was penetrated.

After the Crimean Campaign, organization changes awaited the Legion. In 1855 a special Swiss Legion had been formed by Napoleon III, who had a high opinion of Swiss soldiers, and incidentally wanted to give a command to a personal friend of his. As numbers of Swiss were enlisting in the Legion he considered that it should be possible to form a separate brigade of them, which he proposed should consist of two regiments, each to be of two battalions. The nucleus was organized near Lyons in France, but the original scheme was clearly too ambitious. Recruiting was not up to expectations, so all the Swiss volunteers had to be formed into one regiment.

The Swiss Regiment was primarily intended to fight the Russians, but the war was over before it was ready for action. After some hesitation it was then decided to send it to Algeria, and in July 1856, it disembarked at Philippeville. By the end of the summer of that year the whole of the *Brigade Etrangère* had returned from the Crimea, and was concentrated at Sidi Bel Abbes, under Colonel Chabrière. All the elements of this brigade were lumped together and re-designated the *2me Régiment Etrangère*.

The Swiss Regiment, at Philippeville, became known as the *1e Régiment Etrangère*. The reason why the Swiss Regiment took precedence over the old legionnaires was that its colonel, Ochenbein, was senior to Colonel Chabrière, and therefore demanded the right of having his regiment given the premier designation, and being a friend of Napoleon III as well, he got it.

In the spring of 1857 the French planned to put the finishing stroke to the Kabylia massifs, before devoting their energies to developing the country, so they assembled a force of some 35,000 men for this purpose. This was split into four divisions, the object being that they would converge upon Greater Kabylia from four different directions.

The 1st Regiment, the Swiss, was part of one of the divisions which moved southwards, but was not heavily engaged.

Two battalions of the 2nd Regiment, the veteran legionnaires, were included in a column which advanced from the west. This division, with the Legion acting as the advance guard for most of the way, forced itself into the foothills, but became stuck in front of a large ridge, on which was perched a village called Ischeriden.

The advance on to this enemy position began on June 24th, and was countered by stiff guerrilla opposition. The French reached the valley which lay before the ridge of Ischeriden, where they paused to look up at the defensive positions above them. An open stretch of country had to be crossed before the ridge, a sharp, craggy one, could be scaled.

French artillery opened up on the position, under the cover of which two French Line regiments formed up and moved into the assault, but they were repulsed and had to fall back again. General MacMahon, who was in command of this column, looking through his field glasses, discovered an enemy encampment on the ridge a little higher up than the main position. He pointed it out to the legionnaires, ordered them to take it, and then assault downwards from it on to the defenders.

Advancing in the face of heavy grapeshot (the Arabs had several old-fashioned artillery pieces) in open formation, the legionnaires moved steadily forward, slowly and coolly, until they reached the edge of the escarpment, up which they proceeded to scramble. Without firing a shot they reached the top and took the encampment with the bayonet.

Within minutes they reformed and, still without firing, charged downhill with bayonets fixed on to the main enemy position. Within half an hour of when they started off the legionnaires were in complete possession of the whole ridge, and the defenders had either been killed, captured or fled.

The Legion casualties were 1 officer and 8 men killed, and 3 officers and 87 men wounded.

The Arabs said afterwards that it was the *grandes capotes*, the 'great cloaks', meaning the blue greatcoats worn by the legionnaires, that they feared, which moved relentlessly forward in spite of fire being directed on to them. For a long time after this the legionnaires were known as the *grandes capotes* by the Arabs. They were considered to be slightly mad to wear such garments in the heat of the day on active service, but they did so for the simple reason that in spite of the discomfort it was the best and easiest way to carry them.

The Battle of Ischeriden, a splendid example of discipline under fire, was watched by a number of senior French officers who were deeply impressed by what they saw. Ischeriden was the key to that part of Kabylia and when it fell the hard core of resistance crumbled; but for the next three or four weeks there were skirmishes, after which the fighting died down as the columns converged on the centre of the massifs. At last the French penetrated and quietened this sector.

After the clearing of Kabylia, the 1st Regiment, the Swiss, moved to the Setif area, where for the remainder of the year it was mainly employed on road construction between Setif, Bougie and Bone. It did, however, form part of a small punitive expedition against some tribes which had murdered a French officer, and scattering them, pursued the offenders over the border into Tunisia. It also took part in some minor tax-collecting expeditions.

The units of the 2nd Regiment returned to their depot at the end of July, where they were formally thanked by MacMahon, who inspected them at Sidi Bel Abbes. At the same time news was received that the regiment had been granted a new Colour as a reward for its fighting at Ischeriden. When it arrived the following battle honours were inscribed on it:

'Constantine 1837', 'Mostaganem 1839', 'Mouzaia 1840', Coleah 1841', 'Djidjelli 1842', 'Zaatcha 1849', 'Alma 1854' and 'Sebastopol 1855'.

The scene of its latest exploits, Ischeriden, was not included, as presumably it had not yet been approved as an official battle honour.

The years 1858 and 1859 were quiet as far as Arab revolts were concerned, and were years of static, perhaps confused, thinking on the part of the French authorities in Algeria. Napoleon III did not favour colonizing as such and rather considered Algeria to be an Arab kingdom, or a number of Arab kingdoms—he wished to be an emperor in fact. This attitude caused the out-and-out colonizers to pause, with the result that matters tended to drift aimlessly as there was no firm guiding policy in existence.

After taking part in the Italian Campaign of 1859, the Legion returned to Algeria, the 2nd Regiment, under Colonel Martinez, to Sidi Bel Abbes, and the 1st Regiment to Philippeville. It is true that two companies of the Legion went to Paris in 1860, to take part in the Grand Army Review, but generally the signs were that the Legion was being pushed into the background again. The Emperor's pet scheme for forming a special Swiss Legion had failed and his resultant lack of interest soon began to be reflected in the Legion itself.

At the end of 1861, the 1st Regiment, the Swiss, was disbanded and its remaining personnel sent to Sidi Bel Abbes, where they were posted to the 2nd Regiment, which was at once named the 'Foreign Regiment', the *Régiment Etrangère*. It came under the command of Colonel Butet, who had been commanding the now defunct 2nd Regiment since

October 1859, when he had taken over from Martinez. Colonel Martinez had briefly commanded the 1st Regiment, and then retired from the French service. What happened to him is not known.

Then began a period in the doldrums for the Legion, which, apart from the Mexican venture, lasted until about 1875, when it was renamed the 'Foreign Legion', the *Légion Etrangère*. During a period of some ten years the Legion had 10 commanding officers, and in fact did not get a fair chance to consolidate and progress until 1871, when Colonel de Mallaret began what became a ten-year tenure of duty.

Of the several commanding officers who were appointed, of whom some stayed only for months, some were distinguished soldiers and leaders, but some were less than mediocre. Many were place-seekers, hungry for promotion, and regarding the Legion as a useful stepping-stone, treated it as such. Political influence was frequently at work behind the scenes and used by some to gain advancement. The Legion tended to fade into the background and become something of a pawn when the serious fighting in Algeria was over.

During 1862 the Legion was mainly in barracks at Sidi Bel Abbes, although during this year two battalions went south to take part in an operation against the tribes in the southern part of Oran province. There were a few other skirmishes in which the Legion was involved, but generally matters remained fairly quiet in Algeria.

The Legion left Algeria in 1863 to take part in the Mexican fighting and did not return until 1867, during which year it took part in a few small operations in the southern part of Oran province against dissident tribesmen.

For the next three years there were no large-scale actions and for the Legion remained the monotony of hard marching and plenty of work. Such little action as the legionnaires saw was confined to the south-west sector of Oran province, adjacent to the Moroccan border.

The bulk of the Legion was at Sidi Bel Abbes, but one battalion was sent to Saida, where it moved into existing barracks.

The northern part of Algeria had been pacified to a large extent, and the first and most difficult stage of the French conquest was over, in which the Legion had played a big part.

3

Nineteenth-Century Wars in Europe

Although principally engaged in the fighting in North Africa since its re-constitution, the Legion left Algeria to take part in campaigns in the Crimea, Italy and France.

THE CRIMEAN CAMPAIGN

In March 1854, both France and Britain declared war on Russia, and the hostilities known as the Crimean Campaign began. Marshal St. Arnaud, the ex-Legion officer, was nominated to command the French expeditionary force. As the first task given to the French and British contingents was to relieve besieged Silistria in Rumania, they disembarked at the small port of Varna in Bulgaria. Later the Russians withdrew from the Danubian Principalities, and it was decided to carry the war into the Crimean Peninsula, in southern Russia.

In the first instance St. Arnaud refused to have the Legion in his expeditionary force, although as far as is known he had a high regard for it. The reason is not clear, but he later relented and orders were sent to the Legion to prepare to take part in its first fight in Europe under the French flag.

Each of the two Legion regiments in Algeria, the 1st, at Sidi Bel Abbes, and the 2nd, at Setif, was ordered to produce three battalions, which they did. These units left Algeria separately in June, and joined up at Gallipoli, where they briefly went ashore. These units were merged together into a formation, which was known as the 'Foreign Brigade', the *Brigade Etrangère*.

The *Brigade Etrangère* moved on and as soon as it landed at Varna it walked right into an epidemic of cholera which swept violently through the Legion ranks. Before many weeks had passed the commanding officers of both the 1st and the 2nd Regiments, and nearly 200 legionnaires had died.

When the Allied decision was made to cross from Bulgaria to the Crimea, a Legion *bataillon de marche* was formed of the *compagnies d'élite* of both regiments, and this became part of Canrobert's division, which was probably one of the best in the French contingent. Canrobert had briefly commanded the 2nd Legion Regiment in 1849. At this stage, it was proposed to employ only this one composite battalion of the Legion in action, and the remainder of it was to be used on ordinary line-of-communication duties.

The Allies landed unopposed in Crimea at a small bay near the village of Eupatoria, which was about thirty miles north of Sebastopol, on September 14th, 1854, and the march southwards began, the French being on the right and the British on the left. The French had their right flank resting on the sea, covered by the guns of the Allied ships.

Half-way to Sebastopol was a huge, natural obstacle where the Russians decided to halt the Allied advance. This was a high, rugged escarpment, some miles in breadth, on the south side of the Alma River. It was on these heights, the 'Heights of Alma', that the Russian commander waited with a force of about 40,000 men, well supported by artillery. The position seemed to be almost impregnable.

When the Allies reached the Alma River and realized that the escarpment was held by the enemy, they decided to attack it frontally, instead of outflanking it. This attack began on September 20th, and the French, who were still on the right, were soon heavily engaged as their troops scrambled up the steep tracks and slopes under fire. In the centre of Canrobert's division was the Legion *bataillon de marche*, well to the fore. The initial struggle was fierce and the casualties became heavy as the battalion moved up in the face of the Russian guns. The legionnaires were amongst the first to reach the top of the escarpment and drive the gunners from their positions. A confused struggle on the edge of the ridge ensued and the French were not firmly ensconced there until later in the day, when their artillery was hauled up to support them.

The behaviour of the legionnaires at the battle for the Heights of Alma had impressed Canrobert, as they had been exceptionally well disciplined when under fire. In this fight the Legion unit lost 5 officers and 55 legionnaires killed and wounded.

During the course of the next three weeks the Allied forces moved by a circular route into the area south of Sebastopol. The next battle, the Battle of Inkerman, in late October, was mainly a British action and the French were only relatively lightly engaged, but the leading companies of the Legion battalion were temporarily submerged by the grey mass of Russian infantry. The legionnaires rallied, recovered and successfully counter-attacked the enemy. The battle lasted for ten hours and was fought in mist and drizzle which severely limited visibility.

The Russians withdrew again into Sebastopol, and as winter was approaching, plans were made for a set-piece siege of the Russian naval base. General Canrobert now employed the whole of the *Brigade Etrangère*, and the two regiments, one under Colonel Vienot and the other under Colonel Caprel, played a full part in operations from November onwards, sharing all the hardships of trench warfare. The *Brigade Etrangère* was put into positions to the south-west of the city, where it remained throughout the siege.

During the long winter months there were numerous small raids and counter-raids, either for reconnaissance purposes, to destroy works constructed or dug, or by way of reprisals. One of the most noteworthy took place when the Russians made a strong sortie against the trenches held by the Legion, near an entrenched position known as the 'Quarantine'. The legionnaires resisted well and drove the attackers off. There were several other assaults on their positions, but on each occasion the Legion held on firmly, and in the meantime steadily sapped its way forward towards the enemy.

At the end of April 1855, the Allies took the initiative and began a series of sorties against the Russian trenches which had been constructed as outer defences surrounding the city itself on the southern sides. These culminated in a large attack, which took place on the night of May 1st/2nd, in which the *Brigade Etrangère* was fully engaged. In leading his regiment against the Russians Colonel Vienot was killed. He was the second Legion colonel to fall in battle at the head of his men: Colonel Conrad had been the first.

In this assault a certain amount of ground and some trenches were taken, but at a heavy cost. In spite of Russian counter-attacks the French held on to most, but not all, of their gains. In this assault the Legion lost, apart from Colonel Vienot, 18 officers and over 40 legionnaires killed and wounded.

After this there was a quiet spell for about three weeks while another assault was being prepared. This took place on June 7th, and again the *Brigade Etrangère* as a whole was involved. On this occasion the legionnaires were directed against some Russian defensive works, known as the 'White Works', which they finally succeeded in overrunning after some hard fighting. During the following three months the Allies concentrated upon sapping closer, and the legionnaires came within twenty-five yards of the enemy defences at one point.

The final attack on Sebastopol began on the night of September 8th, 1855. The main French objectives were in their 'right' sector, that is to the south-east of the city. The *Brigade Etrangère* was in the 'left sector', to the south-west of the city, still facing the Quarantine position, which the legionnaires were ordered to contain and compress.

However, in the 'right' sector a detachment of Legion volunteers about 100 strong, carrying scaling ladders, preceded the several French assaulting columns. The ladders were essential to bridge the network of trenches which by this time criss-crossed the whole area. This main attack was only partially successful, as it ran into a Russian counter-attack, which in its turn was also only partly successful. However, the huge weight of the British and French forces together did much to disorganize the defences of the city, and during this night the Russians burnt their fleet and much else besides, before evacuating Sebastopol.

On the morning of the 9th, Allied patrols found the trenches opposite them deserted. On the 10th, the *Brigade Etrangère* entered Sebastopol, where General Bazaine, formerly a sergeant in the Old Legion, was nominated to be the commander.

In the course of the actual siege, the Legion lost through enemy action 72 officers and 1,625 legionnaires killed and wounded. The casualties caused by exposure and sickness had also been heavy. A steady stream of reinforcements for the two Legion regiments arrived from Algeria throughout the campaign.

The winter siege of Sebastopol was an epic of human endurance and fortitude, and the legionnaires suffered in common with all the other besiegers from low temperature, snow, ice, wind and exposure. Particularly was there a lack of fuel, winter clothing and blankets. The ingenuity of the legionnaires was unbounded and showed itself in many ways. As fuel was scarce they constructed ovens, stoves and other economical heating devices which they fitted into their trenches and the underground shelters they built to live in. Each legionnaire carried a *tent d'abri*, a waterproof portion of the section tent, which was put to many uses in an effort to make his existence more bearable.

In Southern Oran Province. The Legion patrol leader checks the route

An aerial view of the famous Legion Depot at Sidi Bel Abbes

The *Brigade Etrangère* did not remain long in Sebastopol and almost at once took part in clearing operations in the surrounding country-side. The Legion column became known as the 'Cabbage Column', owing to the abundance of that vegetable in one of the valleys it cleared, and also, presumably, because of the quantity of cabbages it requisi-tioned. After a long period of static trench warfare, with cramped, miserable conditions, the good food and exercise sent the spirits of the men, already high, rocketing skywards.

After taking part in a number of similar operations, the *Brigade Etrangère* was brought in again and took up winter quarters in the city. There was a grand review of French troops for the benefit of the defeated Russian generals, in which both regiments of the Legion took part.

France was in a genial and benevolent mood and as a measure of reward decreed that all foreigners who had fought for France in the Crimean Campaign who wished to become naturalized Frenchmen were to be given that privilege, and also they were to be allowed to serve in French regiments if they chose to do so. A number of legion-naires took advantage of the first part of this offer, that is to become French, probably having little prospect of ever going back to their own country again, and thus otherwise remaining stateless, but practically all remained in the Legion: few elected to be transferred to another regiment.

One notable character who elected to become French was the old Spanish fighter, Martinez, now a major. He remained with the Legion. He had, incidentally, been a notorious guerrilla in Spain before coming to the Legion, having achieved some fame under his true name of Mina.

After two years' absence, the *Brigade Etrangère*, which was the bulk of the Legion, returned home to Algeria, and shortly afterwards its legionnaires were issued with the Crimean Service Medal, with the clasps 'Alma', 'Inkerman' and 'Sebastopol'.

THE ITALIAN CAMPAIGN

In April 1859, Austria declared war on King Victor Emmanuel II of Sardinia, and France came to his aid. As soon as France decided to intervene, there was no question, as there had been previously, of any reluctance to include the Foreign Legion in the expeditionary force.

Orders were sent to both Legion regiments in Algeria to proceed to Italy and join up with the French contingent.

The 1st Regiment (the Swiss Regiment) was very low in numbers by this time, being less than 600 all told, so it was decided to send it to Corsica to recruit *en route* to Italy. This was a departure from its principle that only Swiss nationals be accepted, which so far had been rigidly adhered to since its formation as the Swiss Legion. Now it hoped to swell its ranks with Corsicans, but after remaining in Corsica for almost a month it had to leave the island, having had little or no success in this field at all. It disembarked at Genoa on May 11th, 1859.

The 2nd Regiment was much stronger, consisting of over 1,500 all ranks, many of whom were veterans of both the Crimean and Algerian campaigns. It proceeded direct to Genoa, where both Legion regiments were put under the command of General Espinasse, who had formerly served as a Legion officer, and became part of the 2nd Division, which was part of MacMahon's 2nd Corps.

Towards the end of May, the French 2nd Corps made a wide flanking movement over the River Po in an effort to trap the Austrians and on June 2nd they neared the enemy. The next day, a large detachment of legionnaires was sent to make a reconnaissance of an important road-rail bridge at San Martino, over the River Ticino, which flows into the River Po. This was a key bridge, being only three miles to the west of Magenta. They found the bridge to have been partly demolished by the withdrawing Austrians, but they scooped up seven artillery pieces that had been abandoned, and captured a corporal's guard which had been completely forgotten by the enemy.

Owing to the state of this bridge it was decided that the 2nd Corps would cross the River Ticino farther to the north over another existing, but smaller, one. That night, the corps encamped at a village called Turbigo, which was about eleven miles to the north-west of Magenta, and on the same side of the river—that is the east side. The French planned to attack Magenta from three sides—the north, the west and the south. The main blow was to come from the north, and was to be delivered by MacMahon's corps.

Magenta was a small but prosperous market town set in a rich agricultural district. It was strategically well sited, as it blocked the principal road into Milan, the capital of Lombardy, which was sixteen miles to the east. Magenta had a big railway station and numerous large stone buildings of different sorts. Everywhere there was a profusion of trees, both in and around the town, which severely restricted visibility.

Early on the morning of June 4th, the 2nd Corps moved off south-eastwards from Turbigo towards Magenta. The two Legion regiments were on the left wing of this advance, which was on a broad front. On the extreme left was the 2nd Regiment, the old legionnaires, under Colonel Chabrière, and on its right was the much smaller 1st Regiment, under Colonel Brayer.

The advance was at first fairly rapid and unopposed, but it slowed down as Magenta was approached, chiefly because the French troops bumped into numerous Austrian outposts which had to be dealt with. The terrain over which the legionnaires moved was highly cultivated in many parts and there were frequent smallholdings, farm-houses and vineyards. 'Bushy-topped' trees abounded everywhere. It was close country in which cavalry and artillery were of little use. It was an infantryman's terrain, and Magenta was an infantryman's battle: the Legion was infantry.

In the Legion sector all went fairly well until a strong Austrian out-post was encountered at a village, called Marcollo, which was about two miles north of Magenta. The Legion, already dispersed, was halted by the enemy fire and wavered a little: there was momentary confusion. The legionnaires of the 2nd Regiment were quickly rallied by Colonel Chabrière, who led them into the attack. The 1st Regiment had already made contact with the Austrian outposts and was engaged in skirmish-ing to the west of this village.

As the legionnaires rushed in to assault Marcollo, Colonel Chabrière, who was leading, was shot dead by a musket ball. He was the third Legion colonel to fall at the head of his men in battle. Fierce hand-to-hand fighting developed and a series of company battles were fought in which the Austrians were slowly pressed backwards to be eventually ejected from the village.

At this point, on the death of Colonel Chabrière, Major Martinez, the old Spanish guerrilla fighter, came to the fore as the dominant personality of the 2nd Regiment. He rallied the legionnaires, breathed fire into them and drove them southwards along the road to Magenta. For the two miles into Magenta it was a running fight through difficult country, as not only were there numerous clumps of trees and ample other natural cover, but there were also many farm-houses and buildings which had to be taken one by one, usually at the point of the bayonet.

Magenta itself was firmly held by the Austrians, but the legionnaires forced their way to the outskirts until their advance was blocked by the enemy at the railway station. They were unable to cross the railway lines and were held up for a while. Artillery fire was tried, but it was of little use to them. Later, as soon as supporting small-arms fire was given from a flank, the legionnaires were able to dash over the vulnerable railway lines to enter the town proper.

Street fighting and the clearing of buildings began. At one stage the Colour of the 2nd Regiment, which was carried into battle, was in danger and was only saved by the legionnaires rallying to it. In this confused fighting on the edge of the town, General Espinasse, the old Legion officer, was killed.

The actual struggle for Magenta was over in about two hours, and by about 9 p.m. in the evening, just as darkness was falling, the last buildings on the southern side were being cleared. The 2nd Corps, which had made the thrust from the north, had practically finished the task before the other two columns had made contact with it. By nightfall all the Austrian defenders were streaming eastwards in retreat.

The legionnaires had taken perhaps the most vital and prominent part in the battle for Magenta, and their casualties had been fairly heavy. Apart from General Espinasse and Colonel Chabrière, the 2nd Regiment suffered over 200 killed and wounded, whilst the 1st Regiment, out of less than 600, lost 5 officers killed and 6 wounded, and over 40 men killed and wounded.

When Magenta fell, the road to Milan was open and the Austrians withdrew without attempting to defend either the road or Milan. Milan was entered by the French 2nd Corps, which had borne the brunt of the fighting, on June 5th.

Martinez was appointed to command the 2nd Regiment and was promoted colonel. The 1st Regiment, the Swiss, which had been reduced to less than 400 effectives, was detached from the corps and left behind in Milan to recruit.

Meanwhile the French army, still with the 2nd Corps in the lead, continued to press the withdrawing Austrian army, which moved eastwards. For over a fortnight there was little contact of note between the opposing forces, during which time rain poured down almost incessantly. Each night, after marching all day through the rain, the legionnaires had to camp in waterlogged fields. Sometimes houses or buildings were available, but more often than not the legionnaires had to sleep on the wet ground.

The French–Sardinian armies marched eastwards in the wake of the Austrians towards the district of Verona and Lake Garda. Contact was made between the two opposing forces on June 22nd, but the Austrians continued to manœuvre rather aimlessly. Whilst acting as the advanced guard to the 2nd Corps, in the early hours of the morning of June 24th, the legionnaires crashed head-on into the Austrian army near a small town called Solferino. It was a chance meeting and both sides were surprised.

Although astonished, and withered by small-arms fire—the Austrians recovered themselves more quickly—the legionnaires stood fast where they were, and thus enabled the remainder of the French force to come up to them. The other French corps took up positions in a line level with the Legion, and then each moved forward to attack independently and take the strategical heights that surround Solferino, and strike at the Austrians in front of them. The fighting was fierce and several heights changed hands several times.

The legionnaires remained in the centre, opposite Solferino, which was situated between two heights and consisted literally of one main street. Slowly the French flanking corps closed in, and as they did so attention was centred on the town itself, which was doggedly defended. The 2nd Regiment fought a stiff action to take a small hill, and then it moved forward step by step until it was halted by a strong enemy position in a cemetery, which was surrounded by stone walls.

The fighting generally died down, and by noon had reached something of a stalemate, as all the available French troops were in action: no reserve was left with which to influence the battle. It was not until Napoleon himself came on to the battlefield about that time, bringing reinforcements with him, that the battle turned in favour of the French.

The fighting lingered on for some hours longer and it was not until late afternoon that Solferino was cleared. This was done as soon as the Legion was able to take the enemy-held cemetery, which had been one of the main positions controlling the defence. By evening the Austrian army was again retreating eastwards, but at some cost to the victors. The 2nd Regiment lost 6 killed and 40 wounded.

It was in this battle that a military observation balloon was used for the first time in history by the French. The legionnaires gazed at it in wonder, whenever they had the time to spare.

After Solferino Napoleon III decided to make peace. The short, gloriously successful war, which had only lasted two months, was over, and the Legion had played a prominent part throughout.

From the previously obscure town of Solferino arose the famous movement known as the International Red Cross. The battle for Solferino had certainly been a hard-fought one and towards the end of the day tempers and feelings on both sides had been bitterly aroused. The victors let their feelings run away with them in their savage moment of victory. Not only were wounded enemies callously neglected and left to die, but in some instances they were sought out and killed: mainly by partisans, it is true. Some prisoners and refugees were also subjected to ill-treatment and a few were shot out of hand. Officers seemed to be largely indifferent, the lingering tradition of the ancient military custom that any city taken by storm was sacked and the inhabitants put to the sword, probably vaguely influencing their thoughts. Perhaps the conduct of the victors, or indeed the vanquished, at Solferino was no better or no worse than that of the victors or vanquished in any of a score of hard-fought battles whose names stud the history books.

However, on to the battlefield at Solferino there wandered a Swiss businessman named Henri Dunant, a civilian, who was profoundly shocked by the scenes that met his eyes, especially the treatment of the wounded and the prisoners. He later recorded what he had seen in a book, which succeeded in doing something to awaken the consciences of the European public to the existing barbarities of warfare. So began the Red Cross movement.

Early in August, the 2nd Regiment went to Paris, where it took part in a grand victory parade, and it is noted that for this splendid occasion the legionnaires were all issued with brand new uniforms.

Over thirty-five decorations were awarded to officers and legionnaires for bravery in this campaign, which indicated that formal recognition, as well as lip-service, had come their way. Previously decorations, had been scarce in the Legion. Now, no longer ignored and unwanted, the Legion began to bask in a brief hour of glory. The Legion list of battle honours was increasing, and now to the names of obscure, unknown places in Algeria, where the legionnaires had fought hard fights, were added names of better-known battles, such as Magenta and Solferino.

THE FRANCO–GERMAN WAR 1870–71

On July 19th, 1870, Napoleon III declared war on Germany, and as there were at the time in Paris, and France generally, numbers of foreigners sympathetic to the French cause who wished to fight for her against the Germans, the Empress Eugénie, to enable them to do so, on August 22nd issued a decree ordering the formation of a '5th Battalion' of the French Foreign Legion in which they could serve for the duration. The Emperor was already in the field with his troops.

This new battalion was commanded by Major Aragao, and was raised in Paris. In the first instance it had nothing to do with the Legion in Algeria, nor were Legion instructors called to train it or to form a cadre for it.

The new 5th Battalion was moved into action quickly, being posted to the newly forming Army of the Loire and was soon engaged in the fighting near Orleans. It distinguished itself particularly in the defence of a village called Bel-Air-Les-Aides, but its lack of training was evident. Although casualties were inflicted on the Germans, the village had to be abandoned.

The fighting then moved to the outskirts of a small town named Bannier, and on October 10th, the 5th Battalion was detailed to hold it. The men resisted the attackers, but gradually the town became sur-rounded by the Germans, and by nightfall the unit was completely encircled and trapped. The commanding officer and 5 other officers had been killed, and there were over 100 casualties amongst the men during the day's fighting. A badly battered Legion battalion was locked up in Bannier, so a break-out was planned during the night. This was only partially successful, although a proportion of officers and men managed to break through the encircling German lines to rejoin the French forces. The remainder were taken prisoner the next day.

In spite of decimated numbers, the 5th Battalion remained in being, reforming under its *Capitaine adjutant-chef*, on October 12th. Some reinforcements arrived and a steady influx of foreigners during this war ensured its continued existence as a separate unit.

Belatedly, the Legion from Algeria was called to the scene. There had been some hesitation about employing it in France at first, but as the situation worsened every man was wanted, and on October 13th two *bataillons de marche* were dispatched from Sidi Bel Abbes to the

Army of the Loire. They then joined the 5th Battalion, which had just escaped through the German lines.

The first action fought by these two Legion *bataillons de marche* against the Germans was on November 9th, at a place called Coulmiers, about three miles from Orleans, where the legionnaires were subjected to intense artillery fire. Generally they had little success to report that day.

The French army was hopelessly outclassed, and that night under cover of darkness the Legion slowly retreated in the face of German pressure. The ensuing days consisted of spasmodic withdrawals in miserable weather, and of fruitless attempts to delay the enemy. The three Legion battalions, grouped together, turned and made a stand at a village, called Cercottes, just to the north of Orleans, on December 4th. For a short time they held the whole village and then lost part of it, but after making a fierce bayonet charge, cleared the Germans out again. This sharp action halted the enemy advance, but only temporarily.

The fighting then moved to another nearby village, named Chevilly, where again the Legion managed to hold up the Germans. In the course of these two fights, the Legion lost 210 men.

With an effort, the French brought a new 'Army of the East' into being, and because of its notable bayonet charge near Orleans and its conduct generally in the depressing retreats, the Legion was selected to serve in it. As its title suggests, the Army of the East moved eastwards to strike at the enemy, the three Legion battalions with it.

On January 14th, 1871 the Legion took part in an action near the town of Besançon, not far from the Swiss border, but this turned out to be inconclusive and the fighting died down. The Legion lost only one officer, who was taken prisoner. However, this was the last battle in this war against the Germans in which the legionnaires took part, and when it was over they remained in the area of Besançon until the end of hostilities.

After the French defeat at the hands of the Germans, civil war broke out in Paris, and the elected National Assembly frantically called in troops from all over France to help to suppress the Paris Commune. The three battalions of the Legion, the two regular *bataillons de marche* and the 5th Battalion, were amongst the troops hastily drafted into the capital.

For several weeks the Legion was engaged in street fighting. Barricades had been erected, which had to be forced one by one, as all were desperately defended. The legionnaires remained together in most of this fighting, and were first billeted in the district of Nanterre, before moving into the fighting area by way of Courbevoie and Neuilly. In turn they fought for and took the Gare du Nord, the Villette, and then the Buttes-Chaumont. The last Legion fight was on May 20th, at the last-mentioned place.

In June 1871 all three Legion units were sent to Algeria. The 5th Battalion, its strength having decreased considerably, was formally disbanded at Saida in December 1871.

4

Other Nineteenth-Century Campaigns

Not only did the Legion fight in Europe, as well as Africa, in the nineteenth century, but it also saw active service under the French flag in countries as far apart as Mexico and Indo-China.

THE MEXICAN CAMPAIGN 1863–67

When Maximilian, the new Emperor of Mexico, landed in that country in May 1864, the military position was that a French force, the only effective one, consisting of about 40,000 European troops, with perhaps up to another 13,000 native auxiliaries in support, held Mexico City and a 'corridor' from it to the sea at Vera Cruz. Opposed to this was the Mexican leader, Juarez, in the north of the country, who had up to 20,000 troops of different sorts under his control, whilst another follower of his, General Diaz, had a smaller force in the south of the country. The French-held 'corridor' was very vulnerable to guerrilla raids, and indeed the whole of Mexico, outside the few cities and towns garrisoned by French troops, was unsafe.

French troops had been actively participating in Mexican affairs since 1862, and back in Sidi Bel Abbes the Legion muttered and chafed at the bit. A war was going on in Mexico and the Legion had not been asked to take part. It seemed that in spite of its proud record and ability it was unwanted. In Algeria, things were comparatively quiet, which made things worse. At this period the Legion was without any powerful advocates who had its interest at heart, so it was overlooked.

Eventually the junior officers could stand it no longer and they collectively addressed a petition direct to the Emperor, asking that the

74

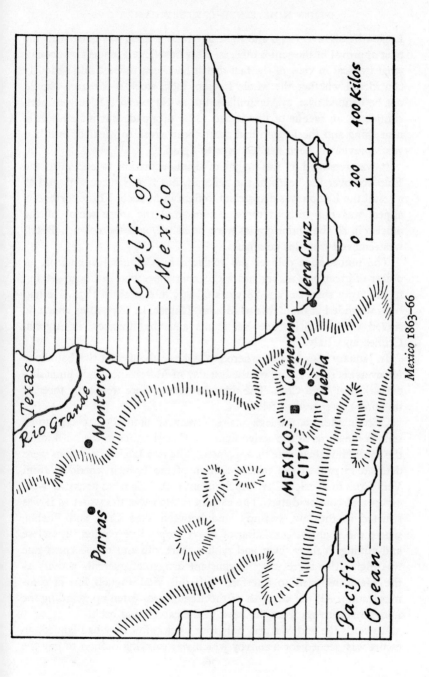

Mexico 1863–66

Legion be allowed to go and fight in Mexico. This was done with the tacit approval of the senior officers. This unsolicited request was somewhat ironical in view of the fact that it had been mooted and seriously considered whether the whole Legion, lock, stock and barrel, should not be handed over to Maximilian, but as Napoleon III had not been completely in favour of this it had to be dropped. But it had been a near thing and the Legion had nearly been given to Mexico, as it had years previously been handed over to Spain.

It was regarded as the height of insubordination to appeal to the Emperor over the heads of the generals, but it was successful, and as a result the Legion was dispatched to fight in Mexico. This unorthodox appeal was not without repercussions, and the more senior of the officers in all the junior grades were punished, and the colonel, Butet, was removed from his command.

The unfortunate colonel was replaced by Colonel Jeanningros, an officer of great personality and wide experience, who had been serving in the army since he was 18 years of age, in fact since 1834. He had been wounded at the Battle of Moulay-Ishmael in 1835, after which he served with French Line Regiments and the Zouaves, in Algeria, Crimea and Italy.

In January 1863 he was ordered to make ready his first two battalions for overseas service, and on the last day of March these two units disembarked at Vera Cruz. The third battalion (there were only three at this time), prepared to follow.

Once in Mexico, the legionnaires somewhat naturally expected to be sent to the scene of the active fighting: that is either to the north or to the south, but they were disappointed. The two Legion battalions were detailed to protect the eastern section of the French 'corridor' from Vera Cruz to Mexico City, which meant that their main activities were escort and convoy duties. The eastern section was the worst as it was situated in the low, swampy land between Vera Cruz and Puebla, where the country, consisting of heavy tropical vegetation, was close and stifling. Yellow fever and typhus were rife and the sickness rate was high. Also there was the constant danger of guerrilla activity as the Mexicans tried to interfere with this vital French line-of-communication. All the strength of the Legion was eaten up guarding the numerous convoys from the coast to the capital and back.

Towards the end of April, only four weeks after they had landed, an escort was needed for a convoy which was carrying bullion to pay the troops in the interior. It was the turn for duty of the 3rd Company of the 1st Battalion, but it had no effective officers, as all were sick. As this was an important convoy that had to get through, three other Legion officers volunteered to go with the 3rd Company, so that it could do its stint on escort duty. They were Captain Danjou, who was the battalion adjutant, Lieutenant Vilain, the pay officer, and Second Lieutenant Maudet.

Captain Danjou was a French officer who had been with the Legion for some time, and had served in it with distinction in Algeria, Crimea and Italy. In the Crimea he had been wounded, losing his left hand, and he wore a false one in its place.

The other two junior officers, both of French nationality as far as is known, had come up through the ranks of the Legion, and each had fought with distinction in several battles. Both had been commissioned as a result of their conduct at Magenta. The 3rd Company had an effective strength of 62 legionnaires, including the *sous-officiers*, and were of the now familiar mixture, being mainly Polish, Italian, German and Spanish.

Owing to the prevailing conditions of unrest in the country it was impossible to keep a secret such as this in Mexico, and the news that a French convoy carrying bullion was about to leave was quickly passed on to the local guerrillas who received the notification some time before it was due to depart, certainly in sufficient time for the local leader, Colonel Milan, to muster a large force with the intention of capturing it.

Colonel Milan was what we today might think of as a 'Territorial officer', who lived in the district and was in charge of the sector. All 'territorial' and 'guerrilla' troops in it came under his command. There were few purely regular formations in Mexico at the time, and most of the units were of a 'territorial' nature, in that they lived and operated in the same districts. They simply mustered when called upon for a particular purpose and then dispersed again to their homes when it was done.

For this task, of intercepting the bullion convoy, Colonel Milan managed to assemble a force of cavalry and infantry, totalling about 2,000. The cavalry were the best troops, having their own horses, and armed with Remington and Winchester rifles. The Mexican infantry was not of such high quality, being mainly pressed inhabitants of the nearby towns and villages: some had rifles, but many had muskets. The

77

standard of training of the infantry was much lower than that of the cavalry.

In the early hours of the morning of April 30th, the 3rd Company started off ahead of the convoy to ensure that the way was clear. A brief halt was made about 2.30 a.m. near a Legion static company position, one of several which had been established at various strategic points along the French-held 'corridor'. Seeing how small Captain Danjou's force was, the company commander offered to let him have a platoon to reinforce it. But Danjou refused and set off again.

The company moved in a formation of two 'blobs' marching side by side, occupying a width of just over two hundred yards, the men being in extended order. Danjou was in the centre, and with his little party were two mules on which were loaded the rations and ammunition. A small rear-guard section followed on some distance behind. French intelligence was not good, as although the legionnaires were always prepared to meet and cope with bands of guerrillas, they had no idea that such a large enemy force was so close at hand.

Just before 7 a.m. Danjou's company moved through the deserted hamlet of Camerone, near a stream noted for its excellent crayfish. This hamlet consisted of a 'hacienda'—that is, a farm house and out-buildings—all enclosed in a courtyard, and there were the ruins of some other hovels nearby. A mile or so through Camerone Danjou halted for breakfast. Fires were made and the water for coffee was almost boiling when the Legion sentry spotted Mexican cavalry approaching.

It was Colonel Milan and 800 horsemen: his infantry was still some distance away. The legionnaires hastily formed square and prepared to meet the charge in their best Algerian fashion. They were caught in the open, but fortunately for them it was not good cavalry country owing to the plentiful clumps of tropical vegetation and waist-high grass. The legionnaires fired volleys from their Minnie rifles, which caused the Mexicans to hesitate. Further firing made the cavalry keep its distance, but Milan, unable to charge directly, instead manœuvred his men closer and began to surround the French company.

Seeing the strength of the Mexican cavalry and realizing how vulnerable his men were against it in the semi-open country, Danjou decided that the best course would be to fight a running action back to the nearest cover, which was the deserted farm house at Camerone, over a mile away, and hold out there. His mules had broken loose in the first mêlée and galloped off with the rations and reserve ammunition, which worsened his prospects. Danjou arranged his men in a wide, square formation and began to retrace his steps. The Mexican cavalry, now dispersed in small detachments, encircled him as he moved and hung on his flanks. The legionnaires deliberately moved through the thickest of the country so as not to present an opportunity for the horsemen to charge them.

Moving painfully and slowly through the tropical undergrowth with the Mexicans pressing close on him, Danjou finally made the farm house at Camerone, having twice paused in 'square formation' to fire volleys to keep the enemy at a distance. In this run for shelter 16 legionnaires had become detached from the main body and were taken prisoner. This left Danjou with a tiny force of only 46 men, of whom a few already were wounded.

The farm house was a two-storey building, partially derelict, and the courtyard was enclosed by a wall with dilapidated lean-to sheds on the inside of it. There was a large ruined barn in one corner of the courtyard. Danjou found when he got there that some Mexicans had beaten him to it and were already in position in the upper part of the house: so his legionnaires were only in partial possession.

At once, with energy and skill, Danjou set his men out and began improving the defences by barricading the openings and reinforcing the walls in readiness to repulse an enemy attack. Then he turned his attention to the Mexicans in the house itself, but was unable to eject them as he could not get up to them. Owing to their positions in the upper storey, a large part of the courtyard occupied by the legionnaires was under their fire. Danjou still apparently did not know that three enemy infantry battalions were fast approaching to reinforce Colonel Milan's cavalry.

The Mexicans dismounted and tried several forays towards the courtyard, but on foot they were handicapped by their heavy cavalry accoutrements, boots and swords, and these were unsuccessful.

By 9 a.m. the sun began to get hot and Colonel Milan called upon the Legion company to surrender, but Captain Danjou refused firmly, and made each legionnaire promise to fight on to the end. The Mexican attacks were renewed and the rate of musketry fire increased. Some legionnaires were killed by the bullets and others wounded. About 11 a.m., Danjou was killed by a musket ball fired from the upper storey of the house.

Lieutenant Vilain took command and he continued directing the defence with determination. By this time the Mexican infantry, with a total strength of about 1,200, had arrived, and as soon as it began to take part in the action the assaults became more deadly to the defenders: but they still kept the enemy at a distance. The heat increased and the men were tormented by thirst as well as hunger. To drink each man had only the contents of his water bottle or wine flask. The number of killed and wounded increased hour by hour.

About 2 p.m., Vilain was killed and Second Lieutenant Maudet took command, seizing a rifle to fire at the enemy. Musket balls rained into the enclosure both from outside and particularly from the upper storey of the house, and the interior of the courtyard was littered with dead, dying and wounded. The Mexicans improved their positions in the house and the legionnaires were reduced to crouching under the walls and behind the barricades, to fire outwards at the succeeding waves of attackers that periodically swayed towards them. It became highly dangerous to cross the open courtyard, but many did so to help wounded comrades.

The Mexican infantry made several assaults but all were repulsed. Another call to surrender was made, but was answered by a rude word. In the afternoon, after another assault had failed, the Mexicans brought up straw and put it near the courtyard walls and set fire to it. Stifling smoke was added to the legionnaires' discomforts. Fortunately, the Mexican infantry was ill-trained and its attacks, once launched, were spasmodic and uncontrollable.

By 5 p.m. Maudet had only 12 men left with him capable of standing on their feet, but in spite of this he rejected another call to surrender. After a brief lull, the infantry massed and moved forward again into the attack. The steady firing of the legionnaires kept the enemy back, but the Mexicans slowly closed in, gaining complete possession of the house and one of the other outbuildings.

These extra disadvantages made the position of the defenders even more difficult, and by 6 p.m. Maudet was left with only himself and 5 other men still able to fight on. When he saw that all was hopeless and such heavy odds were against him, he gave the order to his remaining legionnaires to load and fire. Next, he gave the order to fix bayonets and then, tearing aside one of the barricades, he gave the order to charge. Maudet led his men right into the mass of Mexican infantry and they were absorbed by it. The 6 men were swamped by sheer

Guarding the southern approaches against F.L.N. infiltration

A Legion patrol halts for refreshment

A sudden patrol encounter

weight of numbers. Colonel Milan himself galloped up and just in time prevented his men from killing the surviving legionnaires.

Of the 3 survivors—the other 3 died of wounds—one was Corporal Maine, a future captain in the Legion, who was commissioned on his return from captivity. Another was Corporal Berg, likewise commissioned on his release, while the third was a Polish legionnaire.

The defence of the farm house at Camerone by a small company of the Legion against 2,000 Mexicans was over, but the object had been achieved and the bullion convoy was saved. Hearing the sounds of firing in the distance it had turned back and waited.

The next day, May 1st, Colonel Jeanningros, with a strong detachment of the Legion, arrived at the scene of the Battle of Camerone. Under a pile of dead one living legionnaire was discovered: he had eight wounds and had been left for dead by the Mexicans who had taken off all the other wounded prisoners. This legionnaire was the first to relate the epic of Camerone. Now on every April 30th, Camerone Day, an account of this battle is read aloud to all legionnaires on parade wherever they may be.

Amid the debris in the courtyard Colonel Jeanningros picked up the artificial hand of Captain Danjou. Today it rests in the Hall of Honour at Sidi Bel Abbes, and is ceremoniously taken out annually on parade in front of the 1st Regiment.

At least 300 Mexicans—the exact number is not known—were killed by the Legion in this action, and at least as many more wounded.

The Legion losses can be summarized as follows. Although only 3 legionnaires were standing on their feet at the end of the day's fighting, there were in all 32 survivors of this battle. Sixteen had been taken prisoner in the initial move to the farm house, and another 16 were taken away as prisoners by the Mexicans after the fight, all of whom were wounded, but all recovered. In addition, a further 7 wounded were taken prisoner but they all died in captivity, and this latter number includes Second Lieutenant Maudet who, being an officer, was taken on mule back, together with a sergeant, not identified by name, to a Spanish lady's private hospital, about fifty miles away, where they both died. The sergeant, believed to have been Polish, was one who had been active in the attempts to oust the enemy from the upper storey of the house.

In addition to all the officers, 23 legionnaires were killed. The prisoners were exchanged on a one-for-one basis about a month after the battle, and all were treated reasonably well.

Corporal Berg, one of the last three left standing, and commissioned on his return, had formerly been commissioned in the French army, and as a subaltern had fought in Algeria, and also in Syria, but was cashiered. He then joined the Legion as an ordinary soldier and rose to the rank of corporal, which he held at the time of Camerone. He did not survive long and was killed a couple of years afterwards in a duel with a fellow subaltern. One report suggests that he fought his fellow survivor, Maine, but this is not certain.

From captivity Corporal Berg managed to smuggle a letter out to his Colonel, telling him of the battle and what had happened at Camerone. He ended with the words, 'The 3rd Company is no more, but I must tell you that it contained nothing but good soldiers.'

Of all the scores of battles fought by the Legion, this one is the most highly regarded, and has been selected to be celebrated annually with all the pomp and ceremony that the Legion can give. Camerone Day, on April 30th, is the most important day of the Legion year. When I asked a Legion officer why it was that a defeat had been singled out in this way instead of a victory, he replied that in the Legion it is always the spirit that counts and is remembered, and not so much the deed. To this day the 1st Regiment of the Legion retains the Mexican eagle on its badge.

For the remainder of their occupation of Mexico, all French troops were ordered to halt when passing the farm house at Camerone and to 'present arms'. Today a railway line runs through the courtyard where so many legionnaires fought to the end, and although the buildings, in ruins then, are no longer standing, the outlines can still be traced, and part of the original wall remains in one spot. A memorial to the defence and the fallen defenders was erected by the French on this spot. Each year on Camerone Day a ceremony takes place there attended by French residents in Mexico and Mexican officers.

The epic of Camerone made a deep impression on the French army in Mexico, but in spite of this the Legion remained on escort duty in the most unhealthy part of the country. The yellow fever took a steady toll, and by the beginning of February 1864 the effective strength of the Legion had sunk to 11 officers and 800 men, out of the original figure of over 2,000. Later that month the 3rd Battalion, about 1,000 strong, arrived from Sidi Bel Abbes.

At last Colonel Jeanningros obtained permission both to move his men to a more healthy spot and to take part in active operations against the Mexicans in the field. He at once reorganized his regiment into four small battalions, and in addition formed for scouting purposes a mounted company of legionnaires who could ride. This 'four battalion' organization was unofficial and these units were known by the names of their commanding officers, as his establishment only allowed for three battalions.

Jeanningros also had six small mountain guns, so he formed a battery of legionnaires to man them. Attached to the Legion, and almost a part of it, was a company of Mexican partisans who moved with it and whose task was to provide intelligence about the guerrillas.

The Legion moved off to the higher ground around Puebla, to the east of Mexico City, but still in the French-held 'corridor', where for the summer of the year 1864, it was engaged in desultory guerrilla warfare against the Mexicans. There was only minor skirmishing and no large scale engagement of any note was fought, the role of the Legion being confined to patrolling, reconnaissance work and the inescapable escort duty.

In December that year, the Legion was moved to southern Mexico where French operations were being mounted against the troops there under General Diaz. The legionnaires took part in the marching and the fighting that led to the surrender of this leader in February 1865. There was more marching than fighting involved, as Diaz and his men dodged first this way and then that until contained by the French forces.

Later in 1865, after the southern part of the country had been dealt with, the Legion switched to the north, and its small battalions were dispersed in different places in an effort to bring to battle the bands of guerrillas that roamed through the areas just south of United States territory. In the month of June the Legion battalions took part in a very wide French sweep towards the border of the United States. This had only partial success and most of the Mexicans escaped, some into American territory. The 2nd Battalion occupied the town of Monterey, almost on the frontier of the United States itself.

In April 1865 a 4th Battalion of the Legion was formed at Sidi Bel Abbes, and went out to Mexico later that year. This regularized the position, and thus the Legion, both officially and in fact, consisted of four battalions.

The American Civil War ended in April 1865, and the United States then took an interest in Mexican affairs, openly aiding Juarez. Seeing how matters were going Napoleon III ordered General Bazaine (the ex-Legion sergeant), who was the French officer in command of all the French troops in Mexico, to evacuate all the northern part of the country and to avoid contact with American troops. Monterey was evacuated and the Legion withdrew southwards by stages back into the French-held 'corridor'. As Bazaine began to concentrate his forces at a few key points, Juarez and his followers flooded into the territory the French vacated.

Meanwhile the tradition and example of Camerone had taken root, and the legionnaires intensely disliked withdrawing in the face of the elusive, but arrogant, Mexican guerrillas, whom they tried in vain to meet in a pitched battle. Whilst the 2nd Battalion, under Major Brian, was at a place called Parras, in northern Mexico, preparatory to withdrawing southwards, information was brought in that there was a band of Mexicans in a farm house, known as Santa Isabella, about eight miles distant.

Brian had orders not to embark upon any operations unless he had special permission from higher authority, and certainly not to venture out into rebel-held country unsupported, as French troops were in the act of evacuating the whole area and there would otherwise be danger of being cut off and isolated completely. In spite of these orders, Brian decided that this chance was too good to miss. He and his men had been spoiling for a battle and this would be a good revenge for Camerone.

Shortly after midnight on February 28th, 1866, Brian set off with two companies of the Legion consisting in all of 7 officers and 188 men.

The worst happened: the information was a bait and a trap had been laid. In the darkness, the legionnaires walked unknowingly and blindly into volleys of small-arms fire, and within the first few minutes nearly 80 men had been killed. Brian, leading them, fell dead almost at once.

The command was taken by Captain Moulinier, the senior remaining officer, and he, vowing vengeance, renewed the attack time and time again during the small hours of the morning. Each assault was beaten back by the Mexicans, who were in good positions and well protected from small-arms fire by the walls of the farm house courtyard. Every legionnaire had a 'Camerone in his heart', but it was of no avail.

By 4 a.m. on March 1st it was all over: there were no more legionnaires left standing to fight on: all had been killed, wounded or captured. Only one escaped back to Parras, where the remainder of his battalion was, to tell the story of disaster and heroism, making his way through the numerous Mexican cavalry patrols which were blocking the routes from the place of ambush.

The farm house at Santa Isabella was manned by guerrilla infantrymen, who were supported by cavalry in the background. The cavalry was better disciplined and the legionnaires taken prisoner by it were reasonably well treated and eventually exchanged, but those who fell alive into the hands of the Mexican infantry were all slaughtered as they were taken. The total casualties were 112 killed, which figure included all the 7 officers, and 82 men survived as prisoners: one escaped. The Camerone spirit was there in full measure, but the Legion battalion commander had led his men out in disobedience of orders, and also at the scene of the fighting his initial tactics appear to have been open to criticism.

During the remainder of the year 1866, two engagements stand out amongst the many skirmishes in which the Legion was involved. The first occurred on October 15th, when the 1st Battalion fought an action at a place called Huichapam, when it caught a large force of guerrillas by surprise. There was a sharp fight, and the Mexicans escaped, but not before they had left over 30 dead on the field. A number of prisoners, arms and saddles were taken.

In the second one, the Legion was surprised, when in December a detachment of the Legion Mounted Company, about 50 strong, was surrounded in a farm house at a place called Perral. The Mexican attackers numbered about 500 or more, and they made several assaults in an attempt to overrun the Legion detachment, each of which the legionnaires succeeded in repulsing. Throughout the day the Mexicans were held off until a relief column arrived on the scene.

Generally, the year 1866 was spent concentrating in the French-held 'corridor'. There was much marching and patrolling, but the Mexicans avoided battle whenever they could. In February 1867 Bazaine, with only just over two divisions of French troops under his command, marched out of Mexico City, abandoning Maximilian to his own devices. France was no longer interested in his fate. Maximilian was shot by the Mexicans a little while afterwards.

The Legion embarked at Vera Cruz, and by March had returned to its old familiar barracks in Sidi Bel Abbes, which had remained empty all the time it had been away campaigning. Back in Mexico the Legion left 31 officers and 1,917 legionnaires, who had either been killed or had died of disease, but it took away from that country the tradition of 'Camerone', and all that it meant.

Indo-China 1883-95

INDO-CHINA 1883-95

Since the middle of the nineteenth century, France had been busy colonizing in Indo-China, but although it had consolidated a good record as a fighting corps, the Legion was still kept somewhat in the background, as other enthusiastic French units demanded priority in any campaigns that were going. Thus much of the less romantic garrison duty and drudgery were left to the legionnaires. Colonel Negrier put a stop to this and a depressing period in a backwater came to an end. Negrier raised the Legion to a new pitch of efficiency and, in doing so, he formed a sincere attachment to it and a high regard for the fighting abilities of the legionnaires.

Negrier left the Legion on promotion, in September 1883, and was appointed to command one of the contingents of the French army which were being sent to Indo-China. He was instrumental in persuading the authorities to include the Legion in his command. As a result the legionnaires came to participate in events in the Far East, and to take a full share in the French conquest of Indo-China.

A battalion from Sidi Bel Abbes was made ready and embarked for the Far East, destined for the fighting that was in progress in Tonkin, landing at Haipong in November 1883. From there it moved straight to Hanoi, where it joined the force that was being formed under an admiral to move out against the 'Black Flags' and attack their two principal bases a little way up country, Son-Tay and Bac-Ninh.

China had ordered some local troops from Yunnan to move south and eject the French invaders. These Chinese troops were in fact bodies of Yunnanese irregulars and bandits, who roamed the mountainous regions, periodically raiding down into the cultivated lands and towns of Indo-China. They were known as 'Black Flags', as this was the predominant colour of the banners which each band carried. Generally their discipline was poor and loot was their chief motivation. The various bands were independent of each other and only grouped together temporarily for a specific objective.

This time the Black Flags had mustered a total of about 25,000 men. They were loosely organized, being small units of unequal size, each under its own leader, who only fell in with the master plan—whenever there happened to be one—when it suited his purpose. They were capable of putting up a good resistance at times in terrain of their own choosing, but were unstable and unreliable. Their allegiance to the Empress of China was a fiction, but they eagerly took all the arms and supplies sent to them from China, which consisted mainly of old-fashioned fire-arms, although a few of the more modern types did trickle through in small quantities.

As regards tactics they were guerrillas pure and simple, best at hit-and-run measures, although periodically they could be persuaded to dig their toes in and stand fast. They excelled at ambushes, to which the terrain lent itself well, but they were not keen on, nor could they often be brought into, pitched battles. Their anarchical organization handicapped them when it came to a set-piece attack.

First of all the French admiral marched towards Son-Tay, which was about thirty miles inland to the north-west of Hanoi, on the Claire River. The French force consisted of about 5,000 marines and soldiers, and General Negrier was the senior army officer. The Legion battalion marched with this column.

Son-Tay was a fortified post in that it was a brick-built fortress, constructed in the Chinese fashion, with fairly thick walls and massive wooden gates, surrounded by a dry moat. In addition, there were a few outposts, consisting of rough earthworks-cum-barricades, screening the main positions. Visibility was limited and the countryside was favourable to ambush tactics. The enemy had plenty of small arms of various sorts with ample ammunition, and a few old artillery pieces.

The outer defences covering the fort were overrun by the legionnaires, who led the way, and the French formed up outside Son-Tay to attack, on December 16th, 1883. The Legion was again in front and it assaulted the west side of the rectangular double-walled fortress. A heavy wooden gate was blown inwards by powder laid by them, and the legionnaires were the first men through it. At once they encountered another check in the shape of a second wall and a barricade.

A Legion sergeant climbed the wall with the Colour to stand on the parapet, and all rallied to him. A gap was blown in the inner wall, and the sergeant jumped down in amongst the Chinese. His comrades swarmed through the gap and there was a fierce struggle between the Black Flags and the attackers. The defenders were many times the strength of the French troops, but they soon began to fade away, quietly letting themselves out by the outer gates to disappear into the surrounding jungle.

The French were left in possession of this key fort, but it had been a Legion victory in which the legionnaires had been both first through the outer gate and then first through the inner wall. The Legion lost 10 killed and 48 wounded.

A second battalion of the Legion, which had been formed for the purpose, arrived in Indo-China in February 1884, and at once joined its sister unit, which was still with Negrier's column. The French had now decided on an all-out policy of conquest, and so, having cleared

the Black Flags out of Son-Tay, Negrier marched east to attack their
other main stronghold, that of Bac-Ninh.

On the march to Bac-Ninh the Legion was in the lead, acting as
the advanced guard for most of the way, meeting and dealing with the
patrol and ambush activities of the Black Flags. A number of small out-

A Legionnaire. Tonkin. About 1884

posts screened Bac-Ninh, and these were searched out and smothered
by the legionnaires, who quickly became adept at this form of jungle
fighting, which was a complete contrast to the type of warfare to which
they were accustomed in Algeria. Often in parts of Indo-China, owing
to the density of the jungle and the twisting paths, visibility was down
to a few yards.

89

On arriving outside Bac-Ninh, barely pausing to form up, the legionnaires rushed in to the attack, crashing through the outer defences. They were the first French troops to penetrate the brick-built citadel in the centre of a rather primitive defensive lay-out. Both battalions were to the fore and took part in the short, sharp hand-to-hand fighting. Within minutes the Chinese had had enough and again began to fade away into the surrounding jungle.

The taking of Bac-Ninh occurred on March 12th, 1884, and it was a Legion battle. Legion casualties were 2 killed and 12 wounded.

After Bac-Ninh, the 2nd Battalion moved to a place called Hung-Hoa, and operated in that area, whilst the other, now known as the 1st Battalion, supported by some small mountain guns, moved northwards along the Claire River towards the citadel of Tuyen-Quang, which controlled the approaches from the north in that area. Tuyen-Quang was reached on June 1st, and with only a brief scuffle, the legionnaires were in complete occupation.

This done, the 1st Battalion left its 3rd and 4th Companies there in garrison, and then withdrew to continue patrolling the sectors of lower Tonkin. The bands of Black Flags were ceaselessly roving about the interior of the country, keeping always just out of the reach of the French.

As soon as Negrier's column had left Son-Tay, the Black Flags re-occupied it; so, to prevent this sort of thing happening in the future, it was decided to adopt a policy of leaving garrisons at key points as they were taken.

The Chinese seemed to be consolidating again at Son-Tay, so another column was organized to move out against them, but this had not been able to start off owing to the other activities of the guerrillas in widely scattered sectors of Tonkin. In August the Legion companies at Tuyen-Quang changed over, the 1st and 2nd relieving the other two, whose turn it was to go out on operations.

It was in the month of August that the Black Flags began to flood southwards again in strength. In October, two Legion companies fought a small battle in which they managed to dislodge the enemy from his positions near the Chu River. This succeeded in checking the guerrillas in that sector for a short space of time.

The movement of the Black Flags started again and they moved round Tuyen-Quang, completely isolating the garrison there. Sampans tied across the river south of the position formed an effective boom, which denied the use of the river to the French. At first the garrison was simply cut off and left alone, and as it had ample stocks of ammunition and supplies the authorities were not unduly worried about it.

However, when the Chinese realized how vulnerable Tuyen-Quang was, they changed their tactics and began to close in with the idea of overrunning it. As they were not unified this movement took some time, but it did progress and by January 1885 it was complete. There were perhaps up to some 20,000 Chinese surrounding a French garrison of 390 men. The Chinese force included two or three 'regular' detachments from Yunnan, under local War Lords who had brought them down, being under orders from the Empress of China to press the war against the French.

The first attack on Tuyen-Quang took place on January 26th, when hordes of Chinese launched themselves against the French defences. In this fighting the Legion was smothered by sheer numbers and had to abandon, complete with its connecting trench, a blockhouse which was about 250 yards away from the main citadel. The attackers seemed to have had plenty of small arms and ammunition as a perpetual hail of musket balls and bullets buzzed through the air on the defenders. The attackers were held at the outer walls, but as one wave fell back repulsed another followed after a short interval. This fighting lasted for some hours, but the assaults became weaker and weaker until they finally ceased altogether as the enemy retired to reconsider. Tuyen-Quang was a far harder nut to crack than they had anticipated.

The Chinese changed their tactics, and began sapping.

The French defenders were in a small Chinese-type fort, situated on the south side of the Claire River, on some high ground, and it had a good view of the surrounding area, which was heavily wooded. The fort itself was brick-built and square, having a double line of walls, which were bullet-, but not artillery-, proof. Fortunately, the Chinese had only a few ancient artillery pieces whose penetrative powers were not high. The two Legion companies formed half the garrison, and each held one side of the fortress.

Enemy sapping continued and the trenches crept closer, and when the first Chinese mine exploded on February 12th, they were only about 500 yards away from the outer walls of Tuyen-Quang. The Chinese had moved out under cover of darkness to explode the mine at dawn. They planned that an attack should immediately follow and that the Black Flags should swarm through and massacre the garrison.

This attack in fact started, but was some time getting under way owing to lack of central control and was fairly easily repulsed by the defenders. Only a few Chinese got near the gap that had been made, and they were quietly dispatched by the legionnaires manning the wall near it.

Another mine exploded at dawn the next day, stunning 15 legionnaires. This time the Chinese really attacked in force, attempting to swarm through the breaches in the defences, of which there were now two. They advanced under cover of a hail of musketry fire and the spasmodic firing of the ancient cannon. A few legionnaires had been lifted by the force of the explosion over the parapet to outside the wall right in the path of the advancing Black Flags. Without orders, their comrades rushed out to rescue them.

The 2nd Company of the Legion, which had been guarding the side of the fortress in which this new breach had been blown, was momentarily thrown into confusion, but the legionnaires were speedily rallied by the company commander, and were ready in time to meet the assaulting waves. There was a confused struggle in the breaches, involving hand-to-hand fighting, but although they penetrated the defences, the Chinese were eventually ejected and thrown back by the Legion. The fury of the attack died down and the Black Flags withdrew.

The next few days were quieter. There was both cannon and musketry fire, but the Chinese concentrated on pushing their trenches forward. Then suddenly, on February 21st, there were several explosions, followed by a general attack. One mine exploded under a blockhouse at one corner of the fortress, which was manned by legionnaires. On either side of it were the two Legion companies. The breach made in the wall was immediately blocked by legionnaires who successfully held the leading assault elements. Shortly afterwards, another mine exploded, which blew up about fifty yards of the inner wall, killing the commander of the 1st Company and 12 of his men, and wounding another 21.

The Chinese assaulting troops made for this large gap and the shaken Legion company, but seeing what had happened, the other Legion company turned, and rushed to support it and block this new breach. Yet another mine exploded, causing another breach.

The main Chinese attack was now launched and it hit at the wall with its numerous gaps, which was held by the legionnaires. At all the breaches hand-to-hand fighting took place, and the Legion did good work with the bayonet, ejecting the Black Flags first from one and then from another. The hail of bullets was incessant. After a few more unsuccessful attempts the Black Flags recoiled. Their leaders made fruitless efforts to encourage their followers to resume the battle, but the Chinese were not keen to face Legion bullets or bayonets again. They retired to lick their wounds.

Seeing that the enemy was hesitant and undecided and that there were differing counsels amongst the several Chinese leaders, it was thought that a sharp sortie might demoralize them further and make them relax their efforts. So far whenever the Black Flags had been attacked they had generally not resisted for long. On the night of February 23rd/24th, a detachment of the Legion went out and swiftly cleared a trench, and then hit at a group of the enemy. There was some fighting. The Black Flags were thrown into confusion at the unexpected appearance of the legionnaires amongst them. Two of their standards were seized and brought in triumph back into the fortress.

This had the opposite effect to what was intended, and the Chinese, stung by the impudent sortie, recovered themselves and prepared to resume the attack. From the 25th to the 28th there were three assaults, accompanied by mine explosions: all repulsed. There were now six breaches in the walls of the fort, some very wide, and through them constantly whistled a rain of bullets and musket balls, making it dangerous for the men to cross them in daylight. Many of the defenders were wounded whilst near them. Also, the half-dozen Chinese cannon thundered out periodically, but they were not very vicious.

The legionnaires spent most of their time during the day crouching behind cover and firing at the Black Flags, whose trenches had reached within 100 yards of the outer wall at one point, and at night standing by the gaps ready with fixed bayonets. Night and day, the legionnaires were constantly on the alert to rush from one point to another to reinforce the defences. When the last three attacks were beaten off, the Chinese fell back and relied solely upon sapping, pushing their trenches nearer and nearer.

Meanwhile, when the plight of the garrison at Tuyen-Quang was realized, the column which had been formed to attack Son-Tay was diverted from its original objective and ordered to march to its relief. There was some delay in moving off, but eventually, under General

Negrier, it moved northwards until it met the southern elements of the Black Flags some miles south of Tuyen-Quang, near a place called Hoa-Moc, on March 2nd.

The 3rd Company of the 1st Battalion of the Legion was in this relief columns which also had a few field-guns. For a few hours the Chinese put up a stubborn resistance at Hoa-Moc, and they had to be blasted out of their defensive positions by the French guns. After artillery preparation, in which shells had been liberally used, the men charged, the legionnaires in the van, and succeeded in sweeping the Black Flags aside—but not without loss.

To the north, the legionnaires besieged in Tuyen-Quang heard the distant gunfire and it gave them new heart, as they knew it signalled the approach of a relief column. The Chinese besieging the fortress also heard the gunfire, which decided them on their course of action. They had had enough, the legionnaires were too tough for them, and during the night of March 2nd, they all silently withdrew.

The next day, the 3rd, the defenders saw that all was quiet and that there were no signs of the Black Flags, but they suspected a ruse and waited for a while. Just before noon, a Legion patrol moved out to spring the expected trap and to reconnoitre, when it was discovered that all the Chinese trenches and camps were empty. The enemy had gone, and the French garrison was left alone.

General Negrier arrived late that evening and the siege of Tuyen-Quang was over. The legionnaires had held out for thirty-six days, and had repulsed seven major assaults. The cost had been 32 killed and 126 wounded.

The next day a Legion reconnaissance party moving through the evacuated Chinese lines, came suddenly upon a Black Flag fighter who had been left behind. He was armed, and at once aimed his rifle at the French officer who was leading the patrol, pressing the trigger to fire. As he did so, seeing what was about to happen, a legionnaire pushed his officer aside and was himself killed by the bullet. This splendid example of heroism and self-sacrifice showed both devotion and bravery, and reflected the feelings of the legionnaires towards their officers. It was but one of many similar incidents recorded.

Another new battalion, the 3rd, arrived in Indo-China in January 1885, and at the same time yet another similar new one, the 4th, landed on the island of Formosa. There was now a total of four small Legion battalions in South-East Asia.

94

A formal state of war was in existence between China and France, and on Formosa were numbers of irregular Chinese troops and guerrillas, plus numerous pirates, who, under the wing of the Empress of China, pursued their own sort of warfare against French shipping in a deadly manner. The activities of these pirates caused the French to send a small expedition to deal with them.

The newly arrived 4th Battalion was part of this force, and disembarking on Formosa late in January 1885, walked straight into the fighting on the beaches. Its first fight took place on the 25th of that month, and the legionnaires were successful in driving the Chinese into the surrounding heights overlooking the coastal strip. Two legionnaires were killed.

Then followed a number of smaller skirmishes over a period of three weeks in the hills, in the course of which 1 officer was killed and 2 were wounded, and 25 legionnaires were also wounded.

Next, a small column was organized, in which the Legion battalion was included, to penetrate into some nearby hills. This moved out on March 4th. The Chinese had constructed a series of fortified field works on the high ground, and the legionnaires climbed the heights, charged with the bayonet and overran several of them, driving the Chinese out. This operation lasted three days and during the course of it 7 legionnaires were killed and 30 wounded. It was not possible to estimate the Chinese casualties.

The Legion battalion established itself on this fringe of high ground and paused for breath before going on to sweep through and clear the area, but before it was ready to do so, on March 17th, an armistice agreement stopped hostilities between the Chinese and the French. The Legion unit then marched back to the coast and a few days later embarked for Indo-China, to rejoin the other Legion battalions there. All were then grouped together under the title of *Régiment de Marche d'Afrique au Tonkin*.

In the previous month, February, Negrier had marched with a large column, which contained units of the Legion, through northern Tonkin, but everywhere the Black Flags melted before him. There were a few skirmishes, but not many, and with little opposition he reached the northern frontier with China, where he destroyed a fort controlling one of the approaches.

By the Treaty of Tsiensin, the Chinese recognized a French protectorate over both Annam and Tonkin, after which it was assumed by the French that as Chinese support would be withdrawn from them the Black Flags would return home to Yunnan. But they were reluctant to do so and remained in Tonkin carrying out their depredations. The writ of China was only acknowledged by them when it suited their purpose. The gangs of Black Flags were a nuisance and impeded the pacification.

In Tonkin, the French had been preparing a wide-sweeping campaign in the hinterland with the object of clearing out the Black Flags completely, but the armistice had come into effect before all was ready. As the Black Flags showed no signs of withdrawing to Yunnan, it was decided to launch it and clear them out for good and all. Their main base was Lang-Son, near the eastern frontier of Tonkin, adjacent to China. The 2nd and 3rd Battalions of the Legion, as they were under strength, were formed into a *bataillon de marche* for this purpose. This punitive expedition was commanded by Negrier.

Whilst still some little distance away from Lang-Son he was attacked by the Chinese in strength, near a place called Bang-Bo, where the Black Flags had some defensive works. Coming on to this opposition unexpectedly, the legionnaires, who were leading, walked into an ambush. After a pause to recover themselves they charged with fixed bayonets, successfully clearing the first barricade. Then they were brought to a halt by further defensive works. A hail of musketry fell down on them and in the close country they were at a disadvantage as they could not pin-point the enemy accurately. One or two attempts were made to charge forward but these fizzled out as the legionnaires could not locate the Chinese.

Seeing this, Negrier withdrew a little way, reorganized with the intention of moving round this obstruction, and tried to move along a parallel route. He was still determined to hit Lang-Son hard, being of the opinion that one such sharp lesson would be sufficient to discourage the Black Flags. Whilst he was making this detour, on March 28th, the Chinese attacked again in strength and caught his men in extended column on the march. It happened in close country, and early in the engagement Negrier himself was wounded, and forced to hand over his command to another officer, who decided that the only possible course to take was to withdraw back to the Delta area.

There was confused fighting and the legionnaires, caught unawares to some extent, were split into isolated groups. This withdrawal only got under way with difficulty as the men were unable to break cleanly away from the enemy. Eventually the force gathered into two columns and began to move south-west. The legionnaires formed the rearguard screen to both columns, a position they maintained throughout the movement. All the time the Chinese guerrillas hung closely on the tails of the retreating men, cutting off stragglers. The long withdrawal from Lang-Son was a fighting retreat in which the legionnaires conducted themselves admirably, and thanks to them it was raised above the level of a rout.

Although the war with China had ceased, several gangs of Yunnanese bandits continued to roam about the interior of Indo-China, and the *Régiment de Marche d'Afrique au Tonkin* spent the next few years on column busily patrolling the length and breadth of the country searching them out. There was ample hard marching, but little fighting, as the bandits invariably melted before the French forces only to congregate again when they had passed on. It was only on comparatively rare occasions, when the legionnaires surprised the Black Flags and blocked their escape routes, that a skirmish took place.

There were still bursts of dissidence in one form or another until 1895, when the last action in this phase of the conquest of Indo-China, a skirmish near the Claire River, took place and was fought by the Legion. After this the legionnaires settled down for a long spell of garrison duty in far more congenial circumstances than were enjoyed by their colleagues in Algeria.

In recognition of its work in the conquest of Indo-China and of its work of pacification, the Colour of the *Régiment de Marche d'Afrique au Tonkin* was decorated with the Légion d'Honneur.

5

Africa (1871–1914)

During this period the Legion was engaged fighting in and around Africa, including such places as, not only Algeria, but Dahomey, the Sudan and Morocco, as well as Madagascar. It will be more clear if each is dealt with separately.

ALGERIA

As was perhaps inevitable, the reaction to the French defeat at the hands of Germany in 1870–71 resounded heavily in Algeria, and taking full advantage of French preoccupation and a much reduced garrison, insurrection broke out on a country-wide scale. The Arabs, who had been somewhat sympathetic towards Napoleon III, did not like the idea of a republic.

An incident occurred near Setif which caused Kabylia to go up in flames, there was another near Philippeville, and a son of the long-dead Kader led another revolt in north-western Algeria. In the southern part of Oran Province, which was penetrated but not yet pacified, the powerful Ouled Sidi Cheikh tribe, which had never been subdued but had merely retreated into the foothills when faced by superior forces, now came down again looking for trouble. The rising spread to the tribes living on the edge of the Sahara, where each asserting it was fighting for France against the others, was in fact raiding, looting and paying off old scores. Also, the year 1870 had been one of famine and cholera.

For the first few weeks of this rising the French garrison was on the defensive and only able to take measures to contain the several revolts, which ran wild and unchecked for a little while. However, as soon as the war with Germany was over, French troops returned to Algeria and were available to crush the rebellion. The German victors were glad to see French energy used in this direction instead of against themselves.

The rebels in the area of Philippeville were dispersed and chased over the Tunisian frontier, and then those in north-west Algeria were similarly hunted until they disappeared into Morocco. French troops were sent against Kabylia, and one by one the chiefs submitted. The Legion was used in the southern part of Oran Province to subdue their old enemies, the Ouled Sidi Cheikh. By August, the revolt was dying down, and by January 1872, the last of the rebel chiefs had come in to sue for peace. After this violent spasm the northern parts of Algeria settled down to a period of uneasy calm.

Several expeditions were sent southwards in an attempt to penetrate into the Sahara proper, but they all had only moderate success. The Legion periodically made up punitive columns mainly against the Ouled Sidi Cheikh, whenever they descended from their foothills to make a nuisance of themselves.

Under the German peace terms, France lost the province of Alsace and most of Lorraine, and as a result there were many Frenchmen from those provinces who did not wish to live under German rule, and some of them agreed to emigrate to Algeria to settle there as farmers if land was provided for them. Therefore, when the 1871 revolt was extinguished, as a punishment large sections of fertile land were appropriated from the tribes which had rebelled and given to the *colons*. Several thousand Frenchmen settled on the land in Algeria, and their descendants are still there today.

The French authorities now decided on an all-out policy of colonization, and began to encourage other Frenchmen to come and colonize in Algeria, evolving schemes to aid the impoverished. When this supply dried up, to further this policy settlers were accepted from other Mediterranean countries, and numbers of Spaniards, Italians, Corsicans, Maltese and Sardinians arrived. A group of Spanish immigrants settled in Sidi Bel Abbes, and it is alleged that ever since its womenfolk have made a profession of marrying Legion *sous-officiers*.

In 1871, Colonel de Mallaret was appointed to command the Legion, and he remained for ten years. The Legion, after having a quick succession of commanders, settled down to a period of consolidation.

In 1875, its title was changed from *Régiment Etrangère* to *Légion Etrangère*, the Foreign Legion. This is the title that caught and held the imagination of the world.

Taking advantage of French preoccupation in occupying Tunisia, insurrection broke out again in Algeria in 1881, but this time it was principally confined to the southern part of Oran Province and along the borders of the Sahara Desert. Many Europeans were murdered in the initial uprising, and the Legion was sent southwards to face their old adversaries, the Ouled Sidi Cheikh confederation of tribes, who had been aroused by a marabout. All four of the Legion battalions, under Colonel de Mallaret, took the field.

Almost at once the legionnaires were concerned in a serious engagement on May 19th, 1881, near a place called Chellala. After some hand-to-hand fighting the Arabs were dispersed, but the Legion suffered casualties. After this the legionnaires did not take part in any more big actions for the remainder of the year, but spent their time 'on column', wearily marching from one place to another, unable to bring the rebels to battle.

In July 1881, Colonel Negrier took over command of the Legion. He was an officer of energy and foresight, and he made some innovations and some changes. During the last years of de Mallaret's command matters had tended to get into a rut, especially as for the latter part of it, as indeed for most of the ten years, the Legion had been mainly engaged on garrison duties and constructional work. Negrier took to the legionnaires and they took to him. Under his guidance, the Legion was revitalized and almost overnight it woke from its slumber to spring to life again as a corps that mattered. Negrier had never previously served with the Legion, but had come to it after commanding a battalion of the *Chasseurs d'Afrique*.

At last the Legion had a commander, who not only took a deep interest in it, but also had some influence in higher places. Negrier was destined for moderately high command in the French army, but he never forgot the Legion. For rescuing it from becoming a back number and devolving into a labour corps, the Legion had Negrier to thank more than any other French officer.

One of Negrier's first innovations was to form a Legion 'mounted company', which was a form of mounted infantry, there being two legionnaires to one mule. Each man took it in turn to ride the mule for one hour, whilst the other legionnaire walked beside it: and in this fashion distances of thirty miles or more were covered in a normal day's march.

The rebellious elements that had been suppressed in 1881, smouldered all winter and broke into open flame the following spring. The whole of the southern part of Oran Province and the fringes of the Sahara became alive, and French columns hastily rushed towards the affected areas. As was by now almost customary, the Legion dealt with the Ouled Sidi Cheikh. Especially were the legionnaires active in the pacification of the area around Gerryville.

About this period the French were engaged in mapping the whole of Algeria, and as they extended their effective occupation detachments of surveyors and cartographers spread all over the country, often with the leading troops. Those working in the dangerous areas had to be heavily escorted.

In April 1882, one of these detachments was operating in the sector alongside the Moroccan border, west of Gerryville, and the Legion was given the task of looking after it. It was surveying right into an area not previously penetrated by Europeans, in the centre of the stamping ground of the Ouled Sidi Cheikh. This party was escorted by two companies of legionnaires and one section of the new Mounted Company, a total of about 300 legionnaires in all. There were in addition some French Chasseurs and a few Goumiers, who acted as guides. This party with its escort had halted for the night at a small well, not far from a desolate valley, known as Chott Tigri.

They moved off early on the morning of April 26th, with the Mounted Company in front as the advanced guard, and as soon as the whole party entered the valley of Chott Tigri it ran into a sandstorm. The valley, a long one, was an ideal ambush site, and about 6 a.m. the column was suddenly attacked by a huge force of Arabs, who swarmed down from the hills. It is thought that it consisted of about 1,800 horsemen and about 6,000 Arabs on foot.

The dust was swirling about the surprised legionnaires who were forced to halt where they were and form isolated squares. They hastily fired volleys at the attackers, thus forcing them to keep their distance, but as the visibility was poor the Arabs were able to get fairly close in spite of accurate shooting. The escort and the main surveying party were now split into three separate 'blobs'. The first consisted of the Mounted Company section and some 500 yards behind it was the surveying party with the two Legion companies. The rearguard, which consisted of Chasseurs and Goumiers, with a small detachment of Legion infantry, was further to the rear.

The Arab horsemen made several charges, but were repulsed by the well-aimed volleys of the Legion, but each time the Arabs on foot rushed forward closer under cover of the horsemen's tactics.

The Legion square in the centre managed slowly to move to some higher ground, and then as soon as the sandstorm died down it was better able to defend itself. The Arabs on foot crept nearer, but the square held intact, although there was hand-to-hand fighting at one stage. The members of the rearguard managed to gain the shelter of the main Legion square, although in the process a few were cut off.

The Legion Mounted Company to the front was fighting a battle all on its own, as it was pinned down on unfavourable defensive ground where it had been originally attacked. Numbers of Arabs on foot had infiltrated between it and the main Legion square, thus preventing it from being able to move across to rejoin the main body. Dead mules were formed into a parapet and used as cover from enemy fire. When the two officers were killed, an old legionnaire took command and continued the fight. In spite of several rushes the Arabs were unable to overrun the Mounted Company.

In this fighting, such legionnaires as had been cut off or captured were at once tortured and mutilated by the Arabs, and in this battle there were several instances of men risking being killed or captured, in efforts to rescue wounded comrades, or to recover the bodies of officers or men.

For seven hours the swarm of Arabs, mounted and on foot, buzzed angrily around this tiny Legion force. But when they saw it was not going to be an easy victory, the enemy began to tire. Severe casualties must have been inflicted upon them, but no accurate estimate could be made as all Arab dead and wounded were carried off the field. In the afternoon the baffled attackers withdrew to a distance to lick their wounds, but they remained watching and waiting for any signs of weakness. The Mounted Company survivors were eventually able to join up with the main body.

Then, hastily burying their dead in the sand, a large square was formed with the wounded inside, and a slow withdrawal was begun back the way they had come. Throughout this move the legionnaires were harassed by Arab horsemen on their flanks, who periodically charged the weary men. Accurate rifle fire kept the enemy off and the column struggled painfully onwards. By nightfall the legionnaires met up with the Legion relief column, under Colonel Negrier, which was hurrying to their rescue.

Negrier made a forced march throughout the night to get to the scene of the battle, but when he arrived the enemy had gone. The Legion dead, which had been buried in shallow graves in the sand, had been dug up and their bodies mutilated.

When the roll was called, the Legion casualties in the battle at Chott Tigri were found to be 2 officers and 40 legionnaires killed, and 3 officers and 28 legionnaires wounded. One officer had seven sword cuts and nine bullet wounds, but still survived. At least 3 men were killed whilst trying to retrieve the body of one of the officers of the Mounted Company which lay just outside its square.

The marabout responsible for the rising as a whole, was depressed after his lack of success at Chott Tigri, and he withdrew over the border into Morocco. For the remainder of the year the southern part of Oran Province was quieter.

After this rising Algeria settled down and in the ensuing years the legionnaires had far more work to do than fighting, their activities being mainly centred round the various road construction schemes. The Legion Mounted Company operated near the fringes of the desert proper, being almost constantly 'on column', and was so successful and popular that another two were formed.

The number of battalions in Algeria rose to six, so in 1885 the Legion was reorganized and its title again changed. It was divided into two regiments, each consisting of three battalions. One was known as the *1e Régiment Etrangère*, and the other as the *2me Régiment Etrangère*, but by now the old, familiar name of *Légion Etrangère*, the Foreign Legion, had come to stay. The 1st Regiment was at Sidi Bel Abbes, and the 2nd Regiment at Saida, although the battalions at different times were distributed mainly in western Algeria, out at Tlemcen and the regions adjacent to the Moroccan border.

For the next few years, apart from the occasional incidents in the foothills on the edge of the Sahara where the tribes were not fully pacified, the legionnaires were employed either on training, dull garrison duty or road making.

Without ever seeking it, the Legion began to acquire a world-wide reputation. Information about its feats, its battles, its tough conditions and its endurance, penetrated all European countries, and then farther afield. Rumours were distorted and fables magnified.

Several of the Legion officers, foreign as well as French, as well as a few ex-legionnaires, when they had retired or completed their service, had written their memoirs, which had been published in their own countries. The Legion quickly caught the public imagination and novels centring around it began to appear. Facts were strangely twisted and many authors confused the Legion, a fighting force, with the notorious *Bataillons d'Afrique*, which were the penal units in which French criminals, both military and civil, served and in which conditions were severe. They were mainly used as a labour corps. It was in this latter type of unit that it was probable that abuses and brutalities were practised from time to time, and which, in romantic print, were frequently attributed to the Legion.

As far as Britain was concerned, the Legion burst suddenly on Victorian England when a novel called *Under Two Flags* was published and almost overnight became a best seller. This was the forerunner of other similar romances about the Legion. After this, as to-day, there could then be hardly anyone in the country who had not heard of the French Foreign Legion.

This accidental publicity, which mysteriously attached itself to the Legion, was certainly not sought by France, as the French policy was to operate this corps as quietly and discreetly as possible.

DAHOMEY 1892

Although late in the scramble for Africa, France already had small stakes in scattered parts of that continent, mainly trading posts along the coasts. Two or three of these were in Dahomey, a native African kingdom, wedged between what is now Ghana and Nigeria, then notorious as the Slave Coast. This was no empty title. The French settlements were frequently raided and looted by the Dahomian army.

A treaty was made, but not adhered to, and shortly afterwards Dahomian troops again began to raid the posts and to interfere with French trading activities. This aggravation, coupled with the fact that Dahomey was the notorious 'slave coast', where human beings were both sold into slavery and sacrificed, caused the French to send a military expedition to occupy the country by force.

In April 1892, a force of about 4,000 men was assembled, under the command of Colonel Dodd, and it landed in Dahomey in August of that year. The reputation of the Legion was now established and its good work and adaptability in Indo-China was not forgotten. The

Legion was therefore represented, and a *bataillon de marche* was formed from the two regiments in Algeria. It was commanded by Colonel Faurex, and landed at Cotonou on August 24th, 1892.

Dahomey today is just under 44,000 square miles in size, and was roughly of a somewhat similar size and shape in those days, being an

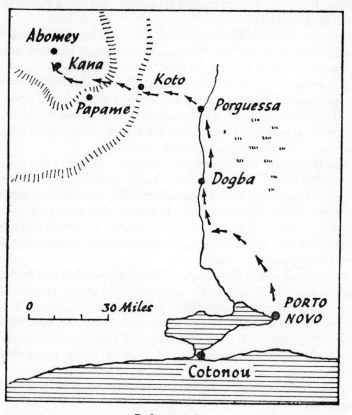

Dahomey 1892

oblong piece of country about 100 miles wide and perhaps up to 400 miles long. The central part of the country consisted of tropical forest, whilst the southern part was a mixture of dense vegetation interspersed with marsh and river. The main scourges of the country, from a European point of view, were the tropical diseases, of which malaria was particularly prevalent.

The capital, Abomey, was some way inland and was protected from the south, or seaward, by a belt of swamp, and then by a stretch of thick jungle through which there were but few paths. Cotonou was the chief port, and Porto Novo had developed into the chief French administrative centre for this part of the West African coast. Ouidah, another important French trading settlement, was about twenty-eight miles from Cotonou.

A few words about the Kingdom of Dahomey may be of more than passing interest. It was founded about the year 1625, and soon became a powerful factor in that part of West Africa, its main activity causing it to become known as the Slave Coast. The army of the king raided the surrounding districts, seizing men, women and children, who were sold to slave traders who transported them to the New World, where they were resold for work on the plantations there. A flourishing business in human beings developed.

The Dahomians also became notoriously blood-thirsty and engaged in the practice of human sacrifice. Large numbers of victims were annually slaughtered, mainly those unfortunates who had been captured but were not suitable to be sold as slaves, such as the old and the physically unfit. It is not possible to determine the number of human sacrifices carried out in Dahomey in the nineteenth century, but there were undoubtedly very many.

The success of the early kings of Dahomey was due to a system of warfare they developed which was based chiefly on surprise. The troops marched in complete silence during the night, unusual in itself amongst West Africans, along little-known routes, or even through the bush, to surround a town or village. A surprise dawn attack followed and invariably resulted in the town or village being overrun and the capture of all the inhabitants, all of whom were carried off, the best to be sold as slaves and the remainder to be ceremonially sacrificed.

The power of Dahomey drooped during the latter part of the eighteenth century, but was revived by an energetic but extremely blood-thirsty monarch, King Gezo, who reigned from 1818 until 1858. He extended the power and influence of his country considerably. All the neighbouring tribes for many miles around lived in fear of his swift, merciless raids. However, after some years of success, in 1851, he was repulsed in battle. He had marched his army eastwards into Nigeria, and was defeated at Abeokuta by the Yorubas, after which he drew his horns in a little and confined his depredations to nearer home.

In that year King Gezo signed a treaty with the French guaranteeing not to attack their trading post at Ouidah, and he permitted the establishment of another one at Grand Popo.

Although blood-thirsty like all his predecessors, Gezo is reputed to have modified the numbers of human beings sacrificed, but upon examination this appears to have been largely on economic, rather than humanitarian, grounds, as slave trading was a very profitable business, and practically every captive, unless very old or deformed, could command a fair price.

The King of Dahomey had his annual blood-bath, an impressive, but ghastly, ceremony, in which it was customary to murder some 500 people. This was the big day of the Dahomian year—a public holiday. There is no way of accurately gauging precise numbers of course, but most accounts seem to approximate around this number. One account suggests that later on this figure was reduced to less than 50, but adds that this was only the number killed for public amusement and that probably untold numbers were still privately massacred within the walls of the mud palace. The usual method of killing the victim was to behead him, the theory being that the more blood there was in evidence, the happier the Dahomians were and the more successful the ceremony was.

The reports of these human sacrifices that filtered through shocked European countries, which had long deplored such practices, but so far no one country had felt strongly enough about the matter to go to the expense of sending an expeditionary force to put a stop to it. Therefore the French had a strong moral ground, as well as an economic one, for their military intervention.

Apart from achieving notoriety by being perhaps the last country in the world to practise human sacrifice openly, Dahomey had another highly unusual feature, in that it had a corps of women warriors, true Amazons. It was a tradition in Dahomey that women fought better than men. At the time when the Legion was marching to meet it, the Dahomian army consisted of just over 10,000 men and about 1,000 women: perhaps more of the latter.

The army, that is the male element, was armed with a variety of ancient and modern muskets and fire-arms, and had been given some form of training by European soldiers-of-fortune and adventurers.

Generally, its efficiency was poor, but owing to the even sketchy training and flimsy organization, was better than any of the adjacent African countries. The fighting spirit of the Dahomian army might have been good in the previous century but it had certainly waned considerably since. The army was still fairly good at night marching, surprise dawn tactics and ambushing, but it could not stand up for long against the disciplined movement and controlled fire power of European troops.

The old warrior, King Gezo, had revived the ancient tradition of having female soldiers in his army and he attributed his success in battle to them. The best women of his country were selected and forcibly taken to serve in the Amazon regiments. In addition, suitable captive women were picked out and impressed. It is thought that at one time Gezo must have had as many as 10,000 Amazons in all. They trained hard all the time, their discipline was strict and they took a prominent part in all battles.

The uniform of the Amazons consisted of a full skirt and a blouse, with a cartridge belt slung either over one shoulder or at the waist. A haversack and a water gourd hung by their sides. Souvenirs of active service frequently dangled from their belts, and took the form of human skulls or bones.

They were divided into small units, each about 400 strong. Female officers were properly appointed, and wore a white head-dress to denote their rank. Each unit had its own 'flag' and ceremonial umbrella, and some had a small detachment of 'drums' for parades. The pick of the corps of Amazons was in the king's bodyguard, which was in two wings, and the best of the fire-arms available were allotted to them. The remainder of the women warriors were grouped together in small units. Apart from the miscellaneous fire-arms, the Amazons were armed with swords, machetes, knives and bows and arrows. By no means all had fire-arms.

The Amazons were selected primarily for their good physique. African women are naturally tough and customarily did all the manual work whilst the menfolk lazed about. All women habitually carried heavy loads on their heads and thought nothing of it. Therefore the pick of such women, when trained, were able to march long distances under adverse conditions, and were usually physically tougher than their male counterparts. Some of the Amazons were quite old.

The Amazons of the king's bodyguard had precedence in the army, and all others had equal standing with the male soldiers, a most unusual feature in West African communities. The units of women were kept apart and always paraded separately from the men, meeting only on the field of battle. Reports vary as to whether they were celibate, and if so, to what degree.

Under Gezo, the Amazons reached a high pitch of efficiency and they took a prominent part in battles, ruthlessly plundering, killing and seizing captives. Their discipline was strict and in fact the corps of Amazons was at one time the only disciplined 'black' fighting body in West Africa.

The king delighted to show off his female warriors in his capital, especially to the handful of Europeans who visited him there at one time or another, and he held full dress reviews in which the Amazons marched past. The king also had a demonstration battle course, in which there were a number of obstacles in the form of thorn fences, and over it he put his Amazons, who charged through the thorn barriers —regardless of cuts, scratches and torn clothing—for the benefit of the observers.

At the Battle of Abeokuta, in 1851, Gezo had some 6,000 Amazons in his army, but about two-thirds of them were killed or captured. After that disaster the strength of the corps seldom exceeded 2,000, and it never really recovered from that blow. In the latter part of the nineteenth century, although the tradition remained, the Amazons steadily decreased in numbers and became primarily the king's body-guard. However, they still figured largely in ceremonies in the capital and also took part in battles, although they were eventually out-numbered by their male counterparts at the rate of ten-to-one. The former strict code of discipline and state of efficiency deteriorated, but for 'black' Africa they were still reckoned as a formidable force in the field.

At the end of August 1892, the French expeditionary force was ready and started to move northwards towards Abomey, the capital. Two small mountain guns accompanied the column. There were no roads, only tracks through the bush, so a large number of human porters were required, and about 5,000 in all were recruited for this purpose, of whom some 2,000 marched with the column, the remainder providing the supply shuttle service. All loads were carried on the heads of the porters.

A small detachment of native scouts led the way, acting both as guides and a protective screen, but the march was slow and exhausting. First it was through swamp, and then the swamp gave way to jungle which closed in around the marching men as they moved along the narrow paths. The French had only imperfect intelligence about the strength, intentions and moves of the enemy, and each night when the column halted, a square was formed and trenches were dug. Attacks were anticipated nightly, and every dawn all expectantly stood-to. By day the French column, like a long snake, wound its way slowly forward.

It was not until September 18th that the column was attacked for the first time by King Behazin's army, at a place called Dogba. Behazin was the reigning king of Dahomey. Suddenly in the dawn the French square was assaulted on alternate sides—a pincer movement—by a horde of Africans, both men and women. It was impossible to estimate their numbers accurately. Salvoes of musketry crashed into the French square, and then an attack followed in which the Amazons led the way, fighting fiercely with spears and machetes.

The first assault was pressed right home with determination and the square shuddered as the waves of Africans hit it. At one point the enemy penetrated part of one side where the Legion was in position, but discipline was maintained and steady firing was kept up. Two companies of the Legion, under Colonel Faurex, moved forward with fixed bayonets to eject the attackers who had broken into the formation. There was a sharp struggle before the legionnaires pushed them all out again. Colonel Faurex was mortally wounded in this charge, which restored the situation and healed the square.

Other assaults followed, but the French ranks remained steady. This fight lasted for two hours, and then when the final assault failed, the Dahomians broke off the action and moved away northwards.

In this battle at Dogba, the first of the campaign, the Legion lost 2 killed, one of whom was the commanding officer, and had 10 wounded. Outside the area of the French square lay 825 enemy dead, a proportion of whom were women.

After reorganizing, the French resumed their advance northwards at the same slow rate along the main bush paths through the forest, continuing for the next fortnight or so without much serious opposition.

The next action occurred on October 4th, at the village of Porguessa when, emerging from the jungle, the legionnaires walked straight into an ambush laid for them. Porguessa is on the north bank of the River Oueme, which was spanned by a small wooden bridge. Fire rained on the legionnaires, there was momentary confusion and the French gave a little ground. The column wavered, but quickly recovered, and the legionnaires rushed forward brushing aside the opposition, which included Amazons, and made their way towards the wooden bridge in three detachments.

The centre detachment of the Legion reached the bridge, and under cover of the small-arms fire from the other two, which lined the banks, forced a passage over the river. Once across, the other legionnaires flooded over behind them. The village was cleared by evening and the enemy retired to the fringe of the forest, but lingered there, spasmodically firing their muskets and fire-arms all through the night. The site of Porguessa was not a good tactical one and so the French force moved to a nearby piece of open ground, where it formed square and settled down for the night.

The next day the Dahomian army hung on to the French formation, although there was no actual attack. The following morning (the 6th) at dawn the Dahomian army tried its favourite tactic and made a rush assault, but the Legion was ready and waiting. The Amazons led the way across the open ground, but the steady volleys of the legionnaires kept them off. At one point the Amazons got to within thirty yards of the French square before they were beaten back again. After about an hour, the Dahomian force withdrew into the forest. When it had gone, many African dead were left lying outside the French formation, including a number of Amazons, who as usual had been well to the fore in all the assaults.

After the clearing of Porguessa the French moved on, but from there onwards were almost in daily contact with the enemy. On both the 9th and 10th, the Legion, when acting as the advanced guard, was ambushed. Again, on the 12th and 13th, the legionnaires were engaged in skirmishing to clear the track ahead, and there was a small toll of casualties.

It was at last known that the enemy had a strong position at a place called Koto, which covered the approach to Abomey, and was about twelve miles to the south of the capital. A messenger was sent forward to ask the Africans to surrender, but this request was refused. Therefore, early the next morning, October 14th, leaving a strong guard on his supplies, Colonel Dodd advanced with his troops in a hollow three-sided square, taking his two mountain guns with him, in the direction of Koto. The Legion formed the front side.

As the French troops neared Koto they were fired upon from ambush, and for about an hour there was confused cross-firing. The French commander sent another message forward to the Dahomians, but the answer was the same. The firing was renewed with vigour. The French troops moved forward, advancing by means of fire and movement towards the enemy, until the 3rd Company of the Legion was close enough to fix bayonets and charge. The legionnaires assaulted and swarmed through the defences. Many prisoners were taken, including some armed Amazons. The small mountain guns had been firing all the time.

In the action at Koto, the French lost over 20 killed, which included the company commander of the leading Legion company and 2 other legionnaires. Also several legionnaires had been wounded.

As he moved towards the capital, Colonel Dodd anticipated he would be meeting stiffer resistance. So far he had followed the main pathways, a policy which had played into the hands of the Africans and one which made his troops vulnerable to ambush.

The column had to be supplied and the ration parties, consisting of long lines of human porters, carrying loads on their heads, provided the shuttle-service between it and the coast, bringing up ammunition and provisions. But they had to be heavily escorted and many were ambushed or their halting camps raided. The strength of the force dwindled alarmingly, and as he expected a stiff struggle near Abomey, Colonel Dodd halted his column to wait for reinforcements before continuing onwards. He used the respite to rest, reorganize and to patrol to gain information.

Patrols were sent out into the surrounding district, and one, a Legion patrol, captured two of King Behanzin's brothers at a village, known as Papame, on October 26th.

After a few days' rest, the column pushed on again without waiting for reinforcements. On November 4th the last fight of the campaign took place near a spot called Kana, which was only a few hundred yards short of Abomey, where the Legion, which was leading, brushed aside the Amazon and male defenders who attempted to bar its way. The Africans were scattered and the road to the capital of Dahomey lay open.

The French column remained at Kana for the rest of the day, and the following morning sent a messenger into Abomey to ask the king to surrender. No reply was given. Early on the morning of November 6th, the legionnaires saw flames rising from the direction of the capital, and the French troops moved hastily forward. Behanzin had set fire to the town before evacuating it.

The legionnaires entered the burning capital to take possession, and going into the king's deserted mud palace, they walked on 'cobbled floors'. The 'cobbles' were the skulls of the victims of human sacrifice, embedded in the earthen floor. Many of the drinking vessels had been fashioned out of human skulls too.

Behanzin was captured two days later, and was eventually exiled, and the French formally declared Dahomey to be their protectorate.

This task completed, the Legion marched back southwards to the coast. Its ranks had been thinned by battle and disease, and when the battalion embarked to return to Algeria, there were only 450 fit legionnaires able to walk on to the ship, although small detachments of reinforcements amounting to over 250 men had joined it since the commencement of the campaign.

FIGHTING IN THE SUDAN

Three great Black African empires had flourished in and around West Africa, had declined in turn and then disappeared. One was the empire of Ghana, which dominated the area between Senegal and the River Niger between the fourth and thirteenth centuries. This ancient name has now been revived and adopted by the Gold Coast on achieving independence, as it is thought that most of the present inhabitants of that country originally emigrated from those regions. Senegal was one of the oldest French colonies, having been acquired in 1637.

The second was the empire of Mali, which controlled the area of the middle Niger from the eleventh to the seventeenth centuries. This name has also reappeared on the map. The other was that of Gao, which included a tract of country around the city of that name, which flourished from the seventh to the fourteenth centuries until it was destroyed by the raiding Moors.

France dreamed of a trans-continental railway running through Timbuktu, spanning West Africa from the Mediterranean Sea to the Ivory Coast. In Algeria this railway crept southwards, but as yet the hinterlands of West Africa, although in the French sphere of influence, were unpacified. They were the haunt of slave raiders, who controlled bands of armed followers, and two of these raiders were particularly notorious characters. One was known as Sultan Ahmadu, who was centred on Segu, whilst the other, known as Samory, roamed the areas of the Upper Niger and Senegal. The latter was especially ruthless and cunning, and led the French Colonial forces a dance for nearly twenty years before he was captured.

Colonel Archinard, the French officer responsible for pacifying the interior of West Africa, requiring some European troops to stiffen his native levies, thought of the Legion. He was of the opinion that ordinary French troops would not be able to stand the pace and do what he asked of them in the pacification role he was carrying out in the face of some considerable opposition from the slavers; accordingly, he asked for a Legion company to be sent to his command. The reputation of the Legion, its general toughness and durability, had reached his ears. This was something in the nature of an experiment, and was carried out about the same time as the legionnaires were campaigning in Dahomey.

A detachment of 120 legionnaires arrived at Kayes, in Guinea, in September 1892, and was at once organized as a mounted company all the men being mounted on mules, unlike the traditional Legion Mounted Companies in Algeria, in which there were two legionnaires to one mule. The notice calling for volunteers had specified that they must be extra fit and if possible under 25 years of age, but had apparently mentioned nothing about being able to ride. However, the legionnaires seemed to have been able to adapt themselves rapidly and this omission does not seem to have presented any obstacle.

This Legion company was divided into two halves whilst still at Kayes, and each moved off 'on column' in the wake of the slave raiders with separate forces. They marched through tracts of fertile country which had been literally despoiled and depopulated. Villages had been burnt, crops razed, houses looted and people carried off. Only a desolate wilderness remained. Here and there was occasionally found alive an old person or even a tiny baby, who had been overlooked by the raiders.

These two detachments operated with French columns in Upper Guinea, Senegal, Upper Volta and the Sudan, and scoured the reaches of the River Niger. They went to the borders of Liberia and then through the districts of Bamako. The farthest point reached was a place called Karo, on the Sassandra River, in the far Sudan. It is recorded that in all they had marched some 12,000 miles, crossed twelve major rivers and fought fourteen engagements.

These engagements were against the armed bands of the slave raiders, who were known as Sofas. The names of the places where these small battles were fought are of little importance, and a complete list would be pointless. One of the more important occurred when a detachment of the Legion killed a notorious raider, named Ali Kari, near Basse.

Whenever possible the Sofas avoided battle and it was only by hard marching, counter-marching and forced night marches that the slave raiders could be brought to battle. Whenever they were cornered they fought well for a time, but they looked for a way out and always slipped away as soon as they could.

The mounted legionnaires operated against Samory and Ahmadu for just over a year in the field, being mainly based for the latter part of that time on places called Kankan and Kerouane. They were then withdrawn and sent back to Algeria. Exactly why their services were so abruptly terminated is not clear. As far as can be seen it had been a very successful experiment, and the job was by no means completed. Samory, for example, roamed the area for another four years before he was finally captured.

Yet another Legion detachment was sent to French West Africa, consisting of elements from both the 1st and 2nd Regiments, and was based on Segu. In 1894, a French colonel and 11 other officers were assassinated in Timbuktu. A punitive column, consisting of this Legion detachment and some other troops, moved against this town. There were one or two skirmishes on its outskirts in which the legionnaires took part, but nothing of a serious nature.

By the end of that year, all the legionnaires had been withdrawn back to Algeria.

BACK TO ALGERIA

In Algeria, in December 1899, a French detachment penetrated to the oasis of In Salah, right in the Sahara Desert, the farthest so far.

In March 1900, a French column, led by Colonel Bertram, the officer commanding the 1st Legion Regiment, moved southward and pushed its way, in the face of hostile tribes, through a defile known as the Valley of Zousfana. Two companies of the Legion were with this column. Bertram was successful in reaching a group of oases, known as Igli, which were in the extreme south-west of Oran Province and on the fringe of undefined territory near the Moroccan border. He planned to establish a base there to strike at the more southerly oases.

The dream of a railway spanning West and North Africa dominated French thoughts, and work on this project went ahead. The railway reached Ain Sefra, and the next point aimed at was Figuig, not far from the Moroccan border.

In 1898, the Fashoda Incident had occurred, and whilst international relations between Britain and France were strained, France soft-pedalled in Algeria and concentrated upon consolidating what she had got. It was not until 1903 that she seriously began to turn her attention to increasing the effective area of occupation; but in the meanwhile, in preparation for this, she had quietly taken possession of several oases fringing the desert, such as Igli, which were good jumping-off points for further penetration, either southwards or westwards.

During these three years the Legion took part in several notable marches and actions. One of these began in April 1900, when a French column leaving Gerryville made a record-breaking march through hostile territory. It contained two companies of the 2nd Legion Regiment, and moved across the empty stretch of desert, marked on most maps as the Great Western Erg, to El Goleah, which was one of the forward outposts that had been established. It then plunged southwards into the desert proper to enter the oases of Timimoun, to carry out a circular movement along the southern foothills of the Great Atlas Range, touching Ghardaia, Laghout and Afloa before marching home again to Gerryville.

Not only was this march through hostile country, but it was through country which was then unmapped, and there was no accurate information about the water points, wells or water-holes. The legionnaires continually ran not only the acute risk of being attacked daily, but of perishing of thirst in the desert. When, in July of that year, the legionnaires returned to Gerryville, they had covered about 1,140 miles in 72 days, an average of about sixteen miles a day, sometimes over very rough going.

The Legion Mounted Companies had their full share of excitement, and one instance was when the Mounted Company of the 2nd Regiment was attacked by a force of some 300 horsemen and 600 Arabs on foot, near a place called Doui-Menai. The legionnaires hastily formed square and were able to hold the attackers off for several hours, until at last they were relieved by a unit of Spahis.

One of the southern oases was known as Taghit, and it had a small French garrison. In August 1903 it had been besieged, and relieved only with difficulty. The tribesmen were particularly lively in this area. The following month, the Mounted Company of the 2nd Regiment fought an action reminiscent of that fought by the legionnaires at Camerone. The Legion Mounted Company was escorting a convoy in the vicinity of Taghit, which was about forty-five miles from Bechar, when it was suddenly surrounded and attacked by large numbers of tribesmen.

The Arabs charged again and again but could not make any impression on the Legion square, which stood solidly for over eight hours. The company commander was killed, as were also 39 of his men, whilst another 47 of them were wounded.

In the same year, Bechar and Kanadsa, both oases near the Moroccan border, were occupied, and during the occupation there was some fighting. The Legion was represented at the taking of both. Bechar has since become better known as Colomb Bechar. Curiously enough, at the fight for Kanadsa a native woman was captured in arms, and was wearing a complete legionnaire's uniform. It was never satisfactorily explained how she came to be in possession of it. Perhaps it was obtained from a deserter, or perhaps it had been taken from the body of a dead legionnaire who had been removed from his shallow grave, or perhaps had been caught and killed.

In June 1903, the French Governor-General was ambushed on the outskirts of Figuig, which was in fact a cluster of oases, and which the railway was fast approaching. As a result of this, the French intensified their activities, and as a reprisal they mounted an attack on a nearby group of oases, known as Zanaga, where it was thought the offenders were sheltering. An artillery bombardment preceded the assault, in which the ubiquitous Mounted Company of the 2nd Regiment distinguished itself.

The heavy blundering columns of the French did not always have the success that was anticipated, and usually they punched away at empty air, as the wily, mobile tribesmen were able to slip away long before the French troops slowly and ponderously arrived. The Muslims were rarely taken by surprise. Also, there was a lack of central direction and the columns and patrols did not move to a set pattern, but often marched aimlessly wherever their commanders thought fit to lead them.

In October 1903, Colonel Lyautey arrived and was appointed to command the area of the southern part of Oran Province. He set about pacifying the sector systematically. First of all the troops in the columns were stripped of all their heavy equipment and baggage so that they could march faster and farther. Also, they patrolled to a master plan. Under the direction of Lyautey the French pushed the rebels out of the Figuig district and gradually cleared the area right up to the Moroccan border. The frontier of Morocco was then contained from three posts, Colomb Bechar, Forthassa and Berguent, from which columns went out to patrol. There were numerous small incidents. The three Mounted Companies of the Legion were normally stationed at these posts and took part in all columns that went out.

For the next two years, 1905 and 1906, this pattern continued, whilst the French increased their control over the unruly tribes in the border areas. Of the several engagements in which the Legion took part, mention can be made of one fought at a desert outpost, known as Fort Chaamba, in January 1906. The Legion defeated a large number of Muslims, inflicting many casualties. This gave the Legion a measure of satisfaction and was some recompense for the many pinpricks and irritations the legionnaires had been suffering for months at the hands of the elusive tribesmen.

For its work in the southern part of Oran Province the Colour of the 1st Regiment was decorated with the Légion d'Honneur.

THE FIGHTING IN MOROCCO

By about the year 1906 the area of the southern part of Oran Province and the adjacent foothills and the desert were quieter. Most of the dissidents had sought shelter over the Moroccan border, from where they periodically raided back into the territory they had previously occupied to make depredations on the tribes which were living more or less peacefully under French control. After a raid they would return to Morocco.

The French now began to take steps to begin the conquest of that country, and better international relations resulted in an agreement being reached between France and Britain over certain colonial spheres of influence. Already previously in 1900 France and Spain had come to an agreement over similar matters in North Africa, which meant, of course, Morocco. Another one was concluded in 1904. These were followed, in 1906, by the Conference of Algeciras, attended by twelve

Morocco

Powers, including France, Britain, Spain and Germany, which did much to determine Morocco's future.

The scene was now set for the French to occupy Morocco.

A short introduction to Morocco will be of interest. The original natives were of Berber stock but they became slightly intermixed with other blood, and all became known as 'Moors', and later Moroccans.

The Moroccan Empire achieved its greatest importance in the twelfth century, when it included Tlemcen, Algiers, Tunis, Tripoli, and parts of Spain and Portugal. The Ottoman Empire, when it rose, rivalled it, lessened its importance, and took bites from it by force, but never succeeded in absorbing or completely defeating it.

The Sultan of Morocco had managed to remain independent of all outside influence. Although it varied, depending upon the strength, efficiency or energy of the individual Sultans, the central government generally had little control over parts of the interior of Morocco, which was inhabited by a jumble of wild, semi-independent tribes. Order was maintained by frequent military expeditions and by playing one tribal leader off against another, coupled with a system of hostages.

Piracy flourished along the coasts, and slavery was legal. There had always been Christian slaves held in Morocco but estimates of numbers vary considerably.

When the French landed in Algeria the Sultan eyed them very suspiciously, and relied upon European rivalry to keep them at bay, playing off one European country against another. He kept ambassadors at most of their capitals. At the turn of the twentieth century, the French vied with Britain, and began to lend him money. This was followed by pressure to gain control of foreign policy and certain other interests.

The Sultan, Abd El Aziz, was both weak and extravagant and played into the hands of the European Powers, especially France, by borrowing huge sums of money. Because of this and other matters he lost the support of the majority of his people. He was also plagued by the activities of Bou Hamara, a Pretender to the Sultanate, who claimed to be his elder brother. Bou Hamara lived in the remote, inaccessible area of the Riff Mountains, and based his activities on the city of Taza.

Morocco is situated on the north-west tip of Africa, and is extremely mountainous in that several of the Atlas ranges run diagonally across it, being the continuation of the ranges from Algeria. In the north the Spaniards had gained a foothold and were endeavouring to increase their influence. On the Atlantic coast are fertile plains, and also inland there are patches of agriculture. In fact the economy of the country rested on agriculture. The capital was Fez, well inland, an ancient seat of learning, remote from the coasts. The population may then have been 3 millions: no one knows exactly.

The murder of a French doctor was the signal to begin the occupation; and at once, as a reprisal, it was decided to occupy Oujda, an oasis town a few miles inside Morocco. This was completed on March 29th, 1907, and was unopposed. The Mounted Company of the 1st Legion Regiment accompanied the French force, which remained at Oudja for the time being.

There was a distinct absence of passable roads in Morocco, and wild stretches of hostile, barren, mountainous country barred the way through to Fez from the east. To force their way by land would mean mounting large-scale operations, which would eat up men and money, and be extremely lengthy. France wanted a swift occupation as she was still not too sure how the other European Powers would react to a long drawn out campaign. Also prestige was at stake, and failure to cut through Moroccan opposition easily and successfully might have unfortunate repercussions in Algeria. Therefore it was decided to wait a while to see what developed.

Not many weeks passed before an incident occurred on the west coast of Morocco at the port of Casablanca, where a joint French and Spanish concern was improving the harbour works and building a railway line. It was alleged that the railway ran too near a Muslim cemetery, and a riot ensued during which some Europeans were murdered, three of whom were French.

In retaliation, after a naval bombardment on August 7th, 1907, a small French expeditionary force landed, consisting of about 3,000 men. It was commanded by General Drude, and included the 6th Battalion of the 1st Legion Regiment, which was itself only about 600 strong.

When Casablanca was shelled most of the inhabitants moved out, but a number of tribesmen from the surrounding countryside came in to loot. The French quickly cleared the town and set up an armed camp on the outskirts. There were one or two spasmodic raids by the Moroccans, but they were not very successful and only caused the invaders to fortify their camp more firmly against such tactics. After a few days the inhabitants of the town began to return.

After the French landing there was a short lull before the reaction set in, and when it did, the tribes for miles around in the hinterland rose with a rush and began to move against them. There is a huge, fertile plain adjacent to Casablanca, known as Shawiya, fringed by foothills inhabited by fierce tribesmen, many of whom were mounted on horseback. Soon armed bands of Muslims started to attack the French camp and French troops whenever they moved outside it.

By September 3rd the Legion battalion was taking full part in the skirmishing. There were many small fights as the campaign warmed up, and the Legion battalion commander was one of the first French officers to be killed in action. This happened at a place called Sidi Moumen, a little way out of Casablanca, to which a reconnaissance force had been pushed. It included two companies of the Legion, and whilst they were at this village they were attacked by a large number of horsemen. Sharp fighting ensued, and the French had to make a fighting withdrawal.

French reinforcements arrived and it was decided to use the Legion in greater strength. At the beginning of September, a Legion *régiment de marche*, consisting of two battalions from the 2nd Regiment, landed at Casablanca. A third one followed a few days later, thus making four Legion battalions in western Morocco. This meant that legionnaires formed more than half the strength of the expeditionary force.

The Legion *régiment de marche* moved straight into operations against the Muslims, and on the 11th the legionnaires were engaged in a fierce fight at a place called Taddert, on the plain just outside Casablanca; and then they took part in another at Sidi Brahim, also a little distance inland, on the 21st.

By the end of September Casablanca and the immediate surrounding district was quieter and the town returned to normal again. Outside it, camps were constructed for the French troops, which had to be protected by sandbags and earth walls, as they were frequently raided, especially at night. Meanwhile the tribesmen began to gather in strength at Mediouna, a fortress on some high ground about fifteen miles inland from Casablanca.

Mediouna was the first test of strength and General Drude, with over 2,000 men, over half of whom were legionnaires, moved inland to meet the Moroccans in October 1907. Two battalions of the *régiment de marche* took part and formed the sides of the square. The hollow square formation, so useful in the flat deserts of southern Algeria, was in favour and was adopted in Morocco; but in broken, hilly country it was unwieldy and only able to move slowly. It was invariably vulnerable to small-arms fire, as the men in the square had rigidly to retain their position and could not take cover from bullets when it was on the move.

The French square forced its way to Mediouna, and there was some fighting just before this place was reached. Firing vigorously, the Muslims faded away as the legionnaires swept through the village to take the fortress. After a brief halt Mediouna was evacuated and General Drude returned to Casablanca. As soon as he had left, the Muslim tribesmen reoccupied the place, which was then used as a base which formed a rallying point for all the tribes in the adjacent hills.

The coolness of the legionnaires under fire and their disciplined precision on the move—such as halting to fire when ordered to do so, and then moving on again in perfect formation regardless of enemy fire being rained down on them—had caught the attention of the war correspondents who were attached to the French expeditionary force. So far the war correspondents had been inclined to turn their noses up at this body of mercenary soldiers, and at first either ignored or minimized their efforts, but gradually their admiration was aroused, and reluctantly the Legion was given some sort of a write-up.

During November and December the French force was largely static, contenting itself with launching a few punitive expeditions which only ranged within a narrow radius from Casablanca. The hollow square formation was strictly adhered to.

In one or two fights the French had not come off too well, and General Drude was subject to some criticism at home: he was especially criticized for allowing Mediouna to be reoccupied after it had once been taken. The newspaper correspondents who accompanied the expedition all forwarded their own particular views to their periodicals as to how the campaign should be conducted. There was no doubt that Mediouna was a most convenient spot for the Muslims to use as a spring-board for their attacks.

Stung by these criticisms, General Drude, on January 1st, 1908, marched out quickly and recaptured this Moroccan centre. There was some hard marching and fighting in this prestige episode, in which the legionnaires again led the way. The Muslims were forced out, and then again Drude returned to the coast. He was relieved of his command, and General d'Amade took over from him. The strength of the expeditionary force was raised to about 7,000 men, and some artillery was added to increase fire power.

General d'Amade adopted a different policy and tactics. He had been attached to Lord Roberts's staff during the Boer War, and had absorbed some of the lessons learned in South Africa. Right from the start he disliked the cumbersome, slow-moving hollow square formations, but favoured smaller flying columns, which could be quicker and less vulnerable. However, he was not immediately able to put these ideas into practice, as he was at once involved in the fighting.

His strategy was to have small columns, constantly out, harassing the enemy. Previously there had been leakages of information, and the Muslims knew the moves and intentions of the troops beforehand, so they were able to prepare, which was a serious handicap to the French efforts. D'Amade was reticent and told no one his plans in advance.

Losing no time, he moved out from Casablanca on January 12th, 1908, with some 2,500 men, and made for Settat, an inland town about forty-five miles distant, which was used as a rallying centre for that sector. It was in the foothills on the far fringe of the coastal plain. Two battalions of the Legion were included, one on either side of the square.

Settat was set on a ridge and was protected by a series of false crests in front of it. After hard marching this town was reached on the 15th, the successive false crests being taken first. Then the legionnaires pushed to the front and led the attack on the town. A Legion company was the first to break into its defences. This done, d'Amade returned to the coast.

Relieved of the burden and monotony of routine barrack life in Algeria, the legionnaires soon happily settled down like old stagers to enjoy the campaign. As if they did not have enough to carry—for they were issued with their own rations which they had to hump as well—they invariably filled the large pockets in their greatcoats with other provender. Current reports state that it was no unusual thing for a legionnaire to have his pockets filled with live poultry, kids or even piglets, as well as other trifles acquired en route and saved for future meals. The tops of the huge packs were often adorned with firewood picked up whilst on the move, and as soon as a halt was ordered, old campaigners as most of them were, fires were lit and coffee was being drunk in no time.

The legionnaires' shooting was good, and its accuracy did much to keep the attackers at bay. In the early stages of the campaign, when all moved in hollow square, the dressing, discipline, steadiness and calmness of the legionnaires was a particularly good example to the other troops. The Legion always moved in formation just as though they were on parade on the barrack square at Sidi Bel Abbes, regardless of whether they were being sniped or whether hordes of Muslims were charging down on them. Solidly, with fixed bayonets, they marched through villages at their slow, relentless pace, killing or capturing those who opposed them, or across the open plain, alternately kneeling down to fire or to meet a cavalry charge. The majority of the enemy were mounted when they went into action, and in addition, they frequently had foot warriors clinging to their stirrups.

At first the legionnaires did not receive the extra active service pay as did the other troops of the expeditionary force, and as they were doing at least their full share of the fighting, they grumbled about this. Somewhat naturally, no doubt. They succeeded in getting this remedied—strangely enough for a body which desired anonymity—through the war correspondents, who were approached unofficially with this complaint. After their initial suspicion, the war correspondents' views had radically changed, and they all came to have a liking and respect for the Legion. Accordingly, they successfully pressed this claim.

After the sortie to Settat, General d'Amade was able to put his new policy and tactics into effect.

During February, there were several combats, the largest occurring on the last day of that month, when a French force, including two companies of the Legion, marched out to meet a body of the enemy which had been located near a gorge of the Mellah River. The enemy was on some high ground on the far side of the river in a good defensive position. The French force splashed across and at once a small detachment of French cavalry charged into the Muslim ranks. The French horsemen cut through the enemy mass, wheeled to form up and charge again, which they succeeded in doing several times, but they were unable to make much impression as the Muslims simply parted their ranks to let them through and then closed ranks again. The French soldiers who were unhorsed during these charges were at once seized and tortured where they fell. As the French charged again through the Muslim mass they met the frightful sight of their fallen comrades being mutilated or burnt alive over fires that had been kindled.

The French cavalry gave up. There was a pause, and then it was the Muslims' turn, and they charged down on the French square.

There were probably over 2,000 Muslim horsemen, each of whom had either one or two foot soldiers hanging on to his stirrups. The legionnaires formed the front of the kneeling square and stood the first shock: the square shook but held its formation, and the steady firing of the legionnaires drove the enemy back again. Darkness fell, and both sides, weary and almost out on their feet, lay down and rested where they were throughout the night.

Early the next morning, the Legion formed up at dawn and charged into the enemy, who broke before its bayonets. The Muslims scattered, and the legionnaires in pursuit cleared the ground before them. Then they stopped to pause for breath before sending out strong patrols to search the surrounding area.

After this success General d'Amade returned to Casablanca. The next action of any note at which the Legion was present was at a place called M'Karto, on March 8th, 1908, and in this battle the French artillery did devastating work.

The following week, the Legion penetrated the foothills to force another Muslim stronghold. A quick, hard march, plus the proverbial reticence of the commander, assisted in this success, as the enemy was taken by surprise. The next three months were spent in steadily expanding the area of influence, in clearing out small enemy nests and in constructing small defensive positions.

By June 1908 almost the whole of the Plain of Shawiya was under French control and the resistance had practically ceased. The Muslims sulked in the hills but seldom ventured down on to the plain. French policy was still cautious and they were not yet quite ready to complete the occupation of the whole of Morocco by force. It was decided that, for the time being, the Casablanca force should be reduced, and beginning in August, the battalions of the Legion one by one returned to Algeria. By October only one was left, which remained partly for garrison duty and partly to assist in constructional work.

Meanwhile, in eastern Morocco there was trouble with the tribes along the frontier, especially with the Beni Snassen, a powerful one, inhabiting the northern border region on either side the Morocco–Algerian frontier. The prefix 'Beni' indicated that a tribe was of Berber stock, and the prefix 'Ouled' meant that it was of Arab origin.

The Beni Snassen were active around Oujda, which the French had recently occupied, and several clashes took place in which the Legion was involved with credit. The conduct of the legionnaires was particularly good in a fight in a pass known as Taforalt, and they were later personally congratulated by General Lyautey. When the Beni Snassen had been quietened to some extent in this district, they moved southwards and began to cause trouble to the west of Gerryville.

There were several clashes, one of which happened at a place called Menabha on the Moroccan border, from which the Legion emerged with honour. Information was received to the effect that there was a large group of armed Muslims in a certain place nearby, and as a result a French column, in which there was an infantry company of the Legion and a detachment of a Legion Mounted Company, moved to attack them. On the evening of April 15th, 1908, this column arrived at the deserted village of Menabha, where there was a ruined fortress and some old buildings, and camped for the night there prior to moving off early the next morning. The halted column was set out in small defensive 'blobs', primarily consisting of sub-units.

In the early hours of the morning, the 16th, it was suddenly attacked by a horde of Moroccan tribesmen, who had accurate information of the moves and whereabouts of this French column. From all sides small-arms fire was rained into it. The assault followed and was directed on to the old fortress and a nearby mound, on which there was a detachment of the Mounted Company. This attack, in the darkness, was partially successful, and the Muslims broke into the camp area, separating some of the groups within their defensive positions.

The Legion company was entirely surrounded, but a wild, blind bayonet charge succeeded in ejecting most of the attackers and doing much to restore the situation. Many men had been wounded in the first rush.

For a little while there was confused fighting. Then a body of legionnaires formed up, moved to a flank and then swept down on the enemy, picking them out with the bayonet and pushing them back. It was still dark. Another sortie by the Legion company drove back the attackers who had managed to creep up to the ruined fortress, and as dawn broke the fighting died down.

When daylight came, the attackers vanished. The Legion had saved the day, but the cost had been high. The Legion casualties were over 120, nearly half their total number.

The next month, on May 14th, the legionnaires played a big part in repulsing Moroccan raiders when a column they were in was attacked at an oasis called Beni Ouzien. The attackers were thrown back.

After these two failures the tribesmen withdrew a little way into Morocco, leaving the French more or less in undisputed possession of the extreme south-eastern corner of that country. Bands of mounted raiders roved through the area but avoided contact with the French, who moved about only in strong bodies.

In 1908, Moulay Hafid, the brother of Sultan Abd El Aziz, proclaimed himself to be the rightful Sultan, and a short struggle between the two ensued, resulting in Abd El Aziz retiring to leave the throne to his brother.

During the next two years the French watched and waited, spending their time in preparation and consolidation. French columns, in which the Legion invariably took part, constantly traversed the border region, which could by no means be thought of as properly pacified.

A number of small engagements took place, of which perhaps mention can be made of one, which was when a unit of the Legion marched to relieve a frontier post, called Bou Denib, which was besieged by about 20,000 Muslims. There was a sharp fight before the post was relieved. In the other actions the Legion Mounted Companies played the most prominent parts, and were seldom omitted from columns of any importance.

Sultan Moulay Hafid was also smothered by loans from the French, but for a time he was left alone as Germany and France eyed each other warily and suspiciously. However, an incident forced the issue, and in April 1911, an appeal went out from the Europeans living in Fez that they were being blockaded there by insurgent Muslims and were in immediate danger. As soon as this request was received in France certain pressure groups persuaded the government to authorize a relief expedition. General Moiner was given 35,000 men and ordered to relieve besieged Fez.

Morocco was certainly unruly, but some reports since have cast doubt upon the alleged seriousness of the situation at Fez, and others are extremely sceptical, being of the view that it was all deliberately engineered and that there was in fact little or no real danger to the Europeans at the time. Whatever the truth was, the fact remained that French troops quickly landed at Port Lyautey, an Atlantic port developed by the French a few miles north of Rabat.

A Legion Section stalk on to an F.L.N. position

Legionnaires taking part in a 'sweep' near the Tunisian barrage

The march on Fez began on May 11th, 1911, and one battalion and a Mounted Company of the Legion took part in it. The French pushed their way steadily eastwards, and in the several actions in which the Legion was involved perhaps the most important was at a place called Lalca Ito, where a French post had been established. The detachment of legionnaires left in garrison was attacked by large numbers of Moroccans, who were successfully repulsed after some hard fighting.

Fez was entered on June 4th, and French troops occupied the city. The French now controlled a triangular corridor from the coast to Fez, and they set about securing it. Lines of blockhouses were constructed on the edges of this territory to resist any attack from the hills. The legionnaires were either employed on building or garrisoning them.

At the same time as the French force was moving eastwards from Port Lyautey, another one began to penetrate from Algeria. Again a battalion and a Mounted Company of the Legion was included in it. This was not successful, owing to the stiff opposition and the difficult country, and did not get very far.

The Legion unit was the 6th Battalion of the 1st Regiment, and whilst it was out on reconnaissance near a place called Ksar d'Alouana, a small part of it walked into a trap. This small detachment, about 35 men in all, moved off towards the village where it was suspected there was a band of armed Muslims. The report was true, but it did not add that the Muslims knew of the approach of the legionnaires. The Legion detachment was allowed to penetrate into a shallow basin near the village and when it was well and truly in the trap, the Muslims opened fire. Pinned down and helpless, the legionnaires held out for five hours during which time they managed to make the attackers keep their distance. When the relief column, consisting of two companies of the battalion, which had been sent to look for the missing men, eventually arrived the Muslims faded away.

Out of 35 men, only 6 legionnaires remained alive. On the bodies of a corporal and a legionnaire were the bolts from the rifles of the other dead men, which they had collected so that if the rifles fell into the Muslims' hands they would be of no use.

When it was seen what the opposition was to the French advance into Morocco from Algeria it was called off for the time being. The year 1911 ended with the French in possession of the strip of territory from Fez to Rabat, and saw the legionnaires feverishly building blockhouses to protect it. The country between Fez and Oujda was solidly blocked.

French negotiations with Sultan Moulay Hafid continued, and on March 30th, 1912, the so-called Treaty of Fez was signed, and a French Protectorate over Morocco declared. This proved to be a signal for a universal native rising against French rule and many Europeans were massacred. General Lyautey had by this time about 40,000 troops under his hand, and he was able to stamp out the revolt step by step, in the areas occupied by the French. The Moroccans did not give in easily and had to be forcibly reduced tribe by tribe.

Reinforcements were sent, which included a Legion *régiment de marche*, and the legionnaires were employed on operations in the French 'corridor' where all energies were bent upon compelling the Muslims to submit. The next phase was to complete the chain of blockhouses for its defence. By August all was fairly quiet as, by brute force, the French gained control, but in the background in the mountains the tribes seethed and simmered.

The Moroccans turned violently against their Sultan for allegedly co-operating with the invaders. French pressure kept the reluctant ruler on his throne for a short period, but he abdicated in August 1912, and then they supported a new ruler, Moulay Youssef. The French moved the capital from Fez to Rabat, on the Atlantic coast. An agreement between France and Spain in November 1912 defined the respective spheres of influence of those two countries in Morocco.

The link-up between Fez and Algeria had not yet been accomplished, and still the stretch of rough, mountainous country, the hard core of which was known as the 'Tache de Taza', blocked the way. Preparations were made to force it at the first opportunity. In eastern Morocco, a Legion *régiment de marche* pushed its way forward from Oujda to occupy a place called Guercif, about sixty miles farther westwards. This was done against stiff opposition, but once there the Legion established a strong post and prepared to make it a stepping off place for the final French break-through to Fez.

The whole of the year 1913 was taken up with countless minor operations along the Rabat–Fez 'corridor', widening and strengthening it; whilst in eastern Morocco, preparations were being made to crack the Tache de Taza, which blocked the route.

By the spring of the next year, 1914, French plans were ready and a pincer movement was initiated when in May the French advanced from both the east and the west on to Taza. Units of the Legion were with both columns. The column moving from the Algerian side pushed through vigorously and successfully, and on May 10th, Taza was occupied by it. The legionnaires had been involved in several skirmishes, but had not taken part in any large-scale battles.

The French column going westwards out from Fez did not do so well, and ran into trouble only a few miles out. There were a number of fights, and the Muslim cavalry, with foot soldiers hanging on to the stirrups, constantly threatened the flanks of the columns. The legionnaires were heavily engaged in all this fighting, and on June 4th they took part in an action to clear the way forward. The Moroccans massed and blocked the route, but the Legion battalion moved into the assault up the craggy hillsides to the rousing sound of its regimental march, which happened to be 'Carolina'. After some struggling, the Legion cleared the way by force.

A most novel incident occurred after this action when the *sous-officiers* and legionnaires of the battalion jointly wrote to the commander asking that their commanding officer, Major Met, who had incidentally distinguished himself in Madagascar, be promoted. Major Met was later made a lieutenant-colonel, but whether as a result of this unorthodox request or not cannot be ascertained. This officer was unfortunate enough to lose a leg when fighting in France against the Germans a few months later.

A further strong point, known as Kenifra, barred the way and was really the final obstacle of any importance before reaching the Tache de Taza. On June 12th, three separate columns converged on it. Legionnaires were in all three. The main assault on the Muslim defensive positions was put in by the Legion, and they were cleared after some hard fighting.

A few days later, the French marched into Taza, and linked up with the garrison already there. The Fez–Oujda 'corridor' was at last open. In many places it was but a thin strip, so at once the French set about widening it and making it secure. Blockhouses were constructed and the Legion was put to work.

This vital link-up had been accomplished just in time, as on August 2nd France mobilized for war with Germany, and the order went out that all offensive operations in Morocco should cease. The troops were told simply to hold what they had got, and to keep the Rabat–Fez–Oujda 'corridor' open.

THE FIGHTING IN MADAGASCAR

Before plunging into the First World War, there is one campaign in which the Legion took part which it will be convenient to fit in at this juncture, and that is the fighting in Madagascar, the island situated in the Indian Ocean, just off the south-east coast of Africa. Because they alleged that the terms of a treaty had not been carried out, a French expeditionary force landed at Majunga, on the north-west of the island in 1895.

A few words about Madagascar will provide the background against which this campaign, in which the Legion played a leading role, will unfold. The island of Madagascar is about 1,000 miles long and 250 miles wide, being separated from the African coast by the Mozambique Channel. It has a high, central plateau, which touches the coastline to the north-west, and which averages between 2,500 and 4,000 feet in height. To the east of this high plateau is a narrow coastal plain, while to the west and south of it is a much broader stretch of lowland. There were hardly any roads at all, the only means of communication across the island being difficult footpaths. Both the climate and the vegetation are tropical and agriculture is the mainstay of the economy.

Tamatave, a small port on the east coast, had an indifferent harbour. The only other harbour of any size worth mentioning was at Diego Suarez, in the north. The landing facilities at Majunga were primitive.

The natives, who were of a mixed negroid stock, practically all wore the 'lamba', their native dress, which consisted of a huge sheet of cloth, usually white, folded around the body somewhat in the style of the Roman toga. Over this 'lamba' was occasionally worn a jacket or even a dress, frequently of European pattern, which produced a grotesque effect. A large straw hat was frequently worn.

There were a number of tribes on the island, of which the dominant one, which inhabited the central highlands, was known as the Hova tribe, whose main enemy, the Sakalava, on the north-west coast, the French had ostensibly come to assist.

The strength of the Hova force was hard to estimate with any degree of accuracy, but may have been as many as 40,000. It was organized into small infantry units, and had been given some rudimentary training by British and other European soldiers of fortune. Two British officers were actually with the Hova army at the time. Discipline was doubtful, and the Hovas did not enjoy a very high

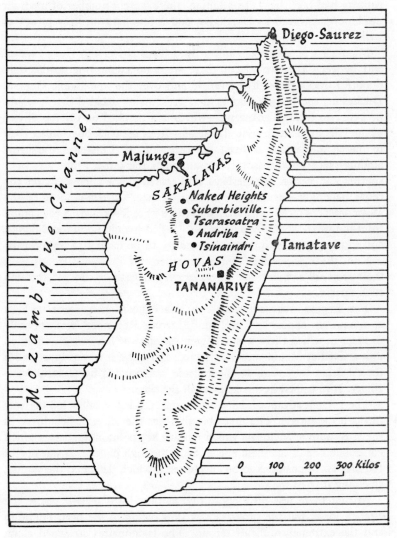

Madagascar

reputation for courage. A small proportion of the Hova army was armed with modern rifles, such as Remingtons and Sneiders: the gun-runners had been busy. In addition, there were a number of medium machine-guns, such as Hotchkiss, and a few light artillery pieces as well.

Majunga was about 350 miles from Tananarive, the Hova capital, and between the two places there were no connecting roads, only doubtful tracks through the jungle and over the mountains. General Duchesme, the French commander, presumably decided that it would be better to tackle Tananarive—which was perched on the top of one of the hills in the high central plateau—from the back door rather than to march and attack it from the direction of Tamatave, the usual landing-place on the east coast; although the latter route was both shorter and better. He perhaps anticipated more opposition on the route he might have been expected to take. Certainly most of the Hova defences faced eastwards, and there were few covering the capital from the west. The Hovas apparently relied mainly upon the difficult, and in places almost impassable, country to be its ally. They perhaps did not think it possible that a large body of European troops with their arms, equipment and accompanying baggage could get through such terrain.

The Legion was represented in this expeditionary force without argument or opposition, and an 'Algerian Regiment' was specially formed, in which there was a Legion *bataillon de marche*. This Legion unit arrived at Majunga on April 23rd, 1895, and it was assigned, with the Algerian Regiment, to the brigade commanded by General Metzinger. It remained in this brigade all the time.

The French advance inland began, and the legionnaires led the way through the jungle. The first objective was the village of Andriba, in the hills south of Majunga, which was at a key point in the passes which controlled one of the main entrances to the high plateau. It was one of the first Hova positions to be encountered which defended the capital, shielding it from the west.

At first there was little opposition as the Hovas melted before the French force, but the progress was slow owing to the heat, humidity and the extremely difficult terrain. The legionnaires struggled along the narrow tracks, mostly in single file. Being the dry season, it was not long before they were all covered from head to foot in reddish-coloured dust which rose up to choke them as they tramped along.

The legionnaires all grew beards and, within days, they had lost their spick-and-span parade ground appearance and had taken on the appearance of old campaigners, their dress and equipment being modified to ensure the maximum comfort and portability.

After a few days' marching, the legionnaires left the Sakalava country and reached the fringes of Hova influence, which had been deliberately made desolate on purpose to delay the invaders. Villages had been burnt and the inhabitants moved, so that neither information nor aid could be given to the French. All supplies had been removed and all crops destroyed.

On June 1st, the Legion, still in the lead, camped at a place called 'Naked Heights', in the foothills of the mountain range they were to penetrate. It was near the junction of two rivers. It was detailed to go forward in small parties to find the best route for the column to follow.

On this day the Legion had its first brush with the Hovas, when one Legion company, taking a small mountain gun with it, came to the River Betsiboka, where there was a ford, which was defended. As soon as the legionnaires appeared, they were fired upon by the Hovas on the far bank, so without pausing, they fixed bayonets, plunged into the river, to struggle across in the face of small-arms fire, up to the arm-pits in water. Dripping wet, they reached the far bank, hauled themselves out of the river and made for the defences. With only a scuffle the Hovas broke and fled, leaving the Legion in occupation.

The Hova troops withdrew to a defended position a few miles in rear, the village of Mevatanana. The position itself was on the top of an almost perpendicular cliff, one of the 'Naked Heights', and gave the impression of being impregnable. It controlled the narrow valley along which the French must pass.

The small Legion detachment followed as quickly as it could and kept right behind the Hovas, but had to halt when it came under fire. By this time the remainder of Metzinger's brigade had come up, and under cover of fire from the small mountain guns, another Legion company quickly swung into position and moved forward to attack from the south. The legionnaires quickly swarmed up the bare end of the cliff and got on to the top of the ridge, where the company flag was planted on the first Hova position, which had been swamped within seconds.

There was only a brief fight as the legionnaires spread along the cliff top to occupy the several posts, and within minutes the enemy had decamped. The Hova soldier was no match for the legionnaire, and in his haste to depart he left arms, equipment and ammunition behind him.

The position as regards rations was now rather difficult as none were to be had from the countryside, which had been made desolate. All food had to be brought forward on the heads of the human porters, so as it ranged forward the Legion had to tighten its belt.

After breaking through the Naked Heights, the column moved onwards without pausing, the Legion still acting as the advanced guard, but it was not until June 6th that it again hit the enemy. This was at a place called Suberbieville, in the foothills, where the Hovas had a blocking position where they briefly attempted to hold and bar the way of the Legion. The Hovas fired on the legionnaires as they approached it, who as soon as they located it fixed bayonets and leapt forward *en masse*, to charge through. Again, within minutes it was all over: the Legion had burst through to the other side and the path ahead was crowded with swarms of fleeing 'Lambas Blancs', as the legionnaires called their adversaries.

At this stage it was obvious that the men needed a brief respite or else they would collapse. The intense strain of tramping in full marching order through difficult tropical country on half rations was telling. Rivers and streams had to be crossed, most of which were infested with alligators, and at night the troops were plagued with mosquitoes and other insects. Fever began to appear and take a fatal toll. Also, the remainder of the French column was badly strung out behind and parts of it were extremely vulnerable to attack.

General Duchesme was having to depend upon a horde of human porters who did not carry a very heavy load and who cluttered up the existing narrow tracks. These conditions meant delay in the ration supplies and had been the reason why the leading troops had been on half rations for some days. Maps of the interior of the island did not exist, but a French officer had secretly visited Madagascar the previous year and had been able to complete a certain amount of cartographical work. This was a useful guide.

General Duchesme decided to stay at Suberbieville for a short while to give his men a rest before pushing on to attack Tananarive. He was very concerned about his poor communications and the lack of tracks capable of taking wheeled vehicles. Indeed, few of the tracks could be negotiated by mules. He therefore decided to build a road fit to take two-wheeled mule carts so that supplies could be brought up far more quickly. It was to run from his base at Majunga along the route he had marched, and was to be continued as the French column nosed its way forward.

Work on making this road began at once and all the troops had to lend a hand. The first task was to complete it as far as Suberbieville, where the head of the column had stopped. Needless to say, the legionnaires played a major part in this work of construction, and on June 12th they were issued with shovels and other tools, and given the most difficult stretch to complete. Under the humid sun they worked with a will and finished their stint in record time.

Fever now burst out and many men died. The Legion suffered from this scourge less than most units. This was attributed to the fact that Legion discipline was stricter and also that the legionnaires clung together and generally did not mix freely with the other French troops.

As soon as the roadway was in a fit state for small mule carts to use it, the French resumed their advance from Suberbieville. This time other troops took over the duties of the advanced guard, as the Legion was left to put the finishing touches to another portion of the road-way.

On June 29th, the French advanced guard met and attacked a Hova position, at a place called Tsarasoatra, where it was reported that there were some 5,000 Hova soldiers in entrenched positions. The Hovas were defeated and withdrew so rapidly that all contact between the two opposing forces was lost for over two weeks. The Legion was not involved in the fight at Tsarasoatra, being still engaged on road work.

Marching through the forested highlands, the French troops of the advanced guard slowed down suddenly and were almost completely immobilized by fever, which created fearful havoc in the ranks. When this happened the legionnaires, whose sickness rate was well below that of any other unit, were taken off their road work and once more the Legion *bataillon de marche* resumed its place at the head of the column. Taking over the lead, the Legion probed eagerly forward along several parallel paths, scouting all of them to discover which was the most suitable for the column to use.

The Legion next made contact with the Hova troops on August 18th, when they set up a small blocking position on a pathway. The legionnaires charged as soon as they came up against it, and within minutes the Hovas were in full retreat. The Legion kept hard after them until a little later it met the main Hova defended position, near a place called Andriba. Here the Hovas intended to make a stand.

The position was a good one and contained a few small artillery emplacements, with mountain guns, which had been sited by a British officer. It is reputed that a battery was actually commanded by one, but there is no substantial evidence to confirm this point.

The position was located by the legionnaires of the advanced guard, and owing to its seeming strength a French battalion following was detailed to take it. Unit rivalry was intense and all eagerly competed for the honour of attacking. It was this French unit's turn, but unfortunately it was so decimated by the ravages of fever that it was physically unable to mount this operation. The two companies of the Legion of the advanced guard were then asked to do the job. The other two Legion companies had been dropped off a few miles to the rear to do a little road constructional work, and so ensure that the roadway kept up with the advance.

On August 24th, the two Legion companies moved into the attack on the Andriba position, along two almost parallel tracks. One company moved to probe and explore the track to the east of Andriba, and in doing so came across two or three tiny, deserted villages, which they burnt. It then crossed over a small river, and the legionnaires were able to scramble up on to the heights to the east of the main enemy position. In other words, they were on the small ridge itself, which was heavily wooded in parts, and jagged and craggy in others.

The other Legion company moved on a track to the west of Andriba, and also came across some empty villages. In them were some supplies, which were seized before the villages were set on fire. These were the first supplies obtained in this manner in the campaign. During the latter part of the movement by this second Legion company, as the legionnaires got closer to the enemy, the Hova artillery opened up and put a good rate of fire down on to them. The ground was lightly wooded so the men were able to take some cover and casualties were low.

Fortunately the legionnaires did not have to endure this artillery fire for long, as the other Legion company reached the top of the enemy ridge just about the same time as the Hova artillery began to fire. The legionnaires turned inwards and moved through the trees along the crest of the ridge. The leading ones commenced to fire their rifles as soon as they saw the Hova positions, advancing at the same time. When they saw the blue-coated soldiers relentlessly moving towards them, the bulk of the Hovas began to retreat. The Hova guns continued firing a few minutes longer, but with only 2 casualties the Legion cut clean through the position. The Hovas decamped rapidly, leaving their artillery, other arms, ammunition and supplies behind them.

The French column remained at Andriba for two days until the roadway reached that point before moving on again. Whilst waiting, the legionnaires were put to work and did a large share in completing it. At Andriba the other two Legion companies came up to join the forward ones.

The column then moved on again, this time with other troops acting as the advanced guard. The track ahead was clear as, without fighting, the Hovas abandoned the territory through which it lay. The Legion was put back on road making.

However, it was not long before it was called for again, and after cutting its way through over two miles of thick jungle, on September 2nd, it debouched in front of the column to hit the main track leading to Tananarive. Once again the legionnaires were in their familiar place in the lead, and they made ready to resume the advance.

On September 10th a detachment of reinforcements from Algeria arrived, consisting of 3 officers and 147 men from the two regiments. They were sorely needed, as the strength of the *bataillon de marche* had shrunk to 19 officers and less than 450 men. The casualties had been mainly due to fever.

Tananarive was still 125 miles distant over mountain tracks, and at the existing snail's pace it would take many days for the whole column to reach that place. General Duchesme therefore planned to form a special task force, composed of the fittest men, which was to leave the others and push on as quickly as it was able. This task force was to carry its own rations and ammunition, and was to go all-out to seize the Hova capital.

When formed it consisted of about 4,000 combatants, plus another 1,500 native porters, the best that could be produced. It was to be entirely self-contained and the twelve small mountain guns were taken along, as well as nearly 3,000 mules to carry them, their ammunition and other supplies.

This was to be a mad race to Tananarive, to hit and take the place by surprise. It was to be a do-or-die effort and anyone who fell out was to be left by the roadside, so it became known to the legionnaires as the *Marche ou crève* Column, which means literally 'march or croak', or better still perhaps 'march or die'. This title became a popular catchword, and since on many occasions it has been cheerfully applied to Legion marches through hostile country.

Over two-thirds of the Legion battalion was chosen, and the Legion contribution amounted to 19 officers and 330 men. The legionnaires were in the first detachment, the whole force of which was divided into three, and again they were continually in the lead on the rush towards Tananarive. These three detachments were in fact small 'brigades', and General Metzinger commanded the leading one.

The task force moved off and on September 15th the French-recruited scouts, who were Sakalavas, who had gone on ahead, came up against Hova defences in the mountains, near a defile known as Tsinaindry. This was the last serious obstacle before reaching the Hova capital. The defensive position itself was an ideal one and con-sisted of about fifteen posts on the top of a steep slope which controlled three main paths where they converged to lead through the pass itself to Tananarive.

The Hova positions covered an open stretch of ground which French troops coming from the west would have to cross. In addition, the Hovas had a few artillery pieces, one of which at once opened up and fired with remarkable precision. It was reputed to be under the direct control of a British officer, but again there is no concrete evidence of this fact.

Only two paths led over the open ground, covered by the Hova artillery, the third one was left open, as the Hovas were of the opinion that it was far too steep to be taken by direct assault by the French troops.

The two leading formations of the task force acted together, and the one on the right attacked the line of dug-in posts on the skyline to the right of the ridge top, moving across the open ground in the face of artillery fire to do so, whilst the other formation, which contained the Legion, was on the left.

As the French troops came into the open the Hova artillery ceased and the enemy opened up with small-arms fire. At the same time, with two companies of the Legion in the lead, General Metzinger's men moved along the third, or left-hand, track. Barely stopping for breath, the eager legionnaires rapidly climbed the steep path, using their hands and rifles to assist themselves up. They came in behind the line of Hova defences. Once on top of the ridge, the two Legion companies spread out and swept through the line of defences. But they met with little opposition, as when the legionnaires reached the crest the Hovas rapidly pulled out, abandoning arms, equipment and supplies.

The Pass of Tsinaindry was the key to the Hova capital, and when it fell the road to Tananarive lay wide open to the French. News that the French had forced this defile caused panic in the Hova capital, and the aged Prime Minister rushed round trying to raise volunteers who would fight to the death, and generally organize the defences of the town against the invaders. The Queen ordered all her subjects to fight to the last.

On September 17th, the French advance continued and daily the distance lessened.

The town of Tananarive was built on a hill, there being a large number of fair-sized brick and wooden houses on all sides of its slopes. The Queen's Palace, a huge wooden house, with four brick towers, one at each corner, was perched right on the very hill-top dominating the town. It had been constructed for her by a Scotsman. The hill-top and its sides were closely wooded and it was surrounded by numerous other similar 'hill-tops', none quite so high, and accordingly visibility was limited.

The most convenient and conventional way of entering Tananarive from Majunga was from the north, but in that direction the town was covered by a series of patches of open, terraced rice-fields, which could prove to be a serious obstacle to delay the attackers. In view of this, General Duchesme decided to make a wide flanking march to avoid them, and instead to hit the town from several different directions.

The task force was divided up into six separate columns which were to move independently, and they were ordered to close in on the town from the east and the south. On September 28th the French columns came in sight of the Queen's Palace, which stood out above the other houses and buildings. As a preliminary to the assault, the mountain guns were brought up to a suitable position.

It was not the Legion's lucky day as the *bataillon de marche* was placed in reserve for the final assault on this occasion, and was in the vicinity of the mountain guns which opened up on the town. As it turned out, although it did no fighting, it saw all the negotiations for the Hova surrender.

After only fifteen minutes' firing a white flag was run up over the Hova Palace and upon sighting it the French guns ceased fire. A few minutes later a grotesque individual in a white 'lamba', wearing a huge straw hat, walking under a large umbrella, with a small escort, came out of the town towards the French commander. He was the secretary to the Hova Prime Minister. The legionnaires sat at a respectful distance and watched proceedings.

The next day was taken up with negotiations, and preparing to move in, and it was not until the following day, September 30th, that the French actually occupied Tananarive. General Metzinger was named commander of the town, and that afternoon a detachment of the Legion was installed in the Queen's Palace on the hill-top.

The Hova army as such disintegrated and disappeared, the men either slipping away into the jungle to their villages where they hid their arms, or simply merging into the civil population. Over seventy artillery pieces of different sorts and vintages were abandoned in the town.

With the occupation of Tananarive the first campaign in Madagascar was over. Only 16 officers and 399 legionnaires were left standing on their feet. During its course the Legion had lost 226 dead in all, of whom only 5 had been killed in action: the rest had died through fever.

Practically the whole way the Legion had formed the advanced guard of the column and it had shown up well all the time. In the whole French expeditionary force only 7 men had been killed in action, so it shows that the Legion took its full share of such action as there was. It must be said, however, that the Hovas were but indifferent adversaries and certainly were not of the same fighting calibre as the natives of Algeria.

The Legion's task over: three weeks later it started to march back along the route it had helped to construct to Majunga. For a change, all the packs and baggage were carried on mules. By December 1895, all the legionnaires, except those in hospitals, were back in Algeria.

In March the following year, 1896, a rebellion against the French

Protectorate broke out in several parts of the highlands, and then rapidly spread to the whole island. It was, of course, primarily anti-French in character, but it was also generally anti-Christian and anti-foreign. Hidden arms were produced from their hiding-places and armed bands sprang up to roam the countryside. The towns were terrorized, isolated French posts were attacked, and Europeans were ambushed and frequently killed.

To enable him to restore order over the whole island, General Gallieni, the French general in charge, asked for more French troops to be sent out, and he asked in particular for the Legion, which he had come to know in Indo-China. He asked first of all for a detachment of some 600 legionnaires who had seen service in Indo-China. Certainly the conditions, climate and country were similar in many respects. In August 1896, a small *bataillon de marche* was formed at Sidi Bel Abbes for this purpose, and its headquarters and two companies disembarked at Tamatave in September. The other two companies followed: all Legion battalions now consisted basically of four companies. The legionnaires were all picked men, under the age of thirty, that is if a legionnaire's age can ever be gauged with any accuracy, and as things were quiet in Algeria there were plenty of volunteers to choose from.

The Legion battalion was split up into detachments which were used to sweep through sections of the countryside to locate the rebel bands which roamed the more inaccessible districts. In the first months the legionnaires saw little action but did plenty of hard marching. The pacification was slow and during the ensuing years there was little fighting, apart from an occasional brush with the rebels. Perhaps three of these skirmishes could be briefly mentioned: there were others, of course, of a similar nature.

One occurred on October 17th, in the first year of the pacification, when the 3rd Company of the Legion battalion was on a reconnaissance operation in the mountains, when near a place called Amnahimazina it surprised a band of rebels and in the ensuing fight the legionnaires killed over 30 of them. This unexpected, but successful, action did much to assist in restoring order in that particular sector of the highlands.

The next fight of importance did not take place until two years later, and the Legion came off second best having run head-on into an ambush. On March 12th, 1898, the 1st Company was on patrol in the region of Vohingezo, making a night approach march in the hope of being able to surprise a rebel encampment at dawn. At about 4 a.m. the leading elements were ambushed, and there was confused firing in the darkness, which lasted for an hour, in fact, until the dawn broke through. When daylight came the rebels had fled, but the Legion company commander lay dead, as did 4 of his men, and another 8 were wounded.

The third fight of which mention can be made was when several groups of rebels had been driven together and confined in an area near the River Manandrave, early in 1900. After a night march the rebel camp was successfully assaulted at dawn, when many of the occupants were killed and most of the remainder were captured. This was one of the actions which finally broke the back of the rebellion, and was literally the last of any note in which the Legion took part.

However, there were still isolated bands of fugitive rebels on the island, and to enforce their submission the French still had to deploy large numbers of troops. Spasmodically, whenever the opportunity occurred the rebels set up ambushes, but these became weaker and weaker. They would fire a few shots and then hastily disappear back into the shelter of the jungle or the hills. In other words, timid nuisance tactics, but several legionnaires were shot in this manner. On June 27th, 1900, for instance, the company commander of the 1st Company was killed in this sort of ambush. He was the second commander of this company to be killed in Madagascar. Another company commander was killed the following year.

As the tempo of the rebellion died down, the legionnaires dropped back into their traditional building role.

Legion reinforcements arrived from Algeria, usually by companies, which either remained intact as they came, or were dispersed to make the *bataillon de marche* up to strength. In April 1900 another complete Legion battalion arrived in Madagascar, and yet another followed the year after, but both came too late as the pacification was nearly completed by this time. Neither saw much action, and were mainly employed on constructional works and road building.

When it was seen that the programme of pacification was almost complete, the French garrison was reduced. From 1901 onwards the legionnaires were sent home in small detachments, or by units. By 1905 all had left the island.

A vehicle of one of the Saharienne companies in a little difficulty

A Legion desert fort from the air

Legionnaires of the 13th Demi-Brigade co-operating with a helicopter against the F.L.N. in the Aures Mountains

Legionnaires of the 13th Demi-Brigade moving forward to attack an F.L.N. position

6

The World Wars

The Legion participated in both the World Wars and gave a very good account of itself in many diverse quarters of the world, both in victory and defeat. Especially did it shine in the First World War. Unfortunately, circumstances did not always allow it full scope and opportunity in the Second World War, but nevertheless, it took part in many heroic encounters.

THE FIRST WORLD WAR

The Legion stepped into the First World War with a good heart, expanded rapidly and took a full part in some of the toughest actions fought. On August 2nd, 1914, the French began to mobilize, and at once recruiting offices throughout the country, especially in Paris, swarmed with foreigners who wished to fight for France against the Germans. Therefore it was decided to form them into *régiments de marche*, affiliated to the two regular Legion Regiments. All the foreign volunteers joined only *pour la durée de la guerre*, that is for the duration of the war instead of for the recognized Legion period of five years.

Each of the two Legion Regiments, the 1st, at Sidi Bel Abbes, and the 2nd, at Saida, were supporting a *régiment de marche* in Morocco, to which they sent reinforcements after having recruited and trained them. In North Africa a few hundred Germans and Austrians were interned, but the majority of the legionnaires from these two, now enemy, countries were content to stay in the Legion. Most of them were in Morocco anyway, so it was decided to send the remainder of them to the two existing *régiments de marche* in that country, where they remained throughout the war. In 1914, these enemy aliens comprised about two-thirds of the Legion strength, which left numbers available to go off to fight in Europe very small.

As the foreigners in France, enlisting for the duration as

145   K

'legionnaires', flooded in each regular Legion Regiment was ordered to form a *régiment de marche* to contain them. These new formations were raised in France, and Legion cadres and training staff were dispatched from Algeria. Sub-units and detachments of veteran legionnaires, to thicken them up, followed as and when they became available and could be spared. Many of the new legionnaires never saw Africa, nor did they ever pass through the barrack gates at Sidi Bel Abbes or Saida, as all the veterans had done.

The cadres from Sidi Bel Abbes were sent to Lyons and Avignon, where small depots were set up, and eventually three new battalions were organized from the volunteers. A fourth was later sent from Algeria, where it had been formed mainly of men who had also joined for the duration only. These four battalions were put together and became the *2me Régiment de Marche* of the *1e Régiment Etrangère*; a long title which can perhaps be conveniently shortened to the '2nd of the 1st' for easy reference. This was based on the Palace of the Popes, at Avignon.

In the initial stages there was some suspicion between the new volunteers who had joined for the duration in France, and the legionnaires who had been drafted from Africa, who had contracted to serve for five years. The two did not mix or get on well together, and this friction lasted for some time until it was dispelled by the comradeship born in the first gruelling battles they fought together.

In the early days few French officers of experience were available. The majority of the officers in these new Legion units were French, but they were largely reservists who had become rusty, whilst of the foreign officers who were granted commissions some were experienced, but others were not. All, however, were enthusiastic.

The training cadres from the 2nd Regiment, from Saida, moved over to France and set up a depot, in the first place at Rouen, to receive and train volunteers, but this was soon moved to Toulouse, owing to the German advance. At Toulouse, three battalions of the new volunteers were organized, to which was added another one, which had been formed in Algeria. All were put together to become known as the *2me Régiment de Marche* of the *2me Régiment Etrangère*, which can also be referred to for brevity as the '2nd of the 2nd'. As in its sister formation, the new and veteran legionnaires did not mix well together at first.

The confusion, bustle, enthusiasm and well-meaning, but sometimes misguided, efforts of those early days at the Legion depots in France can be imagined. Would-be recruits from over a hundred nationalities made their way to them: foreigners were not allowed to serve in French regiments.

Language was another confusing barrier which caused misunderstandings at times. To illustrate this, an incident which occurred in September 1914 can be quoted, when 12 Cossacks in native dress, unable to speak a word of French or even Russian, disembarked and went to the Legion depot at Toulouse, where somehow they were smilingly enlisted. No one at the time could be found to speak their dialect, but this did not seem to hinder proceedings.

The Cossacks were happy for a few days and then their smiles vanished and they suddenly refused to go on parade. All efforts through sign language were to no purpose. More in sorrow than in anger they were confined in the guardroom, where they went on hunger strike. Eventually, a legionnaire who spoke their dialect came along and found out what the matter was. They were indeed Cossacks and had left their country to come and join the French Foreign Legion Cavalry, and now to their horror they found themselves in the infantry. They wanted to be with horses and not have to march about with large packs on their backs. It was sadly explained to them that there was no Legion cavalry, and they were released.

Late in October 1914, the Moroccan Division, into which the two Legion *régiments de marche* had been put, forming together the 'Legion Brigade', was sent to the Front, which had stabilized to some extent by that time, and fitted in a relatively quiet sector near a place called Prunay, which was about thirty-five miles to the south-east of Rheims. It stayed in this area throughout the first winter, right on until the following April.

The first real brush with the Germans did not take place until December 1914, at a spot known as Zouave Wood; although there had been frequent contacts of a minor nature before this date. Already there had been casualties, mainly from patrol clashes, sniping and one or two small German night raids. In fact in November, the previous month, the oldest serving Legion officer, a lieutenant, aged 54, had been killed by the enemy.

The legionnaires of the '2nd of the 1st' and the '2nd of the 2nd' settled down to routine trench warfare.

As the inflow of foreign volunteers for the duration continued, it was decided to form yet another *régiment de marche*, and this became known as the *3me Régiment de Marche* of the *1e Régiment Etrangère*, in short the '3rd of the 1st'. Paris firemen formed its cadre, and the volunteers were organized into three battalions. Few experienced officers could be spared, and the bulk of them were French reservists, many elderly 'dug-outs'. As regards *sous-officiers*, few regulars were available, and any volunteer who had previous military service in other armies or other wars, or claimed he had, was promoted.

The '3rd of the 1st' was sent to a quiet sector of the Front near Santerre, in the Somme Valley, in December. It was then over 2,000 strong, and contained large elements of Russians, Italians and Belgians, who had been resident in France.

The winter was spent in the trenches, and casualties were incurred through patrol actions and raids, although the men were not involved in any big clashes at all. It was a quiet sector but some enemy prisoners were taken and some of his works destroyed. The mud, cold and wet were responsible for even more casualties than the enemy, and through sickness the numbers steadily fell. Many who could not stand the winter in the trenches were discharged: a large number of these had 'reduced' their ages to enlist. No reinforcements in any number were received.

In March 1915 the French agreed to release large numbers of foreign volunteers from the Legion, mainly those who had joined it before their own countries had entered the war. Batches of Russians, Belgians and Italians were discharged, one being over 900 strong: a large group of British were also discharged. This left the '3rd of the 1st' very low in numbers, so it was decided to dissolve the formation. The '3rd of the 1st' had only a short life, and had been allowed to waste away without being able to prove itself in battle.

Yet another Legion *régiment de marche* was formed, thus making a total of four in existence in France at one time. This did not materialize until November 1914, when it was initiated at the insistence of Lieutenant-Colonel Guisippe Garibaldi (a grandson of the famous Garibaldi of Italy, who had fought with his 'Red Shirts' in 1870), who brought a large following of Italians with him into France to fight against Germany. At this period Italy had not yet entered the war. Five members of the Garibaldi family served in this regiment, which was built up to a strength of three battalions. It became known as the *4me Régiment de Marche* of the *1e Régiment Etrangère*, the '4th of the 1st' for short, or more popularly as the 'Garibaldi Brigade'.

In mid-December 1914, without wasting time, the Garibaldi Brigade moved to the Front in the area of Argonne, country which was wooded and split up by deep ravines. The Italians went into action against the Germans about a week afterwards, at a place called Bolante, moving out into the attack through the woods on Christmas night.

The Italian legionnaires spread out and advanced through the trees towards the enemy, who were in strong positions across a ravine. The advance went well until the edge of the ravine was reached. Without hesitating the Italians began to move across it to press home the attack, but they were caught in the centre by German machine-gun fire and halted. Heavy casualties were inflicted within minutes and the Italians were forced to retire, leaving dead, dying and wounded lying in the mud. They were unable to help the wounded or retrieve the dead owing to the deadly sweeping machine-gun fire. This attack failed and the Garibaldi Brigade had to retrace some of its steps. The cost of this first action had been 4 officers and 44 men killed, and over 170 wounded.

The '4th of the 1st' paused and licked its wounds, but its fighting spirit was not dampened and morale remained high. Two days later the Italians were ready again, and moved out into an attack near a place called Courtes-Chausses, a short distance away. Its leading battalion, advancing in the face of machine-gun fire, succeeded in taking some German trenches with the bayonet. The Italians were only partially successful in this assault, but they retained possession of what they had taken. This time the Garibaldi Brigade had 125 killed and 172 wounded. Two members of the Garibaldi family, one the colonel's father, who was serving as a subaltern, were killed.

In January 1915, the Germans began to press forward in this sector, and some French positions gave way in front of the enemy advance, others were evacuated. One important ravine, held by the French, was threatened and the troops holding it became jittery and unsettled, so the Garibaldi Brigade was rushed there to fill a gap. The Italians moved in and held the German advance. As soon as they found their feet, they made an attempt to attack, but this was a failure and they were unable to beat the Germans back. Twice the Italians tried to recover the ground lost by the French, but the Germans had dug-in, and their machine-guns swept the frontage covering their positions.

Italy entered the war on the Allied side in May 1915, by which time the Garibaldi Brigade had lost 429 killed, so the remaining Italians were released to join their own national army.

A spring offensive was planned by the French High Command, and in preparation for it the Moroccan Division was moved out from the sector near Rheims, where it had been for several months, northwards to the region of Arras. During this period the '2nd of the 2nd' had suffered a drain in manpower which the reinforcement rate had not been able to keep pace with, due to enemy action, sickness and the release of detachments of foreigners to join their own armies. The other *régiment de marche*, the '2nd of the 1st', had suffered similar depredations, but not quite to the same extent, and was the stronger of the two.

In May 1915, the '2nd of the 1st' took part in what became known to the Legion as the 'Battle of Artois', while the '2nd of the 2nd' was held in reserve. On May 9th, it formed up at a farm, known as Berthonval, from where it was to advance to break through the German line to its front. A number of enemy machine-gun positions on the skyline faced it.

After a four-hour barrage one Legion battalion jumped up from its cover and began to move across open country. The German machine-guns opened up at the slowly advancing lines of legionnaires. The slaughter started, and men fell like ninepins. The Legion struggled on for some 300 yards before it was battered to a halt, to sink down into the ground. Another battalion moved to join it, but was pinned down.

A third Legion battalion moved off at an angle and was successful in seizing an enemy post, which tended to ease things a little, and enabled the other battalion in front to get forward to overrun some outlying enemy posts on the lower slopes of Hill 140, the Legion objective; but it was not able to get to the top of the hill. German artillery now began to crash down on the men, making their position untenable; and so, unable to hold on to what little territory they had taken, the legionnaires were compelled to withdraw a little way and dig-in. The next morning they were relieved, and slowly and wearily the remnants made their way back to Berthonval Farm.

This battle, the Battle of Artois, had cost the Legion dear. It had taken about 3,000 yards of territory in the face of German machine-gun fire, but of nearly 4,000 officers and men who had commenced the attack, only about 1,800 were able to make their way back to the starting-point at the farm house. Hill 140 still remained in enemy hands.

A fortnight later, the '2nd of the 1st' was again in the area of Berthonval Farm. On June 15th, three times the legionnaires got out of their trenches to move forward into the attack, and three times they were beaten back by machine-gun fire. The German Front had stabilized like concrete.

So far the '2nd of the 2nd' had not been seriously engaged in battle, but was put into the forefront of the attack, when on September 27th, it was given as its objective Navarin Farm, a German machine-gun position. As they rose up out of their trenches the legionnaires ran head-on into machine-gun fire, which withered the ranks. The men struggled on for a little way, but were unable to cross the open ground and advance up the slope to Navarin Farm.

In an effort to encourage the legionnaires forward a trumpeter[1] jumped up and sounded 'Boudin', and other officers and men performed incredible feats of bravery, but it was all of no avail against machine-guns. In the first day's fighting this *régiment de marche* lost over 240 men. For two days the legionnaires were rooted where they were, unable to advance, and when they were relieved their casualties amounted to over 800, out of an original total of some 1,600 going into battle.

In October 1915, the Moroccan Division was briefly withdrawn from the Front, and with other divisions, took part in a review before the French President, King George V of Great Britain, and the Prince of Wales. The two Legion *régiments de marche* took part in this parade and march past, and the well-decorated Legion Colours caused favourable comment. The Colour of the '2nd of the 1st' was decorated with the Croix de Guerre with three 'palms', which meant that the regiment had four times been awarded that decoration. The medal itself and its ribbon, with the 'palms' attached, was pinned to the Colour.

In view of the heavy casualties and of the reduced number of volunteers presenting themselves, it was decided to fuse all the elements of the Legion *régiments de marche* in France together, and this was done in November 1915. The new formation became known as the *Régiment de Marche de la Légion Etrangère*, the R.M.L.E., for short. It remained in this form and under this title until the end of the war,

[1] The Legion always had trumpets, instead of bugles, even in the field.

serving throughout in the Moroccan Division. In the first instance there were only enough legionnaires to make up three battalions. It was commanded by Colonel Cot, an old Legion officer, and it adopted the much decorated Colour of the '2nd of the 1st'.

In July 1916, the Moroccan Division was moved to the Front in the Somme area, and was in time to take part in the first French Somme offensive, which was designed to relieve pressure on Verdun.

It was not until the fourth day that the R.M.L.E. was moved right to the edge of the battle, when it was ordered to advance and capture the village of Belloy-en-Santerre, which had been strongly fortified by the enemy, and was situated on the edge of a wood. After a heavy preparatory French artillery barrage, on July 4th the leading battalion of the R.M.L.E. leapt out of its trenches and 'went over the top'. It did not get far before it was hit with the full force of the hail from half a dozen machine-guns. The line wavered, tried to advance and was then beaten to a halt. The leading companies lost all their officers and one-third of their men within seconds.

A second Legion battalion moved out into the attack towards the objective, going slightly to a flank, which enabled it to make use of some hollows in the ground. By doing this, the legionnaires reached the outskirts of the village, where fighting took place in the gardens and lanes. This was done mostly with the bayonet and grenades. The Legion trumpeters repeatedly sounded the 'Charge' and other calls, and blow by blow Belloy-en-Santerre was taken.

The third Legion battalion followed on and pushed through, managing to get to within about thirty yards of the German main position, but machine-gun fire held it there. That night, the R.M.L.E. stayed where it was, repulsing two enemy counter-attacks. The next day another attempt was made to renew the offensive, but this was unsuccessful.

A thunderous barrage was put down on what remained of the village, and when it was over, there was a heavy silence. All the world seemed to stand still breathlessly waiting. During this lull, the last inhabitant of Belloy-en-Santerre crept out of hiding from amongst the ruins of a house in full view of the watching legionnaires. This caused a cheer and a smile, and was a tonic to morale, as such unexpected insignificant things sometimes are in battle.

It was decided to try again, and on July 8th the R.M.L.E., or what was left of it, formed up to attack. Twice the legionnaires leapt out of their trenches and twice they were knocked back in again. This time there were another 400 casualties.

During 1917, the main French effort was concentrating upon trying to crack the hard German line between Soissons and Rheims, and in preparation for this the Legion moved into a position to the east of Rheims. On April 17th, after several days of artillery barrage which blasted away all the undergrowth and cover, an attack was launched. The ground, battered flat, was muddy owing to heavy rain and the trenches themselves were waterlogged. The slopes were desperately slippery. The objective of the R.M.L.E. was the village of Auberville, in the valley of the River Sippe, and next to it was the village of Vaudesincourt.

The first wave of legionnaires was decimated within minutes by machine-gun fire, and all along the line the French troops shuddered and ground to a halt. The struggle bogged down and developed into a heaving mass of mud and men, trying desperately to force their way forward, trench by trench. Grenades were freely used, and the fighting moved from one dug-out to another, and frequently swayed backwards and forwards. Although it does not seem possible that flesh and blood could stand the pace for so long, the Legion fought on in this manner for six days and six nights before its strength was spent, and through sheer exhaustion, coupled with lack of men and grenades, it came to a standstill. This had been a 'grenade' battle, and the Legion had used over 50,000 of them in this lengthy fight.

For all its superhuman efforts, the R.M.L.E. had only taken two kilometres of ground. Needless to say there were numerous heroic incidents as the legionnaires battled their way forward in small groups. It was a junior leader's battle in which individual initiative played a big part.

On May 30th, Colonel Rollet, who became known as the 'Father of the Legion', took over the command of the R.M.L.E., and stayed with it for the remainder of the war. Colonel Rollet was an old Legion officer who had fought with it in Morocco, taking part in some twenty-one skirmishes and battles. He had left the Legion at the beginning of the war to take command of a French Line Regiment. Rollet was then 42 years of age, and at the height of his energy and enthusiasm: his heart was in the Legion and its morale soared under his guidance.

In Paris on Bastille Day 1917 there was a large military review, in which a detachment of the R.M.L.E. took part. The French

President pinned the *Médaille Militaire* to the Legion Colour, thus making it the most decorated one in the French army, now having six decorations in all pinned to it.

On August 20th, another attack unfolded, and the R.M.L.E. began to advance under the cover of a creeping barrage. The first Legion objective was an enemy position, known as the 'White Works', which it took within an hour. Next, it seized a nearby village, known as Cumiers. Another German position rose up in front of the legionnaires when they reached the far side of the village, which, without pausing in their stride, they cleared with grenades. The legionnaires forced their way forward, until they struck the river at a place called Forges.

These actions became known as the Battle of Cumiers to the Legion, and they had lasted for two days in all. However, unlike most of the previous fights, this had been somewhat more successful, as just over two miles of territory had been seized, at the price of over 350 Legion casualties.

In January 1918, the Legion took part in an attack in the Lorraine area, in which a small advance was made, the legionnaires taking over 100 prisoners.

At the end of March the big German offensive was launched. At first the Legion was not involved, until, quite by accident, on April 24th it became engaged in a heavy fight at a place known as Hangard Wood. The R.M.L.E. was next to the British forces when the advancing Germans struck. Although unexpected, the legionnaires quickly deployed to meet the attack, moving into the wood itself. A Legion battalion, leading the way, charged into a mass of Germans, but being quicker to appreciate the situation, the enemy was able to get his machine-guns into action and inflict heavy loss on the Legion. All the officers of this leading battalion became casualties, and a corporal commanded what was left of one company, and a legionnaire another.

The two other Legion battalions came up in support, and for five hours there was a desperate, almost hand-to-hand struggle in the wooded area. The Legion was successful, as the Germans gave way in the end, and the road to Amiens was securely blocked. This was done at the price of over 850 Legion casualties. The R.M.L.E. remained fighting in the area of Hangard Wood until May 6th. For this action yet another decoration was pinned to the Colour.

Soissons fell to the enemy on May 29th, and as soon as this was known the Legion was rushed, in lorries, to try and stop the Germans debouching, and it took part in the defensive fighting there which lasted for several days. The Legion was engaged particularly in a bitter fight around a feature known as the 'Mountain of Paris', parts of which changed hands several times. The Legion lost 400 casualties on it.

June 12th marked the end of the German Spring Offensive, by which time the Legion losses had mounted to over 1,400 in this phase.

The R.M.L.E. was again made up to strength, before being re-committed to battle, to take part in an attack which began on the night of July 17th, near a place called Villiers-Cotterets. The night was pitch dark and the weather was bad, heavy rain falling all the time. Contrary to their usual method, the French advanced without a pre-liminary artillery barrage, and because of this, took the Germans by surprise. During the night the enemy line was broken, and the next day the advance continued.

The Legion was detailed to seize a piece of high ground, known as the Plateau of Dommiers, and was supported by a number of small Renault tanks. The legionnaires advanced, taking a series of fortified positions that blocked the way. When they neared the objective, the three Legion battalions fanned out and it was taken by an encircling movement.

The next day the R.M.L.E. pushed forward doggedly over a net-work of trenches, taking them one at a time, mostly with the aid of grenades. During the night of July 20th, the Legion successfully with-stood a German counter-attack, and the next morning continued the advance again. The following night, the R.M.L.E. was relieved. It had taken about eight miles of territory, but had lost some 800 men in the process.

The Germans now based their immediate hopes of defence on the so-called Hindenburg Line, which the Allies attempted to smash in an autumn offensive. On September 2nd, the R.M.L.E. moved into action, its objective being a village called Terny-Sorny. This was taken, and some 500 German prisoners were captured, but in the struggle a Legion battalion commander was amongst the dead.

Three days later, on the 5th, the Legion was ordered to occupy a tunnel, known as Vauyaillon, which was in the midst of the Hinden-burg Line itself. Steady fighting followed, which went on day and night without respite, as one by one the German posts and machine-gun nests were stormed and captured.

On September 14th, the legionnaires were almost out on their feet from fatigue and could hardly keep awake.

The strength of the R.M.L.E. had sunk alarmingly owing to casualties, but it was asked to make yet another effort, this time to break through at a place called Allemany. Each of the companies was down to less than 50, and some had no officers at all: but everyone responded to the call. Tired as they were, the legionnaires made a final effort, rushed forward and cracked the enemy position, but it was indeed a last effort. However, they held the gap open and other, fresher, troops flooded through it.

This was the last real battle of the First World War as far as the Legion was concerned, and it was a splendid finish. The R.M.L.E. had been fighting without a break, day and night, for thirteen days, and had taken all the objectives allocated to it. The cost, as may be expected, was high. In this battle to break through the Hindenburg Line, it lost 275 killed and over 1,500 wounded: only about 700 legionnaires were standing on their feet at the end.

Too many facts and figures become dull and tend to bore, but one or two may be of interest to show the extent of the effort the Legion put into the First World War. Some 42,883 legionnaires served in the European theatres of war, of whom some 6,239 were French as far as can be ascertained, the remainder being foreigners from over 100 different countries; 115 officers were killed and so were 5,172 legionnaires; the wounded and missing amounted to five times those figures.

At the end of hostilities, the Colour of the R.M.L.E. was one of the most decorated in the French army, and after the war the legionnaires were given the distinction of wearing a green and gold lanyard on their shoulder (the colours of the ribbon of the *Médaille Militaire*) in place of the red one they had won earlier.

When the official battle honours had been sorted out, the following were selected and inscribed on the R.M.L.E. Colour: 'Artois 1915', 'Champagne 1915', 'Les Monts-Verdun 1917', 'Picardie-Soissinais 1918' and 'Vauyaillon 1918', this last being the vicinity of the tunnel where the Legion had cracked the Hindenburg Line.

THE NEAR EAST

This does not quite complete the whole story of the Legion activities in the First World War, as meanwhile, a battalion took part in a 'side show' in the Dardanelles and the Balkans. A Legion *bataillon de marche* became the 1st Battalion of a formation known as the *Régiment de Marche d'Algérie*, which landed with the French contingent at Gallipoli in 1915. At once the legionnaires were plunged into the bitter fighting that occurred on the beaches following the Allied landing. On June 4th, the Legion battalion was engaged in a fierce battle in a small valley adjacent to the sea, which went against it, but the legionnaires managed to hold out until reinforced by troops arriving by sea in small boats.

About a fortnight later it took part in an attempt to break through the Turkish containing line, but the operation went badly and the legionnaires were savagely mauled. In fact, when this action was over, all that remained of the battalion was about 100 men, under the command of a *sous-officier*. The remnants were withdrawn.

After this disaster, reinforcements partially, but not completely, made it up to strength, and the *bataillon de marche* was then moved to the Balkans, and to Serbia, to join the token Allied force there. But it was too late, and the Allied troops too few to make any difference to the Bulgarian advance southwards. The legionnaires fought in the rearguard all the way back in this retreat, and were engaged in a number of skirmishes. Mention can perhaps be made of one, in December 1915, at a place called *La Dent de Scie*, where the legionnaires held back the attackers for some hours, thus enabling a large body of Serbian troops to escape disaster.

It was withdrawal all the time, and inevitably Serbia fell, the Legion retreating into Greek territory, where the men remained for that winter, and on until the summer of 1916.

In August 1916, Rumania entered the war on the Allied side, which put a new light on events in the Balkans. The Russians pressed hard on the Austrian and Hungarian troops in that area, and the change of pattern enabled the Serbians to advance. The Legion battalion moved with them, taking its place in the advanced guard, which it kept all the time. The legionnaires took part in several actions, which succeeded in driving the Bulgarians back. When Monastir was entered by the Serbian cavalry, the Legion was with it, the only infantry to keep up the pace, but the marching and skirmishing had told, and the Legion lost over 200 men during the advance.

The Legion *bataillon de marche* then stayed on in Serbia, but few reinforcements trickled through to it, and its strength sank lower and lower. Eventually, it was dissolved as a unit at the end of 1917. One small sub-unit of the Legion, however, remained on in Serbia until after the Armistice, seemingly forgotten.

NORTH RUSSIA

There is room perhaps for a brief Legion epilogue to the First World War. A Legion battalion was specially formed and sent to North Russia, its first company arriving there in December 1918. It was at once sent to the frontal area, near a place called Oboserskaia, where it remained static for the remainder of the winter. In March 1919, a second company joined it.

As spring broke, these elements of the Legion were attacked by units of the Russian Red Army, but they were able to hold them off fairly successfully.

At the end of June, yet another company of this Legion battalion, plus a detachment of machine-guns, arrived, just in time to go into action in an effort to block the road to Archangel. There was some indecisive fighting. The majority of the men in this Legion unit were themselves White Russians, who were 'durationists' only.

Towards the end of July 1919, the French disbanded this Legion unit. A few of the legionnaires returned to France to be discharged, but a large body of them immediately went over, as soon as they were released, to join White Russian formations. As a matter of interest, many of the disbanded legionnaires marched off and fought the Reds near Petrograd, wearing French Foreign Legion uniform and badges.

THE SECOND WORLD WAR

When the Second World War broke out there was again the problem of the Germans serving in the Legion to be considered. In the previous World War, this had been satisfactorily solved, and there had been little or no trouble at all.

This time circumstances were rather different. Although disliking and openly condemning the Legion, the Nazi régime had not overlooked its importance or probable use. The flow of German recruits continued, intermixed with whom were a number of Nazi agents or sympathizers who had been deliberately sent to exploit any favourable opportunity. There seems little doubt that plans existed for the German *sous-officiers*, who formed up to 80 per cent of the *sous-officiers* of the Legion, to take control of it forcibly from the French. The Nazi agents in the ranks expected to be able to play on the patriotic feelings of their German comrades and be able to persuade them to carry out this scheme when chance permitted.

The French were aware of this, and several hundred German legionnaires were at once interned. In the course of the next few weeks, and even months, more were arrested as they became suspect of Nazi sympathies. The French at this time were not too happy about the reliability of the Legion for this reason, and there was a distinct reluctance to employ it in Europe, in spite of its wonderful record in the First World War and since.

As soon as war broke out the Legion was glad to enlist men for the 'duration only' again, many of whom joined for idealistic reasons, thus watering down the potential subversive element. Within weeks some 5,000 or 6,000 were enlisted and absorbed into the regular Legion formations in Africa and Syria.

A large number of foreigners living in France also volunteered. After some initial hesitation, it was decided to accept them, and they were formed into three *régiments de marche*, ostensibly part of the Legion. A camp in the Pyrenees was set up, and carefully screened cadres and instructors were sent over from North Africa. The volunteers themselves were also carefully screened, and many were weeded out. Like so many of their predecessors of the First World War, they trained and fought on French soil, and many never saw Africa at all.

In October 1939 the first two formations were formed, and were known as the *21re* and the *22me Régiments de Marche de Volontaires Etrangères*, the R.M.V.E., for short, each of which consisted of three battalions. The officers were practically all French reservists, and the men came from some forty-seven different countries. There was a large contingent of Republican Spaniards.

When these two regiments were made up to strength, yet another was formed, in May 1940, which was known as the *23me Régiment de Marche de Volontaires Etrangère*, the 23rd R.M.V.E. In this latter formation difficulties arose between various factions, and it could not be called a 'happy unit'.

Back in North Africa, the disappointed French Legion officers made representations to be employed in France, and eventually it was decided to form a *régiment de marche* to fight in France. A depot was set up near Lyons in November 1939, and this formation became known as the *11me Régiment Etrangère d'Infanterie*, the 11th R.E.I. This did not turn out to be quite what the old Legion officers anticipated, as it could not strictly be called a true Legion unit in the proper sense of that expression, as over half of the men posted to it were re-called French reservists. Less than half were true legionnaires from Africa. Obviously the authorities were not fully convinced as to its reliability, and so took this unusual measure as a precaution. There was suspicion and uneasiness between the two groups. As soon as it was brought up to strength, the 11th R.E.I. was sent off to the Front in Lorraine.

In February 1940 it was decided to form another Legion regiment on similar lines, and the *12me Régiment Etrangère d'Infanterie*, the 12th R.E.I., came into being. Drafts of legionnaires were sent over from Sidi Bel Abbes, and these were mixed in with drafts of French reservists. There were the same divided views between the French reservists and the legionnaires. Many of the French reservists were disgruntled, objecting to having to serve in the Legion, instead of a French unit. Thousands of foreigners were volunteering, but the recruiting mechanism was slowed down, perhaps deliberately, and this formation filled up but slowly.

Yet another Legion unit was formed, in February 1940, in North Africa, for service in Europe, known as 'Group 97'. This was a true Legion unit, formed from the two Legion mechanized cavalry regiments for mobile reconnaissance in an armoured division. At first it simply had two squadrons of armoured cars, but two others were added a little later. In March 1940 it moved over to France.

Last, but by no means least, was formed the now famous 13th Demi-Brigade, which was destined to become one of the best known regiments on the Allied side. It was formed from volunteers from all units in the Legion, originally to assist Finland. It went first to France, and then, as it had been given some mountain training, was sent instead to take part in the Norwegian Campaign.

The German advance into Norway began on April 8th, 1940, but the 13th Demi-Brigade did not land in Norway until May 6th. On May 28th it went into action against the Germans at Narvik, which is well within the Arctic Circle, and the farthest north the Legion had yet fought. The Legion held the German advance but was badly battered in doing so, one company was overrun, and another lost over 60 men. A retreat was ordered, and the Anglo-French expeditionary force left Norway, the 13th Demi-Brigade returning briefly to Brest. Its morale was high, and it had given a very good account of itself in this sharp encounter with the enemy.

Meanwhile Allied and German armies statically faced each other until May 1940, a period referred to as the 'phoney war', during which period all the new Legion formations had either been sent into the front line, or were in immediate reserve. The hard winter weeded out many of the unfit.

Early in May 1940, the German offensive began, and all the Legion regiments were involved in the subsequent fighting, some disastrously. Dealing with them one by one: the 11th R.E.I. was in a blocking position at a place called Inor Wood, between the Rivers Meuse and Chiers, when on May 27th an enemy attack hit it. For a fortnight the legionnaires stood and fought back, holding up the German advance in this area, the fighting binding together the French reservists and old legionnaires as nothing else could have done. Casualties caused the companies to fall to half strength.

On June 11th, the 11th R.E.I. was ordered to leave its hard-held position in Inor Wood, and fall back in line with the general retreat. The withdrawal continued, and daily the legionnaires moved back, being on one occasion all but surrounded, when it was decided to burn the Colour rather than allow it to fall into enemy hands. The remnants of this regiment mingled with the other retreating troops, but the legionnaires kept up their discipline, which did much to steady a situation which verged on panic at times. At the time of the cease-fire only one-quarter of the men remained on their feet.

The story of the 12th R.E.I. is briefer and less fortunate. It was sent to the area of Soissons, and did not see action until June 6th, when the German attack hit it hard. For thirty-six hours the legionnaires were subjected to a heavy artillery barrage, during which time they were surrounded by the enemy. A break-out was attempted, but less than one-third succeeded in getting clear.

The 21st R.M.V.E. went to the Ardennes area and did not go into action until the night of June 9th/10th, when the defensive position it was holding was assaulted. The legionnaires recoiled, and were unable to hold it, after which they were taken out of the front line and not used again in battle.

The 22nd R.M.V.E. did a little better, being sent to a village near Peronne which it was ordered to take and clear. This was done, but the legionnaires were unable to hold the German counter-attack, which was supported by armour. The fighting went on for three days, during which time nearly half the men were lost.

The 23rd R.M.V.E., lacking training and equipment, was rushed into battle near Soissons, but was not heavily engaged until June 15th, when it was able to delay the enemy armour for two days at a bridge. As the Germans began to surround it, the legionnaires withdrew and joined in the general retreat, helping to collect together the debris of broken units.

The Legion mechanized reconnaissance unit, Group 97, went to the Somme area, making early contact with the enemy on May 18th, and for the next three weeks fought a series of delaying actions as the division retreated. Irritated by this constant withdrawal, on June 9th, in true Legion style, three squadrons of this Group formed up and assaulted the German armour. Outgunned and outmanœuvred by the Germans, the results were disastrous and within minutes half the Legion vehicles had been knocked out. The legionnaires had a chance to withdraw, but instead they re-formed and charged again, this time being completely overwhelmed.

Early in June, the 13th Demi-Brigade had returned to France from Norway, and just before the cease-fire it moved up to Rennes, where it briefly came into contact with the German advanced forces, but the cease-fire became effective before it could be deployed.

By an odd chance, the 13th Demi-Brigade was in the fortunate position of being able to choose whether it joined de Gaulle or stayed in France, as it was so near the Channel ports. Colonel Magrin-Vernerey, who had formed this demi-brigade, was still in command and he elected to go to England to fight on. About half his men followed him, and the remainder stayed behind. In England Colonel Magrin-Vernerey called his formation the '14th Demi-Brigade' for a while, and then reverted to the original title when he learned that the Vichy Government had formally abolished the '13th Demi-Brigade'.

The fate of the Legion survivors depended to some extent upon where they were at the time of the Armistice.

The Germans put pressure on the Vichy Government to disband the Foreign Legion, but this was resisted, and the victors were content to agree to periodic inspections by a German Commission, and to release certain Germans from it. Both these orders were largely circumvented. 'Wanted' legionnaires were either hastily shipped off to Indo-China or sent into the remote garrisons and posts. Inevitably some notice of the coming of the German inspection Commission was received, and when this became known the German legionnaires were sent out on long training marches until they had gone again.

After the fall of France the Legion strength dropped as recruiting sources dried up, and some changes were made. The 4th R.E.I. became known as the 4th Demi-Brigade, and was sent off into the depths of Senegal, after having been filled with legionnaires who did not wish to be handed over to the Germans. The 1st R.E.I. stayed at Sidi Bel Abbes, very much reduced in strength; the 2nd R.E.I. was dissolved, whilst the 3rd R.E.I. remained in Morocco on garrison duties. The 2nd R.E.C. was disbanded, and the 1st R.E.C. remained in existence on a reduced establishment.

About 1,000 Germans were released from the Legion at their own request, and were formed into a special battalion by the Germans: they were not allowed to go home to Germany.

For the next two years life in North Africa was one of humdrum garrison duty for the Legion, which had been left with its elderly small arms and equipment. During this period there was little trouble from the inhabitants either of Algeria or Morocco. The monotony was only varied by visits of the German Commission, with which the French officers delighted to play cat and mouse. Companies of 'wanted' legionnaires marched gaily out into the desert, until the danger was past. Occasionally, however, the Germans did have some success, and the unit of Nazi controlled German legionnaires rose in strength to about 2,000.

An embarrassing problem arose for the Legion. About 6,000 men had joined for the duration of the war, and they felt that when France was defeated in 1940 their war was over, and they wished to be discharged. The Vichy Government would not agree, mainly because most had nowhere to go and would remain in French North Africa to become an uncontrollable liability. They became discontented and mutinous, and efforts to persuade them to contract a regular Legion engagement generally failed, in spite of thinly disguised blackmail.

These 'durationists' were put into large camps, and were pressganged into working on extending the French railway southwards from Colomb Bechar. Conditions were extremely hard, and many died, although a number successfully 'disappeared' from North Africa.

Back in England, the 13th Demi-Brigade was built up to a strength of two battalions, and in December 1940 was used by de Gaulle to win over the French Cameroons. Having done that, it was sent on, round the Cape of Good Hope, to land at Port Sudan in February 1941, where it arrived just in time to take part in a campaign launched against the Italians.

The 13th Demi-Brigade was not actually profusely welcomed at first, but determinedly tagged on behind the leading British troops, who struck inland to seize Kassala. From Kassala, the British force swung inwards and made for the fortified Italian position at Keren, which by the end of February was being nibbled at from all sides. As much because of the shortage of numbers as for any other reason, the 13th Demi-Brigade was brought forward and allowed to have a go. On March 1st, it took part in an attack which completely cleared the Italians from an outlying position. When the final attack went in on the 27th, the 13th Demi-Brigade was present.

Having taken Keren, the British force turned towards the coast, to advance quickly on to the small Eritrean port of Massawa. The 13th Demi-Brigade came along too, having tasted blood, and was involved in the brief struggle for that place.

The legionnaires, who had suddenly become popular, would have liked to have continued with this force to finish the job, but de Gaulle needed them for another task. From May 27th, Syria was considered to be 'enemy-occupied' territory by the British, and it was decided to occupy that country before it could be exploited by the enemy. On June 8th, a joint British–Free French force crossed into Syria from Palestine and Trans-Jordan. One column, containing the Legion Demi-Brigade, struck across the mountains towards Damascus. It was hoped that Vichy resistance would only be token, but this was not so.

The main resistance to this Allied invasion was put up by the *6me Régiment Etrangère d'Infanterie*. The two opposing regiments of the Legion, the 6th R.E.I., fighting for Vichy France, and the 13th Demi-Brigade, fighting for the Free French, faced each other momentarily before they became locked in a deadly struggle, near a place called Damas, in the Syrian hills. The fighting lasted for two days, and as in all fratricidal warfare, casualties were heavy.

Even in the heat of battle, Legion traditions bubbled up. A patrol of the 13th Demi-Brigade bumped into a 6th R.E.I. outpost, which had seen it coming. The guard turned out, presented arms to the officer and then took the patrol prisoner. The guard commander said, 'You are the enemy, but first you are legionnaires.'

Legionnaires of the 6th R.E.I. prevented the Senegalese troops from looting and ill-treating the 13th Demi-Brigade wounded, only to fire deadly bursts of machine-gun fire at the oncoming men of that unit minutes later. Both sides gave full military honours to the dead legionnaires, regardless of which side they were on.

Better and more modern equipment perhaps turned the day in favour of the 13th Demi-Brigade, which brushed aside the remaining opposition to enter Damascus. The fighting continued spasmodically for another fortnight, during which time there were several instances of legionnaires from opposing camps coming into violent and bloody combat with each other. When the Allies occupied Syria, it was turned over to the Free French.

The 6th R.E.I. was dissolved, and its personnel, of whom there remained about 3,000, were given the choice either of being repatriated to Vichy territory or of joining the 13th Demi-Brigade. Roughly one-third joined the Demi-Brigade, enabling it to form a third battalion.[1]

In August 1941, Colonel Amilakvari took over the command of the 13th Demi-Brigade. Amilakvari was a White Russian refugee, a Georgian prince, who had been with the Legion since 1924, and with the Demi-Brigade since its formation. He was a man of immense charm and character, and did much to raise the morale and efficiency of the men.

When the Syrian business had been settled, it was decided that the Free French contingent should join the British 8th Army in the Western Desert, and in February 1942 the 13th Demi-Brigade took up a position, with other Free French troops, at Bir Hakeim, where a defensive 'box' was formed in the desert. Bir Hakeim was the southernmost point of the British defensive line that stretched southwards from the Mediterranean Sea.

In the spring of 1942 an enemy offensive began, and on May 27th the Legion position was attacked by Italian tanks. The legionnaires

[1] Only 2 officers and very few *sous-officiers* left the 6th R.E.I. to join the 13th Demi-Brigade, which illustrates the French cleavage of opinion at this period.

held the assault, and in the afternoon counter-attacked, and the score
at the end of the first day's fighting was thirty-two Italian tanks out of
action.

On June 2nd the Germans took a hand, and after encircling the
'box', attacked with armour, supported by Stuka dive bombers. This
continued for nine days, during which time the men stood firm,
although water was rationed, and food and ammunition supplies
dropped to a low level.

When it was seen that all was hopeless, the Legion was ordered to
break out, and this was planned for the night of June 10th/11th. As
soon as it became dark, a path through the protective minefield was
made, enabling the defenders to make their way through it into the
open desert. Bir Hakeim was successfully evacuated and all contact
with the Germans avoided. The enemy was not aware of what was
happening, and the next morning began to bombard the empty position.
During the siege, casualties had been caused, and as a result the 13th
Demi-Brigade was reduced to two battalions.

In October 1942 the British offensive began, and the Legion was
on the extreme south of the line, under orders to clear an escarpment, known as El Himeimat. By October 23rd the mines had been
cleared, and a Legion battalion assaulted across some open ground.
Whilst it was in the open the Germans launched a counter-attack,
which hit the Legion battalion in the side. The other Legion battalion,
which had been waiting in reserve, saw what was happening, and went
out to meet the enemy. It was a case of the counter-attackers being
counter-attacked.

Cross-fire caught the legionnaires, and the mortar fire rained down
on them as well. The attack hung fire. In his efforts to get his men
moving again, Colonel Amilakvari stood up to urge them on, but
minutes later he was killed by mortar fire, and the attack ground to a
halt. Amilakvari was yet another Legion commander to be killed at
the head of his men.

The 13th Demi-Brigade continued with the British 8th Army until
it reached Tunisia.

Meanwhile, events were taking place in other parts of North Africa,
and American forces landed at Oran on November 8th, 1942. The
Vichy Government ordered resistance, and one Legion battalion moved
out from Sidi Bel Abbes northwards, to halt when it came into contact
with the invaders. The Legion remained passive, although there were

a few scuffles, and the Vichy authorities in North Africa soon capitulated.

When the American landings at Casablanca had occurred, there was an attempt made by some German legionnaires to seize the Colomb Bechar radio station, which was a powerful one, but this was forestalled. It showed, however, that a tiny element of unreliable Nazi sympathizers lingered on in the Legion.

German reinforcements arrived in Tunisia, and in November 1942, Rommel made ready to resist. From the east the British 8th Army was already knocking at his door, whilst to the west both British and American forces were advancing. The Legion did not mean to be missed out, and got ready to accompany the British and Americans. Two Legion *régiments de marche* were quickly mustered for this purpose. One was the *1e Régiment Etrangère d'Infanterie de Marche*, or the 1st R.E.I.M., which was formed from the 4th Demi-Brigade, which had hastily been recalled from Senegal. The other was known as the *3me Régiment Etrangère d'Infanterie de Marche*, the 3rd R.E.I.M. The Legion cavalry managed to rake up a scratch unit, known as the *Groupe Autonome*.

The Legion was waking up and making ready for war again. All was cheerful bustle and enthusiasm. The first blood went to the *Groupe Autonome*, which on January 11th, 1943, attacked a German position near Foum El Gouafel, successfully capturing guns and prisoners, all for the loss of 5 wounded legionnaires. A flying start.

The Germans reacted and decided to broaden their position, aiming to seize the Kasserine Pass, and the 3rd R.E.I.M. walked head on into this offensive, hitting the enemy in the area of a height known as Jebel Mansour. The legionnaires were too eager and pushed too far forward, forgetting that their elderly small arms were no match for modern German weapons. The regiment was almost encircled, and only succeeded in getting clear with the assistance given by Allied aircraft.

The 1st R.E.I.M. went into action in conjunction with the British 1st Army, and met the full force of the German expansion, but although it lost over 300 men, it held on to its main positions. By this time the German offensive was running down, and Legion pressure was able to force the enemy backwards to regain all the lost ground. After this a period of stalemate set in along the western Tunisian front.

To the east, the 13th Demi-Brigade, crossing the border from Libya in February, came up against the German-held Mareth Line. Again, it was on the southern flank, in the mountainous area, and became involved in heavy fighting against the famous German 90th Light Division, around a height known as Djebel Garci. After two days it pushed the Germans out, but by this time it had become reduced to less than 1,200 all ranks.

After being issued with modern weapons and equipment, the 1st R.E.I.M. rushed forward to get to grips with the enemy again, and on May 7th attacked him successfully at the Pont du Fahs, in northern Tunisia. On the 9th the legionnaires pushed on to the town of Zaghouan, where they were halted by fire. But the end was near, and on May 11th there was a cease-fire. During this latter stage of the Tunisian fighting, the regiment of German ex-legionnaires who had left the Legion, or had been taken from it, won praise from Rommel for their conduct. It did not come into contact with the Legion on the battlefield. The men in this enemy formation were mostly taken prisoner, and most of them wished to rejoin the Legion, but for the moment this was not allowed. Later, in 1945, many were permitted to do so.

Once the Germans had been evicted from Africa, all thoughts turned to the invasion of Europe. The Legion strength in North Africa had dropped to well below 10,000, so it was decided that only one infantry regiment, a small mechanized unit and the 13th Demi-Brigade could be supported in the field. Accordingly, the remnants of the various Legion units were fused together into what became known as the *Régiment de Marche de la Légion Etrangère*, which was formally created on July 1st, 1943 (the R.M.L.E., for short). Its selected role was that of being motorized infantry to an armoured division. American arms and equipment were supplied and the men were mounted in 'half-tracks'.

The 1st R.E.C. was also brought up to strength, and given American vehicles.

In April 1944, the 13th Demi-Brigade, reinforced and re-equipped, after a period of hard training in Tunisia, was shipped off to Italy, where it joined the 5th Army, which was fighting its way slowly north-wards in the face of heavy opposition. The legionnaires came in contact with the enemy, and began crawling from height to height, ejecting the Germans as they came across them. The Legion was present in the fighting for Rome, and when it fell the Demi-Brigade

was sent northwards to take an enemy blocking position at a place
called Radicorfani. This was an almost perfect natural defensive work
on the top of an escarpment.

The legionnaires moved into action against it across a line of heights,
but were held off by fire when still some distance from it. Not being
able to advance by the normal approaches, they split up into small
detachments, and, armed with grenades, swarmed up the sides of the
escarpment to bomb the enemy out.

After this the 13th Demi-Brigade was sent to France, landing at
Cavalaire, on the Provence Coast, on August 16th, 1944, being the
first Legion formation to set foot in that country since 1940. The first
objective was Toulon, and the legionnaires took part in the fighting
that liberated that port, after which they turned northwards, moving
towards Lyons. The Legion was engaged in several fights on the way,
and took the leading part in the attack that drove the Germans from
the town. Casualties caused the Demi-Brigade again to be reduced to
two battalions.

The newly formed R.M.L.E. and the 1st R.E.C. formed part of the
5th Moroccan Division, and landed in the south of France in September 1944. Its first task was to penetrate the Haute Alsace, adjacent to
Switzerland. Strong German defences barred the way, being along the
mountain ridges to the west of the River Rhine, between Colmar and
the Swiss border. The key was a pass near Belfort, otherwise there
were few routes over the mountain ranges.

The first contact was made with the enemy on November 2nd,
and for the next ten days the legionnaires were continually in action,
dealing with enemy resistance in the villages through which they
passed. Heavy rains fell during most of this period, turning the ground
into mud, and as the tracks of the 'half-tracks' were of rubber the
vehicles slipped and skidded. The legionnaires had to frequently
hop out to push them up slippery inclines or to lever them out of
ditches.

The Legion closed in on Belfort, and as it got nearer it halted to
prepare for the assault. The 13th Demi-Brigade was brought from
being in reserve to assist, and on November 22nd the first outlying
objective, a village called Montbeliard, was attacked. In this fighting
the legionnaires destroyed half a dozen Panther tanks in the break-
through. The Legion pushed on and took Belfort.

In January, the legionnaires became involved in a furious battle for the possession of some Rhine bridges, which they won, but at some cost. The R.M.L.E. crossed the river and went on alone, unsupported by the armour. There was a sharp fight around a village called Gamsheim, which was taken, but the enemy almost immediately counterattacked. Within minutes one Legion company had been obliterated. Fire was rained down on the men, who held on to what they had taken. Then followed a series of small fights as the French advanced.

Next, the French aimed at Colmar, high on the north end of the mountain ridge. The much depleted 13th Demi-Brigade was again brought forward to assist the R.M.L.E. This was an infantry battle, and Colmar was seized on February 2nd. This was the last action of the Second World War for the 13th Demi-Brigade, which now had less than 1,000 men. It was withdrawn into reserve.

Its odyssey had been a long and heroic one, during which it had become one of the best-known French formations in the world. It had fought in the Arctic Circle, in West Africa, East Africa, Syria, the Western Desert, Tunis, Italy and France. Now it proudly, but sadly, withdrew from the fray. It had come out of the war well, and today its Colour is inscribed with the following battle honours: 'Douala', 'Cheren', 'Massaoua', 'Bir Hakeim', 'El Himeimat', 'Djebel Garci', 'Rome', 'Radicoffani', 'Toulon', 'Lyons' and 'Belfort'. Why 'Narvik' is not included as well is not clear, as the legionnaires fought well in that place, winning what was in fact the first small Allied tactical victory of the war.

The men of the 13th Demi-Brigade were given the right to wear a *fourangère* of the same colours as those of the *Médaille Militaire*, which was pinned to the Colour, yellow and green. One hangs in a place of honour in my study.

After taking Colmar, the R.M.L.E. moved towards Stuttgart, where, on February 15th, it became involved in a series of fights which led to a break-through. On the 19th, it took part in the hardest one, at a place called Lauterbourg, which the enemy held grimly. It had to be taken street by street, and dead legionnaires littered the town before it fell to the French.

After a short lull, this Legion formation, on April 4th, renewed the advance, and entered Stuttgart on the 21st, after which the Legion moved south to the Swiss border. Accompanied by the remnants of the 1st R.E.C., the depleted R.M.L.E. entered the Black Forest, where the Germans still lingered. The legionnaires encountered snipers and ambushes, and they had a particularly hard fight at a place called Friedrichshafen. On April 24th they reached the River Danube.

The war in Europe neared its close, but the Legion forged on through and into Austria, and on May 7th, the date of the cease-fire, it was near Arlberg, which the legionnaires entered the next day.

The war in Europe was over.

In June 1945, at a Victory Parade in Paris, detachments of the R.M.L.E. and the 13th Demi-Brigade were present.

7

Between the World Wars
(1918–39)

During the first part of the period between the two World Wars the Legion was engaged on active operations in Morocco, Syria, and then back again in Morocco, but during the latter part of that time it devolved into little more than a labour corps.

MOROCCO

During the First World War Algeria was comparatively quiet and all energies at Sidi Bel Abbes and Saida were directed towards training legionnaires to fight in Europe. Surprisingly enough, there was a steady flow of Austrian and German volunteers, who were sent to units in Morocco. As many French troops as could be spared had been drained off from Morocco by the end of 1914. The Legion there was reduced to two small *régiments de marche* and two Mounted Companies, and a good three-quarters of their personnel was either German or Austrian.

French policy was to remain static and to concentrate upon holding what territory they actually occupied, which consisted literally of a broad, wedge-shaped strip from Fez to Rabat and Casablanca, and the narrow Taza Corridor from Fez to Oujda. Most of the remainder of Morocco, especially the mountainous areas, was as yet untouched and virtually independent. Nothing was done to provoke retaliation, but there were frequent attacks on French posts and forts. Of the many small actions fought by the Legion, the name of Khenifra stands out. This fortress was continually besieged practically throughout the whole four years of the World War, but it held on successfully until the end.

During the last year of the war Moroccan pressure was increased as efforts were made to squeeze the French out, and a few forts and posts were abandoned. In one of these withdrawals, from a place called Tafilalet, in June 1918, one of the Legion Mounted Companies acted as the rearguard, distinguishing itself by holding off the swarm of Moroccan horsemen who hung on to the retreating column.

There was another Legion fight the next month at a place called Gaouz, in very similar circumstances, and when there was danger of the withdrawing column being cut off, the legionnaires charged with the bayonet to open the way again. In this action, 2 Legion officers and over 50 legionnaires were killed.

When the war in Europe was over the French turned their attention to Morocco, and troops were moved in for the pacification. In the mountainous areas the tribesmen were as firmly defiant and unruly as ever.

Following 1918 the Legion expanded and new units were formed as there was an influx of recruits owing to post-war conditions in Europe. When the R.M.L.E. returned from France it became the *3me Régiment Etrangère d'Infanterie,* and the two existing *régiments de marche* in Morocco, one supported by the 1st Regiment, and the other by the 2nd, were fused together to become the *4me Régiment Etrangère d'Infanterie.* It was decided to make full use of the Legion in the projected pacification in Morocco.

It was thought that there might be a limited use for horsed cavalry in North Africa, so it was decided to form a Legion cavalry regiment, at Saida, which was known as the *1e Régiment Etrangère de Cavalerie,* the 1st R.E.C. The first two squadrons were formed in 1921, and another two followed, but none were ready to go into action for some time.

The build-up in Morocco continued and the Legion units were sent there fairly quickly, but the policy remained static. The French could afford to take matters leisurely, as their military prestige was high. The main French defensive line faced northwards towards the Riff Mountains, the core of dissidence, and from there came frequent raids. At first the Legion was split into small detachments and employed mainly on patrolling, escort duty and building blockhouses.

The most influential Moroccan leader was Abdul El Krim, who made himself secure in the heart of the Riff Mountains in the area adjacent to Spanish Morocco, before spreading out along the northern edge of the French-held Taza Corridor. Krim had been employed in the Spanish government service, and through a series of circumstances had developed into a violent nationalist agitator.

Krim was astute and developed contacts with Europe and gained some European sympathy, but in material terms did not get much support, apart from a few arms and, infrequently, some ammunition. He recruited a few European adventurers, as well as Legion deserters, who gave his followers some sketchy training. They helped him to man the few artillery pieces he had acquired, mostly captured from the French and Spanish, and to train his men to fire the machine-guns. Krim had at least two aircraft, which were of considerable value to him in the early stages of his struggle.

By 1924, Krim had consolidated in the north, and as soon as he thought he was strong enough he turned his eyes southwards. He planned to attack the Taza Corridor along its entire length, where French troops were thinly spread, to cut and block it. It should be noted that the French were also actively engaged elsewhere in Morocco, mainly in the mountain ranges of the Greater Atlas, to the south of Fez, but not to the same extent.

The French, as well as Krim, were preparing, and when the line of protective forts had been completed along the length of the Taza Corridor, they began to push northwards to widen it. During 1922 and 1923 they made several attempts, but without any marked degree of success. The legionnaires took part in all this fighting. Three officers commanding Legion battalions were wounded in action and the list of Legion casualties grew longer. The Muslim opposition was stiff. Capture was dreaded more than death by the legionnaires, as it invariably meant torture and perhaps a lingering death. Bad treatment was the best for which a prisoner could hope. All kept one bullet in their pocket specially to use on themselves in an emergency.

One of its toughest fights was around a mountain known as Tichoukt, when a Legion detachment, acting as an escort to a ration convoy, was completely wiped out after a desperate struggle to try and break through. It was another Camerone.

On another occasion, at a place called Tseghouchen, a Legion battalion fought for twelve hours against superior odds, before crashing through to drive the Muslims back. Many other names could be recited, names of obscure places in Morocco, but names which mean a lot to the Legion, as they are places where the legionnaires fought, were wounded, suffered and died. Scoura, El Mers, Bou Khamoudja,

Ait Maklouf and others sound sweet to the ears of the Legion, although they indicate desolate, inhospitable, barren spots, hardly marked on the map.

In April 1924, Krim began to advance, and as a preliminary he crushed some tribes which had accepted French domination. French troops were sent to their aid, spreading out to block Krim's movement. At first the French did not fully realize the weight of the flood that was bearing down on them, and although they shuddered when it struck them, their defences held. The Legion was fully engaged and helped to bring Krim to a jarring halt. Krim then withdrew a little way, and began to play for time: he was expecting more artillery, supplies and European advisers.

In the following April, he launched his second offensive, for which he had managed to muster some 30,000 armed warriors. He suddenly hit the line of blockhouses along the northern edge of the Taza Corridor with such force that he drove some of them in. The French were overwhelmed and recoiled somewhat. Out of some 66 blockhouses, 9 were overrun and over 30 had to be evacuated. The bulk of the troops in the Taza Corridor were legionnaires.

This swift success probably surprised Krim himself, and he paused wondering what to do next. He made one or two aimless moves, but this hesitation gave the French time to recover and react against him. Reinforcements were rushed into Morocco, and these included two Legion battalions.

For a few days Krim continued to have small successes, but he soon ran into trouble as the legionnaires doggedly dug their toes in. They held him and with an effort seized the initiative. Many of the legionnaires were carrying on the fight independently, being completely isolated. Slowly but surely, the Legion began to force the Muslims to give ground. The two fresh Legion battalions stepped in and one by one recaptured many of the abandoned and captured blockhouses. Especially in the fighting around a place called Taounat did the Legion show up well.

Another notable Legion action took place around a hill known as Astar, which blocked the way of the Muslims. At one stage the Legion was ordered to abandon it, which it did, withdrawing a little way. Disliking this move, entirely on their own initiative the legionnaires went forward and regained the hill, successfully holding it against counter-attacks.

Yet another Legion fight centred around the hill of Mediouna, which was held by the Muslims. The Legion was ordered to take it, and making a night march, a battalion moved off for this purpose. The advanced guard, about 60 men, moving on ahead in the darkness, bumped into the main position, which it thought to be but a small blocking post. Without pausing, the legionnaires attacked up the slopes, using grenades and bayonets. The battalion, following on behind, hearing sounds of action, paused and waited for information. Soon 3 legionnaires returned: all the others had been killed. Roused to anger, the battalion spread out and moved into the assault, still in darkness, but the hill was empty, except for the mutilated bodies of the dead legionnaires.

Bibane, Mghala and Aoulai are some of the places where the legionnaires fought: a longer list could be written. One battalion commander was killed leading his men, and many other officers and men were either killed or wounded. Worse still, some were missing: not all deserters, although there was always a trickle. The Legion casualties amounted to over 3,000.

As regards the actual fighting, the Muslims liked to rush in with their long curved knives to get close in to the legionnaires, who with their long rifles and bayonets were then at a disadvantage. To combat these tactics, the Legion built stone sangers whenever they halted, with breast-high walls over which they could shoot.

By June 1925 Krim's advance was halted. The fact that he had been able to survive so long, fighting on two fronts, was due primarily to the fact that France and Spain were reluctant to co-operate. In August 1925, Marshal Pétain was appointed to command in Morocco, and he was able to persuade the Spanish to agree to making a pincer movement in conjunction with the French.

The French offensive began in May 1926, and as the French troops lined the Taza Corridor to advance, all four Legion infantry regiments were represented. Two squadrons of Legion cavalry were also present, but this was mainly infantry fighting. The movement was well co-ordinated and this time there were sufficient troops available. On a very wide front the French moved in on Krim's mountain stronghold, whilst the Spanish contained and pressed him downwards.

The fighting was on much the same pattern as before, the Muslims holding on until forcibly ejected from their positions. The 2nd Legion Regiment especially distinguished itself in an action at a place called

Djebel Iskritten, and other legionnaires did exceptional work at a spot called Targuist. There were countless other fights along the whole front as the French moved forward.

Weight and precision told against the Muslims, and a few days later, on May 23rd, 1926, Krim surrendered to the French. He realized the hopelessness of the struggle. Krim had hoped that other European countries would give arms, supplies and support, but little had materialized. He was a brave, cunning fighter who had given the Legion plenty of trouble. Two Legion battalions were detailed off to round up the Muslim prisoners, who numbered over 18,000.

This was virtually the end of the campaign, but although Krim had surrendered, the whole area remained alive and turbulent, and for the next few weeks all the Legion units were engaged on mopping-up operations and punitive expeditions. By Christmas 1926, the northern part of Morocco was pacified.

From 1927 until 1932 the bulk of the Legion remained in Morocco, but it was primarily used for constructional work, such as building blockhouses and roads; nevertheless the legionnaires were forever ready and willing to lay down the pick and shovel to take up their rifles to march off into the mountains. The peace was an uneasy one, as the Moroccans never at any time welcomed the French or willingly accepted their domination. It had been a forcible conquest, on similar lines to that of Algeria. No love was lost.

Native hatred welled up and burst out in February 1933, when the tribes simultaneously rose and moved down from the hills to attack the French. This time the French were more prepared and did not give any ground in the initial assaults, as previously, but there was some hard fighting for a short while by the Legion units, all of which were fully involved.

The revolt was disjointed and lacked central control and leadership: it was spontaneous and nationalistic, but entirely unco-ordinated. This made the French task much easier, and by the end of the year the rebellion had been crushed. It continued to simmer violently under the surface for a time, and then subsided. The next year, 1934, French columns traversed the length and breadth of the mountains, and at last succeeded in effectively occupying the whole of the country.

The Legion was active in both the fighting and the working in Morocco, and the conquest of that country must always be closely associated with it. Legionnaires had been in on it right from the beginning, had been present at all stages and had taken part in all battles and operations of any importance.

THE FIGHTING IN SYRIA

The first Legion unit to be sent to Syria, the newly granted French Mandate, was a battalion of the new 4th R.E.I., in 1922. With it went a Legion Mounted Company, with two men to one mule. The first years in Syria were quiet, but in July 1925 the Druse rose *en masse* against the French administration and streamed down from their mountain homes towards Damascus and the coastal plains. The Druse were out for blood, and all who stood in their way were massacred.

The Druse are a fanatical sect, an offshoot of Mohammedanism, which live in the mountains in the hinterland of Syria. They are brave, warlike and have always been difficult to handle. The Turks had left them alone as much as possible.

The small French garrison was alerted, and at once the Legion battalion was sent towards the mountains with the object of blocking one of the routes leading from them. The initial French idea was to attempt to bottle the Druse up and prevent them from erupting into the surrounding countryside.

On July 22nd, the Legion battalion moved in and cleared a village, known as Kafer, to the south-east of Soueida, the main Druse centre, thus firmly blocking the route from that place. In the fighting to take this village the Legion lost 18 men.

A few days later, as soon as the main body of the French troops was available, they attempted to move right into the heart of Druse territory to crush the revolt at the source, but they were too few, the Druse too many and the country too difficult. The French column met with disaster and had to hurriedly withdraw. The Legion was not involved.

This Druse success caused the revolt to burn brighter and to spread, so that soon the larger part of Syria was in open rebellion. The French garrison was forced on to the defensive, and in August had difficulty in maintaining control over the coastal plain.

The Legion Mounted Company was moved, together with the infantry battalion, to Moussiefre, a village near the mountain approaches, which it was ordered to hold. On September 16th, information was received that about 3,000 Druse were approaching. This report was accurate. At dusk the outermost company were attacked, but it had some machine-guns and was in a good defensive position, so was able to repulse the Druse fairly easily.

There was a pause after this setback, but as soon as it was really dark, the Druse put in their main attack, closing in from three sides on to the Legion positions. This was held, mainly by machine-gun fire. One party of Druse managed to get into a position on some higher ground which overlooked part of the village and so was able to pour fire down on one or two of the Legion positions. The villagers produced hidden fire-arms and joined in, shooting into the backs of the legionnaires whenever opportunity offered. One Legion company was in position at the tomb of a marabout, and was the object of a number of assaults throughout the night.

The main force of the Druse attacks lasted for about three hours, and then the fighting died down, when, apart from the action around the marabout's tomb, all was fairly quiet for the remainder of the night. All the Legion positions had held, and none had given way.

The Druse received reinforcements and the next morning again attacked in a resolute manner. Legion machine-gun fire halted the leading waves, but many Druse took cover and crept closer. During the course of the morning other attempts to attack were made, but all fizzled out.

In the afternoon, French aircraft appeared overhead to machine-gun the Druse, and that evening a reinforcement column arrived. But the enemy did not give in easily, and although cut off into small parties, all held on where they were. The firing and the fighting continued until long after darkness had fallen. After midnight, the Druse silently faded away.

When dawn broke the next morning, the 18th, the area around the Legion positions was strewn with men and horses, dead, dying and wounded, and the debris of battle. Over 500 Druse lay dead on the field of battle, and another 500 were captured as they were too badly wounded to crawl away. The total number of Druse dead and wounded who were carried off by their comrades, plus those who managed to crawl from the field, must have been very high. The Legion lost 47 killed and 83 wounded, whilst all the animals of the Mounted Company were killed.

This was the first French success in the campaign so far, and it was a Legion victory which paved the way for the taking of Soueida, which fell on the 24th.

Amongst the reinforcements that arrived in Syria, was a squadron of the newly formed Cavalry Regiment from Saida, which after being used for patrol work on the coastal plain for a while, was sent inland and based on a place called Rachaya, where there was a fort. Here the Legion cavalry squadron fought an action which lasted four days and was one of the major epics of this short campaign. Rachaya was the key to that part of the country, and a large force of Druse mustered in the neighbourhood with the intention of attacking this Legion garrison, rolling it aside and pushing on past it.

On the evening of November 20th, the leading elements of Druse rushed in and made the first assault just as the men were watering their horses. Although unexpected, this attack was repulsed and all the legionnaires manned the walls of the fort, being just in time to meet the main assault as it came in with the falling dusk. It was held by small-arms fire.

During the night, the Druse renewed their pressure and managed to break into part of the fort. After some desperate fighting the Legion was obliged to abandon part of its defensive position.

The next day, at dawn, a Legion bayonet charge enabled it to regain most, but not all, the lost area. During the day the Druse made frequent assaults but they were all repulsed, and the position remained the same: with the Druse maintaining a foothold inside the fort itself.

For three days there was incessant fighting, the Legion squadron successfully holding off a force of some 3,000 tribesmen. Carrier pigeons were sent off asking for aid, the only means of communication the garrison had.

On the third day, a Legion charge, with bayonet and grenade, cleared the Druse completely from the fort, but it was a last effort, as by now the men were thoroughly exhausted. The inside was littered with dead and dying. It looked like becoming another Camerone, and indeed, the French officer in command thought along those lines, as by the end of the third day's fighting the situation was critical as all the grenades had been used and the ammunition supply was dangerously low. The Druse must have been aware of this, and throughout the night kept up the pressure.

On the morning of the fourth day, ammunition was down to some fifteen rounds per man, and had to be used extremely sparingly. Each legionnaire kept one last round in his pocket for himself, as none meant to be captured alive: the Druse women practised fiendish tortures on captured enemy.

The Legion commander decided that if there was no sign of the relief column, as darkness fell, he would make a final, desperate charge out into the mass of surrounding Druse. However, in the afternoon the relief column pushed its way through—just in time. Baulked of their objective by a tiny band of legionnaires, the Druse sulkily faded away. It had been a magnificent defence, but half the squadron had become casualties.

In the November and December of 1925, the Legion was constantly in contact with the Druse, either 'on column', or in a defensive role. It distinguished itself on several occasions, notably at places called Messadi and El Chems.

By the following spring the rebellion had been broken, and the Legion was engaged in no more outstanding combats. The Druse tossed and turned mutinously, but refrained from breaking into open revolt again. By the summer of 1927, life in Syria had returned to normal.

After this revolt, two Legion battalions, a Mounted Company and a squadron of cavalry, remained in Syria. These were grouped together into a formation which became known as the *Régiment de Légion du Proche Orient*, the Legion Regiment of the Near East. Another battalion was sent in 1936, and the formation title was changed to *6me Régiment Etrangère d'Infanterie*, the 6th R.E.I.

THE LEGION IN ALGERIA

Between the two World Wars Algeria was quiet, and there was little Legion activity, the main efforts being concentrated upon training recruits and sending them into Morocco.

Sidi Bel Abbes, the first real home of the Legion, still continued in its role, although when the 2nd Regiment had been formed it had adopted Saida as its depot and home. When the 2nd Regiment moved into Morocco complete it became 'homeless' as the new cavalry regiment took over its barracks. The newly raised 3rd and 4th Regiments were also without roots of their own. For ten years or so this unsettled state of affairs existed, and as each formation was held responsible for its own recruiting, the result was that recruits were frequently 'poached' by one formation or another, and sometimes recruits were 'abducted' straight from the dockside at Oran. The regiments had their own recruiting cadres, which developed press-gang tendencies.

This was eventually sorted out, and in October 1933, Sidi Bel Abbes became the *Depot Commun de Régiments Etrangères*, that is a central depot for all the regiments of the Legion to which all recruits were initially sent. It was made responsible for training and posting them, and came directly under the control of the Inspector-General of the Legion.

1931 was the centenary year for the Legion, and it suddenly woke up to the fact that it was 100 years old. At times its future had been in doubt, but it had survived. Always jealous of tradition, the Legion decided to celebrate the occasion as well as it could. Little or no help was given by the military authorities, and as usual the legionnaires had to provide and improvise for themselves.

Invitations were sent out to ex-legionnaires to attend, and many were able to accept. The 1st Regiment had a magnificent band and corps of drums, and some very impressive parades and ceremonies were held. Incidentally, all the Legion regiments had their own bands, but these varied in quality and strength according to the circumstances.

Most things have happened to the Legion at one time or another, tragic, dramatic and comic, and such a mundane disaster as a railway crash is not excluded. On September 14th, 1932, a troop train, carrying 500 Legion reinforcements from Sidi Bel Abbes into Morocco, left the rails at a place called Turenne, and rolled over down the side of a hill; 56 legionnaires were killed and 217 injured. A handsome monument to their dead comrades was erected by the Legion on the hill-top.

8

Indo-China (1945–54)

Between the two World Wars the Legion formation, which had come to be known as the *5me Régiment Etrangère d'Infanterie*, the 5th R.E.I. remained in Indo-China, where things continued on a more or less even tenor. The outbreak of the Second World War made little appreciable difference for the first few months, but when France fell in 1940, a Vichy French governor was sent to take over.

To the north, in Chinese territory, the Japanese were busy fighting, and in September 1940, owing to her helpless and weak position, Vichy France allowed the Japanese to have military bases in Tonkin, ostensibly to pursue her war against China. In July 1941, the Japanese occupied the southern part of Indo-China. When this happened, the tiny French garrison stood-to and there were one or two brief scuffles between the Japanese troops and the legionnaires, but realizing how chronic his weakness was, the Vichy governor negotiated with them and allowed the inevitable to happen. It was agreed that France would nominally be in control, and that all her troops would retain their arms and have complete freedom of action.

Thus began a four-year period of occupation by the Japanese, who left internal matters of administration as far as they could either completely alone or to the French. During this time the Legion remained static, mainly based on Ventri, Dap Cau and Tuyen Quang, although there were small detachments in other places too. The legionnaires had small arms, but scanty ammunition, with little prospect of obtaining more. They were static because they were powerless to take action against the Japanese army, which, however, was careful not to provoke.

Whilst viewing the Japanese with suspicion, the Legion was no less concerned, the officers especially, with Nationalist China, a doubtful friend on the northern border, which began a campaign to persuade

183

legionnaires to desert into China. This had moderate success, probably due to frustration as much as anything else. Many a legionnaire, afraid of being left out, crossed over into China because he thought the war would be over before he was able to have a crack.

Owing to its isolation and the state of the war, no Legion reinforcements arrived, except a few Germans in 1940, who were hastily dispatched from Dakar, and its strength sank slowly. The majority of time-expired men stayed with the Legion, having little other option, as there were hardly any facilities for returning them. Some took their discharge and made their way to China either to fight against the Japanese or to make their way home. In 1940, the 5th R.E.I. had been about 5,000 strong, but this figure fell to below 3,000.

On March 9th, 1945, Japan decided forcibly to occupy the whole of Indo-China, and disarm and intern the small French garrison. This was a surprise move and all the French units were presented with an ultimatum to lay down their arms. The Legion refused to do this, and there were a series of sharp skirmishes. A few detachments of legionnaires were overrun and a number of atrocities were inflicted upon the unfortunate prisoners.

The 5th R.E.I. consisted of three battalions, and all its sub-units merged together from their several stations during the night of March 9th, and the following day. On the 11th, the Legion began a fighting retreat into Yunnan. The Japanese hastily deployed to block their way, and did manage to ambush the legionnaires on several occasions, but each time the men charged through. There were several instances of heroism as the Japanese were roughly bundled aside. One company commander, leading his company into the attack, was killed by the enemy.

The distance to the Chinese border was about 500 miles and the route lay through difficult country, along jungle paths, across rivers and over steep hills. After fifty-two days marching and fighting the Yunnan frontier was reached, but the legionnaires still had to struggle on for another 200 miles before a motorable road was met with. The remnants of the 5th R.E.I., totalling just under 3,000 men, was allowed to remain in that part of China for the time being. Meanwhile, the Japanese flooded into the whole of Indo-China, clamping that country under military rule, and breaking down what was left of the French administration.

The tide of war swung against the Japanese, and on August 19th,

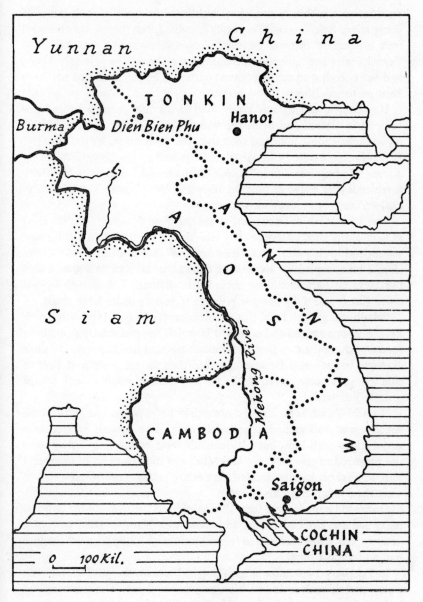

Indo-China

1945, almost within hours, they withdrew the bulk of their army of occupation. A few second-line units remained, but they stood aside and took no part in internal matters. A complete vacuum was left. The French, who had governed absolutely for almost the last fifty years, had not encouraged active political parties. The Japanese had not been keen on them either.

However, a nationalistic party existed, having germinated and developed in China, and upon the withdrawal of Japanese authority, it moved into Indo-China and took over the government of the country. It was known as the 'Viet Minh', and its leader, Ho Chi Minh, set up a form of administration in Tonkin, Annam and Cochin-China, which three countries together became known as 'Viet Nam'. Viet Nam was declared to be an independent state.

The Viet Minh did not want to see the French return, nor it seems at first did it anticipate that they would, but the Potsdam Conference put an end to this idea. The Allies declared that northern Indo-China should be occupied by Nationalist China for the time being, and that the southern part should be occupied by Britain. The British landed token forces and did what was possible to restore order from chaos.

Britain was glad to hand this problem over, and on March 6th, 1946, French troops arrived and occupied Hanoi. They immediately set about re-establishing their authority as though nothing had happened in their absence, but when it became apparent that the restoration of French rule was unpopular and might be hard to enforce, other French troops quickly followed.

Ho Chi Minh was already operating his government with some success, and had gained a large following. The French entered into negotiations with him, but his demands were extreme, and they were not prepared to give way. Ho Chi Minh returned from an unsuccessful visit to France, having decided that active revolt was the only way to eject the French from his country.

It should be made clear that 'Viet Minh' was the name of the political party led by Ho Chi Minh, and that 'Viet Nam' is the name of a country, but I will continue to refer to it throughout by its more familiar name of Indo-China.

In February 1946, after languishing in Yunnan, the 5th R.E.I. began a slow march back to Indo-China, arriving in April. The time-expired legionnaires were returned to Algeria, which practically emptied the regiment, so a few weeks later it was dissolved. However, the Legion did not sever its connection with Indo-China, in fact, far from it, as about this time three other Legion regiments made their appearance in the Far East.

The whole of Indo-China seethed with discontent, and the people were surly and disappointed. The Chinese Nationalists were still in control of the northern part of the country, but their attention was more and more distracted as they became embroiled in their own civil war. In theory, the French sphere of influence consisted of most of Annam, Cochin-China and the southern part of Tonkin, and they energetically set about restoring their authority. As a political policy they decided to support Bao Dai, the King of Annam, which country was the core of Indo-China, but this French puppet was unpopular and his people viewed his relationship with the French with distrust. Bao Dai was kept on his throne by French sub-machine-guns.

Indo-China was full of factions and influential personalities all pulling against one another, each trying to further its own interests. First, and most powerful, were the French, trying to turn the clock back. Then there was the Viet Minh, the only organized opposition, Communist inspired and supported. Then there was the unpopular Bao Dai, collaborating with the French. Then there was the King of Cambodia, who wanted to get rid of the French, but feared and distrusted the Viet Minh—but which the most, he did not know. Then there was the adjacent, elderly King of Laos, who wanted peace and was prepared to run with the hare and hunt with the hounds to get it. There were many other cross-currents, but those were the main ones. Cochin-China, a Viet Minh stronghold, was in open foment. Hatred and bitterness, and the lust for power influenced actions, and all were suspicious of the others.

Once Ho Chi Minh decided upon war he began to make preparations for a lengthy guerrilla campaign, and arms and ammunition began to be smuggled in by sea. Supply dumps were set up within the country, personnel were trained as guerrillas and organized into detachments, and his political agents penetrated the length and breadth of Indo-China preaching the Viet Minh gospel, threatening, teaching, persuading and wheedling.

The French were under no illusion as to the task that faced them, and reinforcements began to pour in. The first Legion formation to arrive was one of those made ready to fight the Japanese, the *2me Régiment Etrangère d'Infanterie*, which had been brought to life again.

It was definitely the 'new Legion' that was arriving, in that there were in its ranks few who had served prior to 1939 or 1940.

The 2nd R.E.I. disembarked at Saigon, in February 1946, and was at once sent into southern Annam, where it was given the task of restoring French authority. The population was actively and hostilely opposed to this and had fled to the hills, leaving their villages empty. In many places, the Legion met with guerrilla opposition, but by the end of May it had succeeded in persuading most of the people to return. But they remained sulky and discontented, and would not willingly co-operate with the French. Everywhere underground the Viet Minh political agents were working on the inhabitants. The 2nd R.E.I. was granted an Army Citation for its work. During three months' guerrilla fighting in southern Annam, it lost over 230 men.

The next Legion formation to arrive in Indo-China was the 13th Demi-Brigade, which disembarked in March 1946. It was sent off to assert French authority in Cochin-China, a land of swamp and river, where it remained for two years. Again, it encountered a sullen population difficult to control and unwilling to co-operate. Under cover the Viet Minh agents were conditioning the people for active rebellion, and the legionnaires suffered a constant drain of casualties due to ambushes and skirmishes.

The third Legion formation to arrive in Indo-China was the *3me Régiment Etrangère d'Infanterie*, which disembarked in June 1946, and was also sent to Cochin-China on a similar mission. This formation had been 're-created' from the R.M.L.E.

The main difficulty at this stage of hostilities, which from a military point of view can be thought of as the 'quiet period of Viet Minh preparation', was telling friend from foe, as the guerrillas wore no distinguishing uniform or badges. Many times unfortunate legionnaires were suddenly fired on by persons they thought to be harmless peasants.

Owing to the adverse situation in Indo-China and the desperate need for reinforcements both to build up the security force and to replace losses, it was decided to take full advantage of the Legion's recruiting boom and to expand it. Sidi Bel Abbes blossomed out and became a gigantic training centre, and the *1e Régiment Etrangère d'Infanterie* became the formation responsible for this.

The Nationalist Chinese remained in occupation of northern Indo-

China, and the fact was that France was only in partial possession of the southern part. A foothold had been gained in Tonkin, where the French occupied the Delta area, mainly Hanoi and Haipong. They also occupied points along the Annamese coastline and parts of Cochin-China—that was all. The remainder of the country, the hinterland of Tonkin, most of Annam and large stretches of Cochin-China had not yet been penetrated. The French had to struggle to retain such small footholds as they had.

The Viet Minh spent most of 1946 in negotiating and in trying to enlist foreign sympathy, but did not neglect preparations for guerrilla war should events turn out to be unfavourable to them.

The first open rupture of any size between the Viet Minh and the French occurred in November 1946, at Haipong. The Viet Minh blankly denied complicity with the current spate of guerrilla activity. The French military came into contact with a large band of Viet Minh which was caught smuggling in arms. Fire was exchanged and a small battle developed. Artillery had to be brought into action before the smugglers were dispersed.

Ho Chi Minh was not dismayed by the outcome of this incident, on the contrary he was encouraged as it had taken a large number of well-armed French troops some time to disperse his poorly armed men. In view of this, he was advised by his military chief, General Giap, to attempt a sudden all-out attack on the French in the Delta in an effort to drive them out before they could effectively build up their strength. Time seemed to be against the Viet Minh.

This first attack by the Viet Minh took place on December 9th, 1946, and was a failure, and the French drove back the enemy with ease. General Giap had mustered several thousand semi-trained men for this assault, and all were armed. Although he had no artillery, even at this early stage he possessed mortars, but he clearly under-estimated the abilities of the French troops and over-estimated those of his own men. Viet Minh casualties were heavy whilst the French hardly had any at all.

However, Giap learnt this lesson well, and until his own army was built up, and he had sufficient artillery, he stuck rigidly to hit-and-run tactics.

This attack on the French was the match which fired off open warfare, and from this moment guerrilla activity was intensified wherever it was possible, and the situation became such that French troops could not venture into the countryside, unless in force or heavily escorted.

The next Legion formation to arrive was the *1e Régiment Etrangère de Cavalerie*, in January 1947, which was sent straight into Central Annam. It was equipped with light tanks and armoured cars, but it did not remain intact as a unit as, in April, it was dispersed in sub-units to perform road escort duties along the roads of Indo-China.

The year 1947 was one of tiny, uneasy guerrilla irritations. Generally the Viet Minh lay low, avoiding action whenever possible, and concentrating on building up their organization. The French spent much of their time searching villages for hidden arms or supplies, and this became a routine task.

In March the 3rd R.E.I. left Cochin-China, which had already cost it some 200 dead, and moved into Tonkin, where it was given the task of patrolling from the Delta to the Chinese border along the coast to the north-east, and inland to Kao Bang. There are a series of high ridges spreading out fan-wise northwards from the Delta, separating the several rivers which flow into it. Kao Bang was on the last one of these, the one overlooking the Chinese frontier to the north-east. The 3rd R.E.I. was also employed on building a number of fortified posts along the main colonial highways for their protection.

In July a detachment of the 13th Demi-Brigade was ambushed whilst on patrol, near Saigon, losing 17 dead and as many wounded. In November a squadron of the 1st R.E.C. surprised a band of guerrillas near a village called Tra-Vinh, killing over 50 of them. That was the pattern of events for the Legion throughout the year.

The next year was spent by the French in making their footholds more secure, and in preparing to expand them. They built strong defensive posts around the towns, and began to erect chains of small, concrete forts at intervals along the strategic routes. The Viet Minh were still cautiously feeling their way along too, but as the year unfolded a more aggressive trend became apparent and bodies of guerrillas, at night, attempted more ambitious ambushes and attacks, especially to the north-east of Haipong.

Of all the Legion formations in Indo-China perhaps the 3rd R.E.I. was the most heavily engaged, as its presence to the north-east of the Delta prevented free Viet Minh access to China. The string of defensive posts along the routes between Hanoi and Kao Bang became the guerrillas' main object. The area flared up and became highly dangerous. When the monsoon rains began in April, the Viet Minh attacks became more frequent, and it necessitated a major road-opening operation to get supplies to Kao Bang and Bac Kan, the main French posts.

General Giap estimated that the Nationalist Chinese were about to evacuate the northern part of Tonkin, and he planned to move in on their heels. In an effort to try and force the French to withdraw he concentrated all his trained guerrillas to strike at Bac Kan. Tactically, the key to Bac Kan was a defended village on the same ridge, known as Phu Tong Hoa, about twelve miles from it. This was an entrenched camp, constructed about the village itself, held by a Legion company from the 3rd R.E.I., consisting of 104 legionnaires, with two light machine-guns.

The Viet Minh guerrillas closed in on Phu Tong Hoa, and after a period of reconnaissance along the ridge, made ready to attack. It is not known with any degree of accuracy how many men Giap used in this assault, but he did have about ten heavy mortars. On July 25th, in the evening, after a heavy shower the Viet Minh opened up with their mortars on to the Legion post. At first the whole weight of it was directed on to the west side of the defences, which were in the form of a square, with a sand-bagged bastion at each corner. Mist covered the hills and visibility was poor.

As darkness fell there was a lull in the mortar fire, but instead of attacking as the Legion expected, the enemy simply turned his mortars on to the main entrance and began blasting away. Both the Legion officers had already been killed, and the radio set put out of action, but not before warning of this attack had been passed back.

About 9 p.m. that night the Viet Minh attacked in the darkness, and by sheer weight of numbers the successive waves of attackers succeeded in swamping three out of the four corner bastions. The fourth held fast. Minutes later the legionnaires counter-attacked and recaptured one of the lost posts at the point of the bayonet. This meant that the village position was now shared by both the Viet Minh and the Legion, each holding two corner bastions.

For over an hour there was fierce fighting, during which the legionnaires recaptured the third bastion from the Viet Minh, thus leaving only one remaining in enemy hands. Then the moon rose, the moonlight being of advantage to the legionnaires who could now see to shoot. They soon drove the enemy out of the remaining bastion, and once again the whole position was theirs. All this fighting was directed by the *sous-officiers*, there being no officers.

After this, for half an hour, the Viet Minh fired their mortars and small arms into the post, but the Legion fought back. But half an hour was enough, and the attackers then withdrew silently into the surrounding jungle. Giap's offensive had met with a check, and the French post remained intact. At dawn the next day over 40 enemy dead lay outside the defensive wire. The Legion company had lost 23 killed and 33 wounded, half its strength.

When the commander of the 3rd R.E.I. learned of this attack he himself led the relief force. Briefly warned of his arrival, the Legion guard turned out in ceremonial dress to receive him, just as if it were a normal routine inspection visit.

It was a dramatic and heartwarming sight, and it was described to me by the commander of the 3rd R.E.I. himself. The line of 10 legionnaires stood stiffly for a moment and then 'presented arms', their red fringed epaulettes, white képi covers and blue cummerbunds making a splash of colour against the background of jungle foliage. The trumpeter sounded the salute, the guard 'shouldered arms', and the guard commander, a sergeant, stepped forward to report to his colonel.

General Giap continued concentrating his men in this area, and French convoys to the Kao Bang and intermediate posts were frequently ambushed, the road was cut and bridges were blown. War material was reaching the Viet Minh from Red China, and Giap contented himself with merely keeping the pot boiling until he was stronger.

In November 1948, yet another Legion formation arrived in Indo-China, this time the 1e *Bataillon Etrangère Parachutiste*, the 1st B.E.P., which had been formed in Algeria. It was sent to Tonkin and was used at first in an ordinary infantry role. A little later a second unit of Legion paratroops arrived at Saigon, the 2nd B.E.P., and this was sent to Cambodia, acting in an internal security role.

In April 1949, the 1st B.E.P. concentrated in the region of Vietri, and formed the spearhead of a French column which on May 12th forced its way into Tuyen Quang, the old Legion post, against Viet Minh opposition.

Meanwhile, the 1st R.E.C. remained in the marshy areas of Cochin-China, where it formed an amphibious group, being equipped with old

Legionnaires of the 13th Demi-Brigade patrolling in the Aures Mountains

Patrolling Legion Cavalry near the Tunisian barrage

American 'Alligators' (light amphibious armoured vehicles) which proved to be very useful in that type of country. The 1st R.E.C. was successful in cutting off several bands of guerrillas as its peculiar vehicles gave it mobility over both land and swamp.

When, in 1949, the Chinese Communists drove the Nationalists from the mainland, they were able to give Ho Chi Ming more material aid, which included artillery. This extra quantity enabled Giap to form 'regular' formations. The Chinese also lent him instructors. By this time Giap had several thousand trained guerrillas under his hand in Tonkin and just over the border in China, over and above the cadres scattered throughout Indo-China and the part-time volunteers. He wisely stuck to guerrilla tactics.

In November 1949, the old *5me Regiment Etrangère d'Infanterie* was revived as a formation. It was employed in Tonkin on escort duty and constructional work.

The French began to recruit and train local Viet Namese, who had previously not been considered to be suitable material, and a number, in complete sub-units, were sent to be attached to the Legion, everyone assuming, quite correctly, that the Legion would be able to assimilate them successfully. Soon most Legion formations had these Viet Namese units attached to them.

By September 1950 Giap estimated that he had sufficient artillery and that enough of his 'regular' units had reached the standard of training necessary to be able to clear the French completely out of Tonkin. As a first step he hoped to clear them from the Kao Bang ridge, the one adjacent to the Chinese frontier, then from a parallel one, and to force them back to the line of the Red River. The French had garrisons at Kao Bang and other points along this ridge, the chief being Langson. The key defensive post between these two places, also perched on the frontier ridge, was Dong Khe, held by two companies of the 3rd R.E.I.

Giap decided to hit Dong Khe and break through at this point in strength. Early on September 16th, the Viet Minh encircled the position and began shelling. This continued throughout the day, during which time a proportion of the defences were dismantled. There were four main sand-bagged bastions, which formed the pattern of the defensive lay-out.

The next morning, under cover of mortar fire, the waves of infantry attacked. It has since been estimated that Giap had about twenty of his 'regular' battalions on the ridge, of which about six were directly concerned with this assault. The enemy broke through the outer wire perimeter and, gaining a foothold, drove the legionnaires from one corner bastion. The fighting lasted for several hours and the defenders were steadily pressed backwards, losing another corner bastion. Then a third one fell. By the end of the day all the defenders were cramped into the one remaining defence work. Already there were over 40 Legion dead and nearly 100 wounded.

By nightfall the wire had been penetrated everywhere. As soon as it was dark the legionnaires counter-attacked and recaptured one of the bastions. The fighting continued on throughout the night, and during the hours of darkness this one particular bastion changed hands no less than eight times, but it was finally lost when the legionnaires were driven out just before dawn.

As soon as it was daylight it was seen that most of the shelters and trenches had caved in. The legionnaires were still resisting but were cramped into the last defensive post. During the morning the Viet Minh used incendiary bombs to set fire to the remaining defences to drive the legionnaires out. Seeing that all was hopeless, the Legion decided upon one last gallant sortie. All those capable of standing, formed up together and charged out into the surrounding mass of Viet Minh infantry, which contained Dong Khe. The majority of the survivors were able to make their way through the jungle to link up with other French posts.

It was another Camerone.

When Dong Khe was attacked a strong column went out from both Kao Bang and Lang-Son to try and crush the attackers in a pincer movement. The column from Kao Bang contained most of the 3rd R.E.I., whilst the other had the 1st B.E.P. To shorten a sad story, both were ambushed and ran head-on into Viet Minh fire, suffering terrible loss. Sub-units were scattered, and only with difficulty gathered together again. Two complete Legion battalions were written off in the fighting on Kao Bang ridge.

The whole frontier ridge had to be abandoned and the French forces withdrew westwards over the next one, parallel to the line of the Red River. It was a desperate fighting withdrawal, in which the Legion units acted as the rearguard screen. Viet Minh casualties must have been heavy as the infantry charged forward in mass after the then prevailing Communist pattern. It was sheer mass that defeated the French in this action, together with the fact that Giap had developed good radio communication with his units.

The 1st B.E.P. suffered 90 per cent casualties and was disbanded: it had been sacrificed to cover the retreat back to the Red River.

Apart from the terrific boost to morale this success in the field had given the Viet Minh, it gave Giap the distinct advantage that he had a firm base to work from, lying adjacent to the country which was supplying him and helping to train his men. It is thought that he had about thirty 'regular' infantry battalions, and at the end of 1950 Giap began to organize them into divisional formations and to prepare for positional warfare. Elsewhere guerrilla activity was intensified.

French morale drooped after this defeat at the hands of what they thought of as ill-equipped and ill-trained guerrillas. The shock to military pride caused a defensive attitude of mind to develop. At night the majority of troops shut themselves up in their posts and pill-boxes, which lined the routes, and thus the whole countryside was turned over to the Viet Minh, who were able to roam freely about as they liked and to intimidate any pro-French natives.

Under the leadership of Marshal Lattre de Tassigny, the French recovered from their period of depression and went over to the offensive again, having some small success in clearing parts of the Delta area.

The pattern of the war remained much the same. In January 1951 a patrol from the 13th Demi-Brigade surprised a band of guerrillas and killed over 200 of them. This regiment fought another successful defensive fight in the December, and a number of Viet Minh dead lay outside the post when it was all over.

One battalion of the 5th R.E.I. fought a good action at a place called Noi Thon, in October 1951, when a large Viet Minh force was located there. One company assaulted from the north and another from the east, and in spite of checks due to mortar fire, the position was taken after a stiff fight. The legionnaires, in the face of small-arms fire, charged over the bamboo palisades.

The 1st B.E.P. was re-formed in March 1951, and with the 2nd B.E.P. took part in several parachute drops. The paratroops took part in the fighting around Nglia Lo, a key defensive position on the ridge between the Black and the Red Rivers. Nglia Lo fell on October 18th, 1952, the occasion being just as if a sea dyke had been breached, and the whole line of French fortified positions on the ridge collapsed.

A fighting withdrawal had to be made, which was covered by the Legion paratroops. Another slice of Tonkin had fallen to Giap.

In April 1953 Giap invaded Laos with at least two of his 'regular' divisions, and when the monsoon broke he evacuated, returning to northern Tonkin with the valuable opium crop. The fact that Giap was able to carry out such a manoeuvre upset French calculations, so it was decided to establish a strong 'centre of resistance' to prevent such a move happening again. The place chosen was Dien Bien Phu, a village at the junction of three tracks in northern Tonkin.

Meanwhile the pattern of the fighting for the Legion elsewhere remained the same: sweeps, road escorts, searches, patrols and small operations, wherever they were. The Legion did its full share of the constructional work.

In fact the many and varied skills of the legionnaires had been eagerly sought by one and all, and this resulted not only in the formation of several specialist Legion companies for particular tasks, but also that legionnaires, in ones, twos or small groups, were lent to units or bases as technicians, mechanics, builders, plumbers and cooks. Individual legionnaires were scattered throughout Indo-China performing jobs for which they were qualified, and they mixed with and came into personal contact with the French army to an extent never known before.

There sprang into existence several Legion motor transport units, and river transport units as well. One Legion *ad hoc* company had fifteen armoured boats in which it transported men and stores along the Mekong River. Another Legion company was formed and used as an air supply unit, another packed supplies to be dropped from aircraft, and another serviced helicopters. One ran the armoured trains in the Delta. The Record Office at Sidi Bel Abbes admits that it does not know exactly how many of these specialist Legion companies there were in existence; it records over thirty, but thinks that there were several more.

In November 1953 the 1st B.E.P. dropped by parachute and secured Dien Bien Phu. The airstrip was repaired, and troops and supplies were flown in. In the following weeks the force was built up to some twelve infantry battalions, its strength eventually reaching over 14,000. The defences were carefully laid out and it developed into a huge sprawling entrenched camp. The defended localities, mutually supporting, were well sited and well dug-in, and heavily wired and mined. All were given names, but it will be sufficient only to mention those which were held by the Legion.

By December four more Legion battalions were flown in; in January 1954 another arrived, and in April, the 2nd B.E.P. dropped in by parachute, which meant that out of the twelve battalions garrisoning Dien Bien Phu, seven were of the Legion—over half.

As to their dispositions, one battalion of the 3rd R.E.I. held a posi-

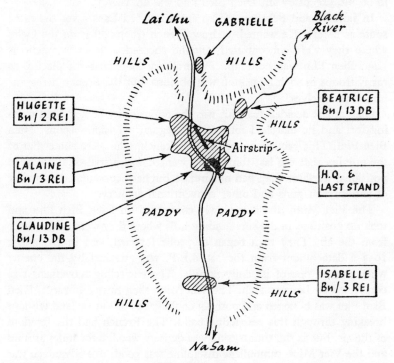

Dien Bien Phu

tion, detached to the south, known as 'Isabelle'. One battalion of the 13th Demi-Brigade held a position on the south-west of the perimeter, known as 'Claudine', and another battalion of the same regiment held a position to the north-east, known as 'Beatrice'. One battalion of the 2nd R.E.I. held a position on the north-western part of the perimeter, known as 'Huguette', and the 1st B.E.P. were in mobile reserve.

Another battalion of the 3rd R.E.I., plus its Mortar Company, arrived later and was detailed to hold a position on the western perimeter, known as 'Lalaine'.

Dien Bien Phu was in the centre of a huge 'bowl', fringed by low, wooded hills which overlooked it on all sides. The site itself was of no tactical importance. There was no land communication between this French garrison and the Delta, as the routes all led through hostile territory infested with Viet Minh guerrillas. Nothing could get either in or out, except by air. Dien Bien Phu was an 'island'.

In January and February, Giap again invaded Laos, over the same route as before. He wanted to draw French troops off from the Delta where they were concentrated, and he succeeded to some extent as Dien Bien Phu was built up. The military foolishness of placing so many troops in such a position was obvious, but the French had committed themselves.

Giap at last decided that this was the opportunity he had been waiting for, and he marched four of his 'regular' divisions against Dien Bien Phu. This vaguely surprised the French, who were somewhat of the opinion that the last thing Giap wanted was a trial of strength in positional warfare. Giap had no aircraft, but had accumulated a number of anti-aircraft guns and other conventional artillery.

The Viet Minh divisions slowly converged on Dien Bien Phu and took up positions in the surrounding hills where they were under cover from the air. They then began to probe forward, and in December 1953 a detachment from the 1st B.E.P. was attacked by the enemy when out on one of its daily patrols. The encircling movement was completed by January 11th. The Viet Minh then turned inwards. Dien Bien Phu was besieged and nothing could get in or out by land without breaking through this restricting band. The French had the freedom of the air, but as the countryside was densely wooded for miles around and the Viet Minh camouflage discipline was good, this advantage was largely nullified.

Giap began to close inwards, at the same time bringing his anti-aircraft guns into play. The French were surprised at the number he had and their accuracy. The dropping of napalm bombs on the Viet Minh positions and saturation bombing seemed to have little effect. When the Viet Minh reached the open country within the 'basin', they began sapping forward in the old-fashioned way. The ring tightened and by the beginning of March the Viet Minh trenches were about two miles from the outer defences of Dien Bien Phu. At night Legion patrols went out and filled them in but it was a losing battle.

The French welcomed what was to be a test of strength. For years they had been fighting an elusive enemy with whom they could seldom get to grips. They anticipated that Giap's precious 'regulars' would batter and decimate themselves against such strong defences. The fighting at Dien Bien Phu can roughly be divided into the following phases: the initial attack, the second attack, a period of encroachment and then the final assault.

The Viet Minh trenches got closer and closer, and the French aircraft were unable to neutralize the enemy anti-aircraft guns. Next, Giap turned his field artillery, of which he had recently received a quantity, on to the French positions, and the first attack was preceded by a lengthy, and heavy, Viet Minh bombardment. This surprised the French by its density and accuracy. The Commanding Officer of the 13th Demi-Brigade and several legionnaires were killed by it.

At dusk on March 13th, waves of Viet Minh infantry assaulted 'Beatrice', on the north-east, held by a battalion of the 13th Demi-Brigade. It was a mass infantry attack, pressed forward regardless of casualties. The enemy penetrated right up to the outer defence wire, and after a little while the Viet Minh dead draped the wire, masking the fire of the legionnaires. The Commanding Officer of this battalion and 6 other officers were killed, and the Legion that night suffered over 400 casualties. Later that night 'Beatrice' was lost: it was simply swamped and the Legion fire was neutralized by the solid 'wall' of enemy dead.

Similar tactics and methods were tried at the same time against 'Gabrielle' and 'Isabelle', but both held fast and the Legion successfully drove off the attackers. At dawn the next morning both sides paused and there was a mutual unofficial truce to enable the combatants to recover their dead and wounded: the first of its kind in the Indo-China fighting.

After this first massive attack which had dented the French defences, the Viet Minh resorted to sapping again, whilst their artillery pounded away at the defences of Dien Bien Phu. There was another attack on March 25th, when 'Lalaine', held by the legionnaires of the 3rd R.E.I., was attacked by two 'regular' Viet Minh regiments. There was particularly fierce fighting and parts of the position changed hands as many as six times. The enemy gained a firm foothold, and the legionnaires could not eject them. The position was eventually swamped and lost.

By this time all in Dien Bien Phu remained below ground in daylight, and it became a repetition of trench warfare reminiscent of 1914–1918. At night the legionnaires raided out into 'no-man's land', filling in trenches whenever they could, whilst by day the French aircraft searched for the enemy with napalm and cannon.

The second main attack began on the afternoon of March 30th, and lasted until the morning of April 4th. The Viet Minh trenches had eased nearer and the French defences were more constricted. The airstrip was out of action, and the enemy had gained a foothold on one corner of it. Nothing could now get in or out by air. Dien Bien Phu was completely besieged and isolated. French helicopters made some daring trips to take off wounded, but the Viet Minh anti-aircraft artillery soon put a stop to such flights.

Swarms of enemy infantry continually moved against the French defences during the hours of darkness for six long nights. The Viet Minh seemed careless of casualties, but the legionnaires held fast on to all their positions.

Next came the period of encroachment which lasted for about three weeks. When the main attack failed to overwhelm the French 'centre of resistance', the Viet Minh settled down to sapping closer. The French were staking all on the successful defence of Dien Bien Phu, and realizing somewhat belatedly that Giap had at least four divisions creeping up to them, flooded in last-minute reinforcements by parachute. The 2nd B.E.P., some 700 strong, was dropped in during the night of April 9th/10th. Also, other volunteers were called for, and several hundred legionnaires from the 3rd R.E.I. and the 5th R.E.I., all non-paratroopers, were dropped—for the first time in their lives—on to Dien Bien Phu by night.

The final Viet Minh assault began on May 6th, by which time all the French artillery had been silenced, except for a handful of guns near the Command headquarters. At dusk, on all sides waves of Viet Minh infantry rose up and moved inwards. It was a mass attack, pressed relentlessly forward, despite casualties. 'Lalaine' was hemmed in and partly overrun. Legion counter-attacks could make no impression. The legionnaires fired and hurled grenades, but these efforts were neutralized by the blanket of Viet Minh dead draping the defensive wire.

A little after midnight 'Lalaine' fell. The legionnaires had asked for permission to make a break-out and this was granted. In true Camerone style, the survivors banded together and tried to break through, but they were dragged down by sheer weight of numbers. Other defensive posts on the outer perimeter had also fallen during the long night of fighting, and when daylight came the next morning, the 7th, the defenders were compressed into a small space around Command headquarters. To the south, Legion-held 'Isabelle' remained defiant.

There was a lull during the day during which the French air force tried to assist, but was not successful. As night fell, again all along the line Viet Minh infantry rose up and moved forward, constantly renewing the attacks whenever they faltered or were held. Ammunition was becoming scarce, and the end was in sight. The legionnaires made countless counter-attacks, and several positions and parts of positions changed hands frequently, but one by one the defended localities were lost.

Just before dawn the next day, May 8th, Dien Bien Phu fell.

'Isabelle', held by a battalion of the 3rd R.E.I., held on a little longer, and then after destroying everything of value the legionnaires formed up to break out, hoping to fight their way southwards, but when they did so sheer mass weighed them down before they had gone many yards.

The defence of Dien Bien Phu is a military epic, and the defenders showed heroic courage of a very high order. That it was not a victory was not the fault of the legionnaires or the French soldiers. Both had fought long and well.

During this siege, 1,500 had been killed and over 4,000 wounded, of whom over half were legionnaires. The remainder, nearly 9,000, were marched off into captivity, with the wounded.

Whilst the lengthy struggle for Dien Bien Phu was in progress, efforts were made to prevent Viet Minh reinforcements making their way there, and French columns traversed the country, but to little purpose. Guerrilla activity was intensified everywhere in the attempt to keep the French forces occupied elsewhere.

On April 20th, a battalion of the 2nd R.E.I. fought an action in which over 100 enemy were killed, but the previous month this unit had lost men in an unsatisfactory encounter. During the first quarter of 1954 the 5th R.E.I. was concerned in several skirmishes in the Delta, suffering over 420 casualties.

Dien Bien Phu signalled, and was in fact, the end of the war in Indo-China. It had been a long-drawn-out fight, but General Giap had out-generalled the French Command. In July 1954 the French signed an agreement to evacuate.

With the other French troops, Legion units were sent back one by one to North Africa. The bulk of the Legion prisoners taken at Dien Bien Phu were exchanged about a month later, a few lingered on for some time longer in Viet Minh hands, and several were repatriated to Europe through Red China.

The French war in Indo-China had lasted nine long years, and the Legion had been in it right from the start and had stayed on right to the bitter end, taking a very large share of all the fighting. Four Legion regiments of infantry, the 2nd R.E.I., the 3rd R.E.I., the 5th R.E.I. and the 13th Demi-Brigade, as well as the 1st R.E.C. and the two B.E.P.s, were involved, plus the numerous companies of specialists, such as engineers, builders, air supply, transport and work-shops, which were scattered throughout Indo-China.

The Legion sacrifice can be seen from the fact that 314 officers and 10,168 legionnaires were killed, and over three times as many wounded.

9

Algeria (1954-60)

We now return to Algeria, the home of the Legion, where a bitter, protracted struggle has been in progress since November 1954, throughout which the Legion has played a prominent part. At the time of writing it is still being fiercely waged, so for very obvious reasons this chapter must be brief and of a somewhat general nature.

The last country-wide revolt in Algeria had occurred in 1870-71, after which the country settled down under French rule. There were isolated risings in different parts from time to time but these became fewer as the years went by. The various native agitators had difficulty in keeping the tribes together for any length of time and consequently had only a brief period of success before they were eclipsed. Tribal rivalries barred a cohesive, nation-wide attempt to throw off French authority.

However, after many years of seeming placidity, in May 1945, a nationalistic revolt broke out, which took the French by surprise. A number of Europeans were murdered before it was brought under control. These nationalistic stirrings had probably been prompted by the events of the Second World War.

France had never done much to encourage nationalistic aspirations in Algeria or allowed much scope to ambitious Muslim politicians. They preferred to rule through the local chiefs and village headmen, and had either ignored or underestimated its force. The initial revolt of 1945 had been rather spontaneous, although widespread in character, and once the French recovered from the momentary shock they quickly suppressed it. The leaders were forced underground and began to work to build up a subversive organization, which grew in strength until it numbered over 3,000. Most of its members were raw and inexperienced and the French police soon unearthed it, scattering the Muslim plotters.

In spite of the changing wind and the fact that an irresistible wave of nationalism was sweeping over Africa, the French still looked over the heads of the Muslim Algerians, and did little to help or encourage their nationalism. During the ensuing months and years, the Muslim leaders slowly built up a strong, vigorous underground movement which became known as the Algerian National Liberation Front, the 'F.L.N.'. Active support was given by certain countries abroad, mainly Arab ones in the first instance, and arms, ammunition and supplies were smuggled into Algeria. Egypt and Tunisia in particular both helped in the early stages of this struggle. With this aid the Algerian nationalists prepared to fight for 'freedom'.

The Algerian War, as this campaign can be conveniently called, can be said to have broken out on November 30th, 1954, when some thirty detachments of F.L.N. fighters struck simultaneously at the French at diverse points throughout the country. Again, the French were somewhat taken back. Exultant and slightly surprised at their easy successes, the F.L.N. were carried away by their enthusiasm and for several months had things much their own way. Being able to more or less strike where it pleased, the F.L.N. quickly broadened the scope of its operations to include practically the whole of northern and central Algeria. Overnight it seemed to develop and swell, and its strength rose by stages to a maximum reputed figure of about 90,000, about half of whom were fighters, whilst the other half were active workers.

The F.L.N. fighters were fairly well trained in guerrilla warfare, and armed with a variety of small arms and explosives: a little later mortars were added to the armoury. From the very beginning the F.L.N. stuck rigidly to guerrilla tactics, concentrating upon ambushing small parties of French troops, and upon acts of terrorism. They avoided battle with the French army and merged into the Muslim population whenever hard pressed. Using these tactics the F.L.N. fighters managed to establish themselves predominantly in the mountains and a few other inaccessible parts of the country. Also, in the towns, especially Algiers, the F.L.N. terrorists were busy. In each of the years 1955 and 1956 the number of 'incidents' was over 8,000.

At the same time the F.L.N. developed a campaign of intimidation to prevent the Muslim inhabitants from collaborating with the French, and it occasionally hit out at sections of the population which were not fully co-operative with them. All Muslims were not, especially in the early stages, in full sympathy and agreement with the F.L.N., its

ideals and methods, but because of the fear of reprisals and atrocities
on their families, all were apprehensive of working against it and co-
operating with the French. Large sections of the country became unsafe, especially at night, both for the French and for the peaceful
Muslims.

At the local elections in 1956, over 60 per cent of the population
did not vote and the French were forced to suspend the local councils.
One of the local Muslim politicians, named Ferhat Abbas, quickly
came to the fore, to become the leader of this movement for a free and
independent Muslim Algeria. He directed the F.L.N. policy from
exile.

During the first months of this revolt, the French garrison was very
much on the defensive, being largely unprepared for such a wide-
scale insurrection, but once its magnitude was appreciated, reinforcements began to arrive, and within eighteen months the number of
troops was built up to about a quarter of a million.

It was not until the beginning of 1956 that the French were really
able to do something about quelling the revolt, and even then the
politics of Paris were reflected in Algeria, resulting in uncertainty and
indecision. Little positive was achieved and throughout that year small
bodies of French troops were wastefully dispersed about the country,
engaged in scrambling awkwardly after the nimble, elusive F.L.N.
fighters.

It was to this scene that the Legion units from Indo-China returned
to join up with those already in North Africa. After initially running
down in strength, mainly through the discharge of time-expired legionnaires, the Legion began slowly to built itself up again. The various
units filled out.

In keeping with the then prevailing military policy, the Legion sub-
units were at first dispersed far and wide into the danger spots, where
they spent their time patrolling and searching, both by day and night,
in an effort to bring the F.L.N. to battle. Their skirmishes and brief
contacts with the enemy were many, and not always successful. In 1956
and 1957 particularly the Legion suffered from rebel ambush tactics,
and its casualty list grew long.

The shortage of French troops in Algeria generally caused a somewhat defensive attitude of mind to develop, which resulted in them
being kept in their barracks at night. This meant that sections of
the countryside were virtually given over to the F.L.N., who were

accordingly free to move about under cover of darkness, and to terorrize the local inhabitants. There were, of course, many Legion and other French patrols out at night, but not sufficient to control the areas effectively.

In 1957, there was again an alarmingly high number of 'incidents', particularly of bomb-throwing in the towns. To try and cope with this form of subversion, French reservists were recalled and French divisions from NATO were sent over to Algeria, where the size of the garrison rose to over 400,000.

Still no positive military policy was formed and French patrols aimlessly roamed the countryside. In a few places the F.L.N. were in all but open control, and having gained a hold on the local population, it was almost impossible for the French to gain surprise. French aircraft constantly flew over the country during the daytime, but the F.L.N., still sticking to guerrilla tactics, lay low in daylight and took to moving only at night. French casualties mounted steadily, causing the tendency to shut themselves up in camps and towns to become more pronounced.

In the towns bombs were thrown daily and shots fired, curfews were imposed and military patrols roamed the streets at night. Algiers especially developed into a hotbed of terrorism, averaging at one period over twenty 'incidents' a day. In 1957, it was swept clean by General Massu, who commanded a French paratroop division, in which there were units of Legion paratroops.

The Arab League countries openly supported the F.L.N., and as Tunisia and Morocco gained their independence, so were they able to step up their assistance. The western part of Tunisia developed into a huge F.L.N. base, training camp and refuge. Arms, many of them ex-British, poured in from Egypt.

There was uncontrollable infiltration across the long Algerian–Tunisian frontier, and in an attempt to stop this, an electric fence was constructed. This proved to be fairly successful, but not completely so, and another one was built parallel to it to give the first 'barrage' depth. This double Tunisian barrage stopped large-scale movement across the border and did much to curtail rebel supplies and reinforcements. This caused the F.L.N. to turn to sympathetic Morocco, where it began to develop an alternative base and training ground. To prevent infiltration from Morocco the French constructed a similar electric barrage alongside that frontier.

When General Challe became the Commander-in-Chief of Algeria he collected together the wastefully dispersed French troops, concentrating them with the intention of clearing the various rebel black spots one by one. His main plan was—as soon as the two frontier barrages

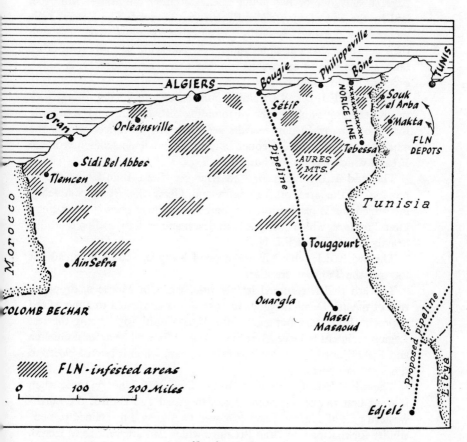

Algeria 1958

were complete and the F.L.N. in Algeria largely cut off from Tunisia and Morocco physically—to sweep down from the north, securing the country as he went. The inhabitants were removed from certain sectors, partly so that they would not provide background into which the F.L.N. liked to be able to merge whenever hard pressed, and partly to remove the source of food supply. The F.L.N. in the field lived on the country and needed little in the way of supplies except for ammunition.

Most of the Legion units from Indo-China returned directly to Algeria, only one or two going briefly to either Tunisia or Morocco, and by the end of 1957 all had concentrated there. The Legion regiments have remained basically in the same locations since, although their sub-units have at times ranged far and wide in support of other units and to join in operations in other parts of the country. A rough order of battle might be as follows:

The 1st R.E.I. is still a training unit, based on Sidi Bel Abbes, with several training camps in the surrounding district. Although a training formation, many Legion recruits see early active service, as into the adjacent foothills there frequently venture small detachments of the F.L.N. which have to be hunted.

The 2nd R.E.I. went first to Morocco from Indo-China before moving to the area of Ain Sefra and Gerryville. It is completely motorized and is responsible for controlling a huge portion of southern Oran Province, which contains both desert and endless, rolling foothills, heavily infested with F.L.N.

The 3rd R.E.I. settled in and around Kabylia, and then spread out towards the Tunisian frontier.

The 4th R.E.I. resumed its old title, when in Morocco, dropping that of the 4th Demi-Brigade. In 1956 it was converted to a motorized regiment, but it did not move into Algeria until 1957, being the last Legion regiment to leave Morocco. It stayed for a while around Guelma and Biskra, until in 1958 it was re-equipped, when it moved closer to the Tunisian barrage.

The 5th R.E.I. did not leave Indo-China until January 1956, when it went first to the Tlemcen sector, to guard and control the northwestern part of Algeria. Later it moved to Arzew, but retained responsibility for that part of Oran Province which was adjacent to Morocco.

The other infantry regiment, the 13th Demi-Brigade, returned to Algeria in July 1955, and for three years was in the Aures Mountains. In 1958 it moved a little northwards to make its base at Bougie, from where it went frequently on operations back into the mountains to the south of that place.

Of the two cavalry regiments, the 1st R.E.C. returned from Indo-China in January 1956, going first to Tunisia. Later, when it was

A Legion mortar section on the alert

A Saharienne company on parade

The Colour Party of the 4th R.E.I.

moved into Algeria, it was sent to patrol the Tunisian barrage which was under construction at the time. In fact, both the cavalry regiments are engaged on this task now, the 1st R.E.C. patrolling north from Tebessa and the 2nd R.E.C. to the south of that place. Both are equipped with heavy armoured cars.

The 1st B.E.P. expanded slightly and in February 1955 became known as the 1st R.E.P., moving to Zeralda, where it still remains. In December 1955 the 2nd B.E.P. became the 2nd R.E.P., and was established at Philippeville. Both regiments have patrolled and operated extensively in the mountains to the south of where they are stationed.

The four gaily-uniformed Saharienne Companies must not be forgotten, and they patrol the southern fringe of the mountains bordering the Sahara Desert.

As regards the strength of the F.L.N., it was estimated that there were in 1958–59 at least 15,000 armed and trained fighters in Algeria, and at least as many more active helpers closely associated with them. Practically the whole of the Muslim population supported the F.L.N., either actively or passively, willingly or unwillingly. In neighbouring Tunisia there were at least 10,000 trained fighters, and several bases and other installations, whilst there were at least another 5,000 guerrillas in Morocco. The two electric frontier barrages have curtailed free movement of large bodies of F.L.N. from one country to another, but have not stopped it altogether, as small parties still succeed in slipping through, whilst the larger ones take the longer detour around the southern extremities, where they can infiltrate through the foothills.

In spite of the fact that the French had about half a million troops in Algeria in 1959 and over 400 helicopters to help search out the enemy, the F.L.N. formations could not be trapped or forced into battle in any decisive actions, and only limited numbers were killed and captured. The mountainous areas and the ranges of foothills can hide whole divisions, let alone small units of guerrillas, and as the F.L.N. for a long time operated in units about 40 strong it can be realized how extremely hard they were to find, and even harder to bring to battle. Surprise was seldom possible owing to the advance warning of the approach of French troops given to them by the Muslim population. In both 1958 and 1959, the number of 'incidents' still numbered between 3,000 and 4,000.

In 1959, the F.L.N. experimented with small 'commando sections'

209   O

of about 6 men, but they have since abandoned this and are now developing units of 'company' size.

The casualty figures in the Algerian War are undoubtedly very heavy on both sides. No really complete accurate figures are available and estimates vary considerably, depending upon who gave them out. For example, the French admit that 12,000 French troops have been killed in Algeria between 1954 and 1959, but they are silent as to their number of wounded. The French claim that Muslim casualties may have averaged over 30,000 a year. The Muslim estimates are very much higher. The true figures are obscure as yet. About one and a half million Muslims have been 're-grouped', and another half million 'displaced' in the course of the struggle, whilst there are about 200,000 Algerian refugees in Tunisia and another 100,000 in Morocco.

The Legion casualties have been estimated as being as high as 1,500 a year, killed and wounded. This may, in fact, be an over-estimate, although in one year they were certainly over 2,000.

That the Legion has been heavily and fully engaged in battle can be guessed from the alleged casualty rate, whilst the fact that it is still heavily engaged can be deduced from a few examples of the results of 'incidents' in which the Legion has been involved in recent months. They are a selection taken at random and are representative of what the Legion is doing in Algeria.

On Camerone Day in 1959, the 2nd R.E.I. lost a captain killed and another 11 wounded during operations in the hills which lasted for three days, in which the Legion killed 31 rebels and took 43 prisoners.

During 1959, the 3rd R.E.I. claimed to have killed 462 rebels, took 664 prisoners, and captured 12 medium machine-guns and over 320 other sorts of fire-arms, many of British origin.

The 4th R.E.I. on one day captured 25 rebels who were trying to infiltrate through the Tunisian barrage, and later in October 1959, the same month, took part in another sharp action along the same barrage in which it killed 44 rebels for the loss of 4 Legion dead.

In February 1959, the 5th R.E.I. from Arzew moved into central Oran Province and during five weeks of combing the mountainous areas killed 63 rebels and took 36 prisoners, as well as seizing a huge pile of arms and explosives.

The Legion paratroops have been continually in action, mainly in the mountains, and the 1st R.E.P., in 1959, claimed to have killed 972 rebels for the loss of 42 dead and 97 wounded legionnaires. In a two-day action in June 1959, the 2nd R.E.P., patrolling near the Tunisian barrage, killed 29 rebels and took 27 prisoners.

The Legion cavalry regiments have had their share of action, being concerned mainly with dealing with attempted infiltration through the Tunisian barrage. In the course of 1959, for example, the 2nd R.E.C., the *Dauphin Etrangère*, killed 383 rebels.

Even the Saharienne companies have their share of excitement, and, for example, the 3rd C.S.P., in April 1959, in a skirmish on the edge of the Sahara, killed 13 rebels and caught 10 others.

And so it is still going on into 1960. The Legion has been intimately involved in fighting the F.L.N. since November 1954, and hardly an action has been fought or an operation of any magnitude carried on without elements of the Legion being included.

The fighting against the F.L.N. in which the Legion was particularly associated at the beginning of 1960, centred around the Aures Mountains, which has always been a black spot of Muslim resistance, owing both to the nature of the terrain and the warlike, hostile attitude of the inhabitants. In January 1960 three units of the Legion took part in 'Operation Binocular', a sweep in the Constantine district, which had some success. Another large-scale operation of a similar nature took place in March, and at one stage there were no less than elements of six Legion regiments engaged in action at the same time.

Even if such a thing were possible, it would be beyond the scope of this book to attempt a brief, impartial sketch of recent military and political events in Algeria; or to speculate on the future—and the future relationship—of Ferhat Abbas' Free Algerian Provisional Government and de Gaulle's Fifth Republic. The issues are complex and involved; passions run high; on every side resentment and bitterness are so ingrained that peace negotiations will almost certainly be stubborn and protracted.

In Algeria, still war-torn and tormented, the Legion bears a lion's share of the fighting, patrolling, searching, guarding and convoying. Almost daily legionnaires from over fifty different countries are dying there for their adopted country. One incident may be mentioned; though, happily, there was no bloodshed. It was to Legion paratroops that de Gaulle turned early in 1960 when the regular French troops virtually refused to take action against the insurgent *Colons* in Algiers who defied him over the dismissal of General Massu. There can be little doubt that the Legion's presence was one reason for the insurgents' sudden surrender, after which they were given the choice of standing trial for civil insurrection or of joining the Legion to fight the F.L.N. Many had been tacitly allowed to slip away, and of the 780 who gave themselves up only 420 were accepted—mainly for medical reasons. They were formed into a separate unit and attached to 1st R.E.P., but in fact only served a few months before being quietly discharged. Disaster was averted, but it had been close to civil war.

Whatever view is taken of the issues involved in the Algerian situation, whatever the political outcome may be, one thing at least is certain —that the Legion is serving, and will serve, with *honneur*, *discipline et fidélité*.

10

A Few Facts about the Legion

The publication in this country in the mid-nineteenth century of the novel *Under Two Flags*, by Ouida, roused the interest of the British public in the French Foreign Legion to an unusual degree, and this has been maintained ever since, aided by a spate of novels, memoirs and the perennial escape stories of deserters, and added to in more recent years by both the cinema and television. Over the years fact and fiction have become hopelessly mixed up. This publicity and interest has always embarrassed the French authorities, who were never keen to advertise their body of foreign mercenaries. Their reluctance to answer any questions about the Legion or the legionnaires has given impetus to lurid fiction. All assumed that the French had much to hide.

Rumours of brutality, ill-treatment, callous neglect and suffering, mingle with those of heroism, endurance, devotion to duty in adverse circumstances and glorious victories. Common sense and a knowledge of fighting-men decree that the two conflicting aspects are directly contradictory of each other, and both cannot be completely true. One does not naturally produce the other.

Where then is the truth, what is fact and what is fiction?

A short account of some of the facets of the Legion, past and present, and of the legionnaires, as well as a few other matters of general military interest may help to dispel myths and enable a fairly accurate picture to be formed.

ORGANIZATION AND STRENGTH

The Old Legion was organized on the pattern then prevailing in the French Infantry of the Line Regiments, and each battalion consisted of eight companies and a small headquarters. Each company had an establishment of 112 men, and was commanded by a captain, there being at different times between 2 and 5 officers per company. The battalions were commanded by a major; and a colonel, or sometimes even a lieutenant-colonel, was in command of a regiment, which was close knit.

The Legion was unusual in that right from the beginning it formed *compagnies d'élite*, each battalion having a company of *grenadiers* and one of *voltigeurs*. These consisted of picked men, the best in the unit, and in this respect the Legion was ahead of the remainder of the French Line Regiments. The *grenadiers* were the shock troops of those days, the commando, and usually the men were the biggest and strongest in the battalion. The *grenadier* company was expected to lead any attack, and weight and height were important. The *voltigeurs* were the scouts or the skirmishers, who protected the battalion when on the line of march and frequently went on ahead of it. The *voltigeurs* were more agile and were selected for their toughness and ability to use country. The remainder of the battalion was known as 'infantry of the centre', and formed the solid body of the unit.

However, when the New Legion was formed its battalions did not have *compagnies d'élite* at first, and it consisted simply of ordinary infantry companies. As a reward for its conduct at the taking of Constantine, this privilege was restored to the Legion, by which time most of the French Line Regiments had them. There still remained basically eight companies in each battalion for a number of years, of which two or more were *compagnies d'élite*. There seemed to be no set number, and some battalions eventually had three, or even four, *compagnies d'élite*. Also, some Legion battalions at times had either more or less than eight companies in all.

In 1847, the Legion formed its first *bataillon de marche*, or 'marching battalion', which was an *ad hoc* formation assembled for a special purpose. This was a continuation of Napoleon's idea of bunching together the best elements of a battalion or a regiment temporarily to perform a set task, the theory being that all would send only their best men to represent them as unit prestige and honour were at stake, so there would be an absolute minimum of indifferent men.

During the years the Legion formed innumerable *bataillons* and *régiments de marche*, all being assembled for a particular job, after which the officers and men in them reverted to their original units. Quite frequently in the earlier days the *compagnies d'élite*, for example, were formed into a *bataillon de marche*, as for instance in the Crimean Campaign.

In 1868 there was a reorganization in the Legion, the *compagnies d'élite* being abolished. Each battalion then consisted of eight ordinary infantry companies, each of slightly over 100 men. The ranks and titles of *grenadier* and *voltigeur* disappeared, and in their place was instituted the rank of *légionnaire de première classe*, or First Class Private, a rank equivalent to that of lance-corporal, which remains in existence today.

This pattern was followed for a while until it was gradually superseded by smaller battalions, each of four companies only, which persisted until the early 1900s, when extra companies of infantry were added in some units, as well as transport and administration companies.

The battalions sent to the Far East in the 1880s consisted of four companies, and averaged each only about 600 men. But the number of personnel began to rise slightly, and the battalion sent to Dahomey, for instance, was just over 800 strong. Then battalions seemed to settle down to having a strength of between 800 and 900 all ranks. Each Legion regiment usually consisted of three battalions, but this figure was by no means constant and some had more, depending upon circumstances. The regiment in Indo-China had four battalions, and at one time the 1st Regiment had as many as six.

The first establishment of the Old Legion had been provisionally set at 6,000, but after that there does not seem ever to have been a fixed one. The strength of the Legion had fluctuated considerably, depending primarily upon the forthcoming flow of recruits and the current needs of France.

The New Legion began with 800 men, but grew fairly rapidly until it reached the 3,000 mark, after which, during the conquest of Algeria, although it nearly reached 7,000 at one stage, its average was in the region of 5,000, or less. Its strength was just over 3,000 when it went to Mexico, but before that it had been less than 2,000, when it had gone to Italy in 1859. By the 1870s it had stabilized in the neighbourhood of 6,000. From that date onwards, there was an increase until the early 1900s, when it topped the 10,000 mark. During the First World War it was filled with war-time volunteers, but although thousands flocked to join and were accepted, owing to its high casualty rate its overall strength was always well below the 9,000 mark.

In the course of the Moroccan fighting of the 1920s the Legion strength rose to over 25,000, but when Morocco was pacified it fell off to below 15,000, to perk up again on the outbreak of the Second World War, when it shot up to 26,000 within weeks. After the defeat of France in 1940, the Legion sank down to 10,000, and then below that figure. Even after 1943, when France joined the Allies in active fighting, this figure was not much bettered; and the Legion, especially towards the end of the war, had great difficulty in keeping its units in the field in Europe up to strength.

The 13th Demi-Brigade, when with the Free French Forces, reached the 2,000 mark slowly, and always had difficulty in passing that figure, even when sent to Italy. Generally, as far as the Legion was concerned, there was a distinct shortage of recruits in the latter stages of the Second World War compared with the First World War, as many who might have volunteered had already committed themselves elsewhere.

When the Indo-China fighting developed, this position changed quickly and the Legion strength shot up to some 20,000. By 1950 this figure had been nearly doubled, and it is thought that at its peak, about 1953-54, it reached 65,000. This number was drastically reduced, beginning in 1955 on the return to North Africa, and fell to 20,000, but as the Algerian fighting developed it recovered and has swelled since, in spite of heavy casualties incurred. Today (1960) it is about 30,000 strong, perhaps a little more if anything.

It was the French army practice to group two regiments together and call them a brigade, and this was for long their basic strategic formation in North Africa and other overseas theatres, excluding Europe. During the conquest of Morocco it was found that the brigade, or even the regiment, was too unwieldy, so it was decided to experiment with the battalion as the basic army unit in the field. This proved to be quite successful at first, although later, when the French force was increased in size, it was found to be more convenient to use the regiment. For a time the battalion commanders had great powers of control and personal influence, and the Legion battalions became popularly known by the names of their commanders, rather than by their official designations.

Just prior to the Second World War, whenever a regiment was detached or used alone it was known as a *demi-brigade*, half-brigade. One Legion regiment changed its title to the *4me Demi-Brigade*, for instance, and of course, the famous *13me Demi-Brigade* still retains its title.

Between the World Wars the infantry regiment of the Legion became officially known as a *Régiment Etrangère d'Infanterie*, of which, in 1939, there were six in existence, the first four being in Morocco and Algeria, the fifth in Indo-China and the sixth in Syria.

The Legion itself, since its formation, held a somewhat undefined status, and for many years was not included on the French Army List of Regiments, being regarded as a sort of irregular corps of vague standing. It certainly had no social glamour. By decree, it was not to be employed in Metropolitan France except in time of war. It was not until 1931, its centenary year, that it was formally included in the Army List, and then it was placed just below the *Bataillons d'Afrique*, the French penal units, and just above the Native Colonial units and levies of different kinds.

It was at the same time compensated to some extent, and upgraded from being a 'nobody's baby' to having a general officer appointed to represent it at the War Ministry, known as the *Inspection de la Légion*, in other words an inspectorate, the general officer in charge periodically inspecting all the Legion units and reporting on them to the War Office.

This position was improved still further after the Second World War when, in 1950, a decree created the *Groupement de la Légion Etrangère*, G.A.L.E., which virtually made the Legion an independent corps within the framework of the French army, giving it a somewhat similar position and status to that enjoyed by the U.S. Marine Corps. This has since changed slightly in form and title, but not very much. The Legion is now controlled by the *Inspection Technique de la Légion Etrangère* in Paris, an inspectorate headed by a general officer, with a small staff.

Generally the Legion had always been predominantly infantry, although in the very early days legionnaires were called upon to handle and fire small mountain guns in the initial conquest of Algeria. The first Legion artillery battery was formed in Mexico, when it was given a small number of mountain guns, and sufficient ready-trained gunners, who had learned their trade in other national armies, were produced from the ranks. This battery functioned for a time, but was disbanded when the Legion left Mexico.

During the latter stages of the conquest of Morocco, another battery simply came into existence: it just happened. There were more 75 mm. mountain guns than French gunners to man them, and the Legion was able to step in and provide the skilled men. Another two batteries

Legion Mounted Infantry. About 1924

came into being in southern Algeria in 1935, but were never employed in action, being disbanded in 1939.

The Legion achieved some fame for its very special type of 'mounted infantry' in the North African fighting. It was not until 1853 that the Legion was first used in a mounted infantry role, when a detachment in Algeria was hastily mounted on camels in order to penetrate quickly southwards into the Sahara. In 1881, Colonel Negrier, when in command, formed a mounted infantry company on entirely new lines, which was known as the 24th Legion Mounted Company. It was organized and operated on the principle of two men to one mule, and each legionnaire took it in turn to ride whilst the other marched alongside him. In this manner they covered distances of thirty miles, or more, in the twenty-four hours, day after day. The mule carried rations for itself and the two men for twelve to fifteen days. The men dismounted to go into action.

This experiment was extremely successful, and the Mounted Company accomplished a number of forced marches and fought a number of surprise actions. After a trial period other Legion Mounted Companies were formed on the same pattern, one of which remained in existence until 1939.

The legionnaires fighting in Europe at the end of the Second World War were also employed as mounted infantry, being mounted in American armoured half-tracks. Again, in Indo-China several Legion units became lorried infantry on occasions. Today, in Algeria, some units of the Legion have gone a step farther, from camels they passed to mules, from mules they progressed on to M.T., and now they are frequently carried by helicopters. Many legionnaires are now quite accustomed to being flown into the scene of operations by air.

As regards cavalry proper, in Mexico a Mounted Company was formed, which was in fact really a squadron of light cavalry, all the men being mounted. This was used mainly for scouting and reconnaissance work, and was disbanded upon leaving Mexico. It was not until after the First World War that the idea was revived, when it was thought that there might be a limited use for horsed cavalry in North Africa. Accordingly a regiment was formed, known as the 1e *Régiment Etrangère de Cavalerie*, and full use was made of the many White Russian recruits who had previous cavalry experience.

Its squadrons were used individually, both in Morocco and Syria, but the day of the horse on the battlefield was over. The horsed cavalry squadrons were used for patrol work in Syria, whilst in Morocco their use was even more limited. Presumably the French had ample native cavalry available, and as the legionnaires were of far more value as infantry, the Legion horsed cavalry was not developed.

Mechanization came but slowly to the Legion, and its first motorized transport company was not formed until 1933, when an existing Mounted Company was converted to operate in southern Algeria on the fringes of the Sahara. By 1939, this was still the only Legion M.T. company, although a handful of motor vehicles had been officially given to Legion units. A few desert-going lorries and patrol cars were used, but it was not until 1940 that the Legion formed its first Mechanized Patrol Company to police the wide open stretches of the Sahara Desert. This was formed by the 1st Regiment, and continued to operate as such throughout the period of the Second World War. It later became known as the *1e Compagnie Saharienne Port de la Légion*.

The 1st C.S.P.L., operating as a mechanized patrol company, was so successful that others were formed after the war, the second in April 1946, and the third in February 1949. A fourth was created in August 1955, and it took on the traditions of the old 24th Legion Mounted Company.

The Legion cavalry was ahead of the infantry in the matter of mechanization, and in 1929 two squadrons of the 1st R.E.C. were converted to a light mechanized reconnaissance role. Other squadrons followed, so that by 1939 the whole regiment had become mechanized, and on the outbreak of war there were few horses left. The *2me Regiment Etrangère de Cavalerie* was formed that year and was mechanized right from the start.

There was a reorganization of the Legion infantry regiments in 1957, when, instead of consisting of a number of battalions, each was divided into ten companies, of which eight were infantry, one a heavy mortar company, and the other an administrative one. The 'battalion' as such disappeared. Each of the companies was designed so that it was easily transportable by air. The regiment itself was still split up into three 'combat groups', but these were not of fixed strength, and any number of companies could be put together into a combat group for a particular task.

Not to be forgotten are the Legion parachute battalions, of which there are now two. The first was formed near Sidi Bel Abbes just after the Second World War, and was then sent off post-haste to Indo-China. As there were ample volunteers who had previous para-trooping experience in other armies, another battalion was formed as well.

The system of supply and administration, with but slight variations, was the same for the Legion as for other French units, so there is no particular point in discussing it specially. However, perhaps a brief word about the supply system in Morocco may be of interest. There the French army had no organized service and supply corps of its own, and all rations were brought right up to the front-line troops, even when in action, by a civilian firm, known as the *Compagnie des Transports Marocains*. The Legion was also fed by this civil organization.

At first in Morocco, the Legion used mules to distribute rations and ammunition within the battalions and to company posts, but as it built roads it adopted and used a small mule cart, often pulled in tandem fashion by the two mules. These were largely unofficial, but most convenient, and each regiment in Morocco had up to about thirty of them.

Today the Legion in Algeria has six infantry regiments, five of which are divided into three combat groups, two cavalry regiments, with heavy armoured cars, each of between three and five squadrons, two parachute battalions, and in Madagascar there is an infantry battalion. In addition, there are the four independent Saharienne companies.

Sidi Bel Abbes is the central depot for the whole of the Legion, and is the seat of the 1st Regiment, which is a training formation, responsible for training recruits, posting them to units, re-postings, records, promotion boards and discharges. It is also a transit depot. There are a small number of small training camps scattered around Sidi Bel Abbes, under its wing. There is also a small depot at Oran, another at Marseilles, and a small detachment at the *Inspection Technique*, at Fort Vincennes in Paris.

ARMS AND EQUIPMENT

In the Old Legion the men were armed with long, muzzle-loading muskets of limited range and doubtful accuracy, which were discharged in volleys by word of command. Usually the front rank knelt and fired first, and then the rear rank fired standing over its head. As reloading took so long, the current French tactics were to fire and then charge immediately with the bayonet.

A long bayonet was carried by all the legionnaires, and in addition the men of the *compagnies d'élite* carried a sabre. In Spain these sabres gradually disappeared. All the officers wore swords. White pipe-clayed cross-belts supported the bayonets and sabres. The men carried a huge pack on their backs, on the top of which was a rolled-up piece of their 'section tent'. In Spain a haversack and wine flask, both worn by the side, were added and retained.

The New Legion when it was formed still had the same old-type muskets, but after 1842 it began to be issued with a newer model of a percussion, breech-operated weapon. The rate of fire was still slow and reloading was cumbersome. Somewhat naturally in those days the legionnaires relied in battle more upon bayonet fighting than shooting. The legionnaires marched off to the Crimean Campaign still armed with this weapon.

A leather waist-belt, with a cartridge case which was worn squarely on the front, had been adopted in Spain and was retained. In the Crimean Campaign they were the only French troops to wear such a case in such a position, and it resulted in the Russians nicknaming them the 'Leather Bellies'. Officially, it was to hold bullets and powder, but reports indicate that it did duty to carry the many odds and ends soldiers accumulate when on active service. The large pack was retained and grew heavier as more items were attached to it.

The Swiss Legion, when it was formed in 1855, was issued partly with ancient muzzle-loading muskets and partly with more modern weapons. Its other equipment was elderly, being dug out from mobilization stores in France. The Swiss Legion never wore the cartridge case on the front of the belt.

Before moving off to the Italian Campaign, in 1859, all the legionnaires were issued with the new Chassepot rifle, which brought them up to date in terms of small-arms fire power on the European battlefield. In Mexico, the legionnaires were mainly armed with Minnie rifles: breech-loading weapons, which held and fired a single shot at a time. Each man carried sixty rounds of ammunition in his pouch. The 5th Battalion of the Legion, raised to fight in France in 1870, was given a mixture of old muskets and newer Chassepot rifles.

Beginning in 1875, the legionnaires were issued with the new Le Gras rifle—replacing the Chassepot model—which they carried for the next thirty years or so, after which the Lebel gradually took its place. In the early fighting in Morocco the legionnaires complained of the poor steel of the long, slim bayonet, the end of which turned up like a fish-hook when it struck something hard. A number of Mauser rifles were issued about the turn of the century.

When the Le Gras rifles were issued, to hold the ammunition for them Colonel Negrier designed a special pouch, which was worn high up across the front of the chest, a position where it could be got at more conveniently than from the leather case on the front of the belt, especially when the man was lying down behind cover. This became known as the *Cartouchière de Negrier*, and was worn for a few years, especially in Indo-China and Dahomey, and then discarded. The old leather cartridge case on the front of the belt gave way to two smaller, similar ones, worn on the belt, but slightly to each side. This leather equipment is still in use in the Legion, and can be seen at Sidi Bel Abbes, worn both by recruits in training and by the sentries on the main gate.

During the First World War, in France, the legionnaires wore the same equipment and had the same arms as the ordinary French Line Regiments, including a steel helmet. Grenades seemed to be always favourite with the Legion, but the men also experimented with trench mortars and machine-guns during their spell in the trenches. After the war, the French light machine-gun was introduced into all Legion units. The Legion cavalry, when formed, were armed with a sabre and a short carbine.

Prior to 1943 little or no new equipment was issued to the Legion, but from that year onwards a supply of American material was received, which included armoured vehicles, trucks, arms and other equipment. Also, after the war France obtained large stocks of surplus war material, of which the Legion was given a share, especially when the Indo-China fighting was joined. Mortars, 120 mm., 81 mm. and 61 mm., became integral weapons, as did the bazooka.

Since then the new Belgian FN light machine-gun had been issued to the Legion as a standard weapon, and the French version of our Sten gun is carried by all junior leaders in the field. Some units have automatic rifles.

During the Second World War, American light tanks, armoured cars, half-tracks and lorries were sent to the Legion, and more have been received since, especially when in Indo-China. Many—but not all—of the armoured vehicles in use today by the Legion cavalry are of U.S. origin.

Today, in 1960, the arms and equipment are a contrasting mixture of old and modern. The paratroops and Legion units on field operations have the modern material, whilst the older is reserved for training and garrison duty.

UNIFORM

When the Legion was first formed the men were dressed in the same uniform as that worn by the French Line Regiments at that period, which was basically a tight-fitting blue shell jacket and red pantaloons. A blue greatcoat was worn too. The head-gear consisted of a huge shako, with a large brass eagle on the front and a heavy brass chin-strap. A black leather stock was worn tightly round the throat. Epaulettes of the men in the companies of the centre were of plain blue, whilst those of the *grenadiers* were large ornate, red-fringed ones, and those of the *voltigeurs* were yellow.

The uniforms of the officers varied, as seconded French officers wore their own, whilst the foreign officers wore a uniform similar to that of the men, but with more gold braid in evidence.

Months of marching, working and fighting in Algeria caused this dress to be modified, and the shako was quickly abandoned in favour of a lighter cloth cap, of vaguely similar shape. As was habitual in the French army for many decades, the greatcoat was worn on the march regardless of the season of the year or the heat. The men obtained looser clothing by the simple expedient of wearing a jacket a size too large.

In Spain, no clothing replacements arrived and local material was used. The red trousers gave place to white ones, and before long most of the men wore sandals obtained locally. A beret was adopted as the head-dress, and the black leather stock was left off and its place taken by one of blue cloth.

The New Legion wore traditional French uniform, but regimental distinctions appeared, such as badges and buttons. The small red and blue cloth cap came to stay for a long time. Officers left off their great-coats and began to wear a belt outside their tunics, a departure from the then military fashion. They wore a wide variety of hats, seemingly no standard pattern being insisted upon. The officers early adopted the habit of carrying canes.

The legionnaires fought in this dress, or variations of it in the Crimea, Italy and Mexico, although in the latter country it was again modified as all replacements had to be obtained locally. In Mexico a huge straw sombrero was tried out at first as protection against the sun, but this was soon left off as the men preferred their cloth caps. A blue cummerbund was adopted, and has been retained ever since. The

Swiss Legion was an exception at first, being dressed in rifle green, which it retained whilst in France, but when it was shipped over to Algeria this was exchanged for the traditional Legion uniform of blue and red.

The uniform of the Legion in North Africa hardly changed until after 1914, being basically, a blue jacket, red trousers and a blue greatcoat. The cut varied slightly, and at times the trousers were of off-white material. In Morocco the legionnaires were likened to 'blue-backed beetles', from their habit of fastening back the frock of their coat so that their knees had full play when on the march, which, when viewed at a distance, gave them this appearance.

When taking part in Colonial expeditions to Indo-China, Dahomey and Madagascar, the legionnaires started off in their North African uniform, and then replacements invariably came from marine sources. The marine uniforms were white, and for example, by 1900 the legionnaires in Indo-China were all in white drill when on parade, but with Legion buttons, badges, epaulettes and sash to set it off.

During the First World War in France the legionnaires wore the standard blue uniform of the French army, which gradually changed to khaki. At first the Legion was identical in dress to any other Line Regiment, but regimental differences soon appeared, such as buttons and badges, and then the blue cummerbund was worn over the great-coat.

After the First World War, back in Algeria the Legion reverted to the old pattern of blue tunic and red trousers. There were large stocks of this type of clothing in the French stores and so little new came the way of the legionnaires. The newly formed cavalry were dressed in a similar manner, except the men wore riding boots and breeches. The squadron in Syria was dressed in khaki, as was later the 6th R.E.I. In North Africa a summer uniform, of either white or khaki drill, began to appear, especially as a fatigue dress. The legionnaires in Indo-China adopted a kind of khaki drill uniform also.

On the outbreak of the Second World War when first formed, the 13th Demi-Brigade was issued with special dress for fighting in cold climates, and a certain amount of khaki uniform was issued to other units. Otherwise for the first three years of the war, things remained much the same. From 1943 onwards, Allied stores and material were received, and the legionnaires were soon clad in battle-dress. Khaki as a colour for active service came to stay and the conventional battledress was eventually generally adopted. The general colour scheme of service uniforms changed to green in Indo-China, but is now back to khaki again in Algeria.

The legionnaires today wear a khaki battle-dress during the winter months and a lighter khaki drill uniform of somewhat similar cut in the hot weather. In the desert, the 'jellaba', the striped Arab robe, is worn, which blends well with the desert and foothill background. The Legion paratroopers wear their mottled jumping suits.

The famous *képi blanc*, or white cap, just appeared. Through the years it kept bobbing up spasmodically until the Legion was practically forced to adopt it as the official head-dress. It seems to have made its first appearance in the 1840s, when a white cover, with an attached neck cloth, was worn as protection against the sun. This was unofficial and disappeared after a while, spontaneously breaking out from time to time during the conquest of Algeria. White cap covers and neck cloths, especially the latter, were worn in Mexico.

In the 1880s, a khaki cap cover was issued, which with constant washing and the sun, bleached almost white. Raw recruits, issued with a deep khaki-coloured cover, hastily scrubbed and scrubbed until it faded, in the hope that they would be mistaken for old campaigners. From then onwards, the *képi blanc* was worn by all legionnaires in Algeria, but it was really off-white in colour. The true *képi blanc* was not taken into official use until 1939, and was worn on parade for the first time when a detachment of the Legion marched through Paris. Since then it has become the symbol of the Legion.

The white neck cloth is still occasionally worn, but has never been official. Only the legionnaires wear the white *képi* cover, the *sous-officiers* wear the blue *képi* without it.

Other hats worn by the Legion at different times include the solar topee, the steel helmet, the beret and the bush hat.

The stock, worn tight, persisted until the Second World War, after which military fashions changed, and the collar and tie became the vogue. In 1945 the French had a large surplus stock of green ties, and as no one else wanted them, they were given to the Legion. The Legion took them, wore them and has since adopted the green neck tie as its very own. Now no other French regiment wears one of that colour.

It is perhaps on a ceremonial guard at the main gate of the Depot at Sidi Bel Abbes, or on a Camerone Day Parade, that the legionnaire looks his best. He wears his *képi blanc*, a bubbling relic of the conquest of Algeria, his leather equipment is a reminder of the penetration into the Sahara, his blue cummerbund is from Mexico, his red-fringed epaulettes are souvenirs of the Legion *grenadiers* of old, and the white gloves, green tie and anklets are added for smartness. There is plenty of 'bull' in evidence when the Legion is on parade.

A 'Saharienne'

The romantically dressed *Sahariennes* must not be overlooked, as they have adopted a uniform, both serviceable, appropriate and striking. The men wear sandals, black baggy trousers, white drill tunics and flowing blue cloaks, to which a splash of colour is given by the red epaulettes and blue cummerbund. Bandoliers of ammunition across the chest, with the rounds visibly glinting, gives a rakish touch to their appearance.

THE OFFICERS

In the Old Legion there was a large percentage of seconded French officers, and they outnumbered the foreign officers. Again, when the new Legion was formed, for many years the proportion of French officers remained high, and it was not until the 1850s that this began to change. From then onwards influxes of foreign officers caused the French officers frequently to be outnumbered.

Direct commissions in the Legion were granted by the King of France to foreigners for a variety of reasons. In those days the Legion had little glamour and no social appeal, and these persons were mostly needy and impoverished, and relied upon this patronage almost as a last resort. Some had formerly held high rank in their own national armies but had been compelled to leave their own countries either for political reasons or because they had been defeated in battle, and owing to French sympathy for their cause, commissions as junior officers were given to them in the Legion.

Also serving from time to time were a small number of foreign aristocrats and even occasionally members of minor royalty, who were either in exile or disgrace. When Napoleon III became Emperor a number of republican officers came to serve with the Legion, their principles refusing to allow them to serve in France under a monarch.

Little is known in any great detail of the foreign officers of the earlier days, except for the occasional note of a duel, and it is not until after the 1850s that more information is available. There was, for example, a wide disparity in ages in the different ranks, subalterns of 20 years of age served alongside subalterns of 60 years of age, also there were both young and old captains. Some of the foreign officers stayed for several years, whilst others hardly tarried, several were killed in action, many were wounded and a few were decorated. As regards the French officers some were sent to the Legion for disciplinary reasons; others went because rank and inducement were offered; others to obtain active service experience; and yet others used it as a stepping-stone for promotion. Few were true volunteers in the early days.

For a number of years at least half the officers were foreigners, but most held low ranks, it being most unusual for them to rise above the rank of major. A few foreigners were commissioned from the ranks, usually as a reward for gallantry in battle. One was Martinez, the

Spaniard, who rose to command a regiment, and other examples were Vilain and Maudet, heroes of the Camerone fight.

Of the French officers of those days who served with the Legion and who later rose to high command, can be mentioned Marshal Bazaine, who was a sergeant and then an officer in the Old Legion; Marshal St. Arnaud, who was a captain at the taking of Constantine in 1837; Marshal MacMahon, who commanded the 2nd Regiment in 1842; General Canrobert, who commanded the 2nd Regiment at Zaatcha in 1849; and General Negrier, who commanded in 1881. One other French officer can be mentioned from the point of view of interest, as he fought against us during the Boer War and was killed in the Transvaal, when holding the Boer rank of general. He was Colonel de Villebois-Mareuil, who commanded the 1st Regiment in 1895.

During the Franco–German War of 1870–71, a number of distinguished foreigners served as officers in the Legion for the duration only, one of whom, a subaltern, was the future King Peter of Serbia. Of the other foreign officers deserving a mention—the list is long—was a German subaltern who served with the Legion in Mexico, winning a decoration for gallantry, who in 1870, on the other side of the fence, watched his former corps being bombarded by German artillery. He was Milson Von Bolt, an Uhlan major, then serving as a staff officer to his cousin, Prince Frederick Charles.

During the First World War a large number of foreigners were granted commissions for the duration, many of whom had been officers in their own national armies, but most of these left immediately after the Armistice. A tiny handful stayed on with the Legion and a few others were accepted because the war rendered them stateless. The White Russian ex-officers formed the bulk of the latter class. Several of them had held high rank in the Imperial Russian army, and one at least was a major-general. They were granted commissions as subalterns in the newly forming Legion cavalry.

This influx raised the proportion of foreign officers to over half, but during the ensuing years many of the White Russians dropped out, and the proportion again declined. By 1939, it was below 25 per cent. The fighting in Morocco had attracted a few, but the dreary monotony of garrison duty and labour afterwards did not encourage them to remain. One of the more distinguished foreign officers of this period was Prince Aage of Denmark, a cousin of King George V, who served in the Legion as a regimental officer for nearly twenty years, until he died in 1940. Another regimental officer was Prince Louis II of Monaco.

During the Second World War a number of foreign officers served in the Legion, but not nearly as many as in the previous one. However, after the war there was a large influx, mainly of Poles, Czechs and those from countries similarly placed, who were granted commissions as junior officers. Many still remain in the Legion. This influx raised the proportion to over 50 per cent, but it has fallen since, and now hovers about the one-third mark.

Practically all the senior officers are French, and always have been, and it has always been the exception rather than the rule for a foreigner to command a regiment. Today the number of foreign officers appointed to the senior ranks is restricted, and their chances of promotion are not good. The Legion allows for one foreign colonel and one lieutenant-colonel only, then one major to each regiment and one captain to each battalion, or combat group. The remainder have to serve as subalterns, and all tend to be elderly by our standards.

A small but steady flow of foreign officers is maintained by granting commissions to men from the ranks. Any legionnaire who aspires to a commission in the Legion is encouraged to try and assisted to study, but all applicants have to pass the equivalent of the G.C.E. (in French), a step which defeats most foreigners. Even so a handful do succeed and are commissioned each year, but again their age tends to be high for their rank. Foreign Legion officers generally only have jurisdiction over their own men.

The French officers are seconded, but once with the Legion, if finally accepted, stay for long periods. The days of using the Legion as a stepping-stone are over. Today, the standard of the Legion is high in professional circles, and it has the first pick of the officer cadets passing out from St. Cyr.

There have been many distinguished and colourful, as well as slightly eccentric, French officers in the Legion, of whom one may be mentioned, General Rollet, who had commanded the R.M.L.E. in France with distinction in 1917–18, and who became its first Inspector-General. He was known as the 'Father of the Legion' and did much to raise its prestige. Rollet was a small, peppery character, of slightly unorthodox habits, but very popular with the men, and a host of anecdotes are told about him.

He would help a drunken legionnaire back to barracks and smuggle him past the guard, yet would deal severely with a man brought in front of him on a trivial disciplinary charge. He would sentence a legionnaire to detention, during which time he would receive no pay, and would then lend him money to send home to his family. Rollet reputedly wore no shirt under his tunic, his 'cuffs' being supported by threading a piece of string through the arm-holes of his tunic. These occasionally broke loose at unexpected, embarrassing moments. He was a live-wire, constantly dashing here and there, and he remained the Inspector-General until he died at Sidi Bel Abbes in 1941.

THE MEN

The Legion claims that at almost any given time men from over fifty different nations are serving in its ranks, and that this figure went up to just over a hundred in the First World War, when foreigners flocked from all over the world to fight for France. These claims are probably correct, as few nations have not been represented in the Legion at some time or another.

A few days after it was formally established, Frenchmen were banned, by decree, from joining the Legion, and with the exception of such periods as the two World Wars, this has remained in force. If he wishes to join the Legion, a Frenchman usually passes himself off as either a Swiss or a Belgian, which in the early years a great number did. It is only after some years of good service, if a French legionnaire declares his true nationality, he is allowed to stay on in the Legion, otherwise he is discharged. This sort of confession until recently was never encouraged.

The pattern of nationalities in the Old Legion has been given, and for some decades the Spanish, Polish and Italian groups were the largest. The state of Europe was reflected in the personnel serving in the Legion, and in turn the Italians, Russians, Austrians and Germans formed the largest national group, depending upon the unsettled state of their homeland. As French units were formed in Algeria and other French possessions, the number of Frenchmen in the Legion declined.

By 1857 the Germans had become the largest group, a distinction they have generally, but not always, maintained ever since. The other large national groups at that period were the Belgians, Italians, Russians and the Poles, whilst there were a fair sprinkling of Greeks, Portuguese, Dutch and others from Central and Eastern Europe.

It is recorded that there was a solitary Chinese legionnaire at Sidi Bel Abbes for some years, who kept his pigtail, which he sometimes wore curled up inside his hat and at others hanging down his back. There seems to have always been an unofficial and unwritten ban on negroes, and although many another dark-skinned man was accepted, the coal-black legionnaire was a rarity. Another rarity through the years has been the British legionnaire, although as far as I can gather, the Legion was seldom without one or two.

After 1871, the percentage of Alsatians and those from Lorraine rose, and remained very high for a few years, eclipsing the Germans. On the other hand the German element dropped down to some 20 per cent, and then by 1885 even lower, to 12 per cent—its lowest for years. But that was the turning-point, and since then the Legion has held a fascination for some Germans, frequently those from comfortable middle-class homes. It is rather inexplicable that so many Germans in normal times should choose to take service under the flag of a country so many of them dislike. The German authorities were vaguely disturbed at this persistent number of their young men going into the Legion and did their best to discourage them. Partly, it hurt national pride that the young men should elect to serve a foreign power, and partly because it deprived the Fatherland of the services of a conscript.

By the 1900s the German contingent had risen to some 40 per cent, about where it wavered for some years. Today it is reputed to be nearer 60 per cent. It is also believed that today up to 80 per cent of the *sous-officiers* in the Legion are German. After the First World War, the influx of Germans and Austrians was heavy, and included many seasoned soldiers of good character, who went to make up the bulk of the two new Legion regiments that were formed, the 3rd and the 4th. They did much to improve the reputation of the Legion and to give it an air of respectability, as well as raising its standard professionally.

After the Russian Civil War, there was an inrush of White Russian refugees. Again, owing to the disturbed state of Spain in the 1930s, there were always large numbers of Spaniards coming into the Legion, and these swelled in 1939, when the Republicans lost the Civil War.

Before the Second World War had ended, the Legion was busily recruiting any nationality it could get, and in 1945 it began to expand seriously, accepting many enemy aliens. The Legion units sent off to Indo-China were largely composed of Germans and Italians, many of whom had but recently been fighting against the Allies. Some of these men had distinguished service in their own armies, and were a great asset to the Legion professionally.

Many foreigners who had collaborated with the discredited Vichy régime were also accepted, and all inquiries about them were met with silence. Also, the French openly set up recruiting offices in the part of Germany she occupied, and encouraged foreigners of all sorts and shades to enlist. There were looks of disapproval from her allies as France recruited such large numbers of former enemy aliens who had not been properly screened, especially as many of them had been politically active during the war. There is little doubt that many minor war criminals disappeared into the ranks of the Legion.

The Germans allege that Dien Bien Phu was a German battle as the Germans there far outnumbered the French.

The decree that men of the same nationality or speaking a common language should serve together in the same company was adhered to for the first twenty years or so, but it was not a success. Colonel Bernelle's experiment of mixing the nationalities up together in Spain was a great improvement. Off parade there were perpetual factions and quarrels, which were a bane and a problem. Brawls amongst men of the same nationality were as common as fights between men of different companies. Duels were by no means unknown amongst the men as well as the officers. Keeping men of the same nationality together fanned parochial differences and squabbles, as well as unhealthy rivalry between companies.

Over the years it was found by experience that a man fought better in action when he was beside one from another country, national honour was unconsciously involved and each felt that he was representing his country on a foreign field, and so fought his best. When grouped together by nationalities this did not always occur. Unofficially, the 'mixing' of nationalities together began in Algeria, and by the time the Legion went to the Crimea this original rule was no longer strictly adhered to. By the time the Legion went to Mexico this decree had become a dead letter, although it was not formally repealed until 1875. Since then it has been tacitly understood that no one national group should exceed 50 per cent of a company's strength, but whenever the German element has been exceptionally high, this has not always been possible.

This principle has been kept to ever since. There has only been one brief departure from it, and that was in the First World War, when groups of nationals presented themselves to serve France in the Legion provided they could all stay together. In their initial surge of enthusiasm the authorities allowed this, and companies were formed of Greeks, Poles and Czechs, who were allowed to serve under their own national emblems in one of the Legion battalions. It did not work, as any old Legion officer could have told them, and before long factional fights burst out. The battalion had to be dissolved and the 'cocktail' well shaken up again. Nowadays, the 'cocktail' is judiciously mixed at the Postings Office at Sidi Bel Abbes, and it is held that the fighting quality of the Legion is largely the result of this careful, and secret, blending of nationalities.

No thought seems to have ever been originally given as to whether legionnaires were willing to fight their own countrymen. The Legion battalions were shipped to the Crimea, complete with Russian legionnaires, and at this stage no attention had been paid to this problem. At Barbastro, in Spain, in 1837, this sort of fratricidal warfare had worked only too well, and the French military authorities presumably thought it would continue to do so—that is if they thought about it at all. The fact remains that Russian legionnaires went to Russia to fight their fellow countrymen under the French flag, and as far as is known they did so with little or no trouble. The only step taken was to break up the Russian groups and distribute the men amongst the companies.

The same thing happened in Italy, in 1859, and the Austrians in the Legion went with it and were expected to fight their fellow countrymen. In Mexico the position was similar and the Spanish legionnaires had to fight against the Spanish settlers there. It was not until 1870 that this matter was seriously considered, and when the Legion went over to France that year to fight against Germany it left all the German legionnaires behind in Africa. However, it was not until 1910 that the Hague Convention, forbidding the compulsion of foreigners to fight against their own country, was accepted by France.

During the First World War, the Germans and Austrians in the Legion remained in Morocco, where they served well, doing a good

234

job for France. Surprisingly enough, throughout this period there was a small, but constant trickle of Germans, Austrians and even a few Turks, to enlist in the Legion. In the Second World War conditions were somewhat different and many of the serving German legionnaires were interned, although once they were screened many were allowed to continue to serve.

The reasons that caused the men to join the Legion do not seem to have changed much over the years. There is not much known in detail about the legionnaires of the early years, as none were great letter writers or diarists, but it appears that practically all had a very compelling and personal reason for joining, which was probably either political, criminal, domestic or economic.

The oppressed and war-torn countries of Europe provided a steady intake of recruits, which has continued since without ceasing. There has rarely been complete peace in Europe. Famine, poverty, economic depressions and other misfortunes were compelling motives in many cases. Men deserting uncongenial wives has been a far more common cause than is generally realized. The novelists like to picture a man joining the Legion to 'forget' some very attractive, but unattainable, woman, which may have been true in a few instances, but it is not nearly so frequent as the man who wishes to forget a woman for the very opposite reason. Love of adventure seems to have seldom come into the picture.

Early accounts describe the Legion as containing many picturesque ruffians and gay vagabonds, as well as disappointed men and unsuccessful adventurers: it had its share of the devil-may-care as well as the sullen, the proud and the touchy. Amongst this exciting, motley sample of humanity was a sprinkling of cashiered officers, both French and foreign.

About the 1870s we come to know a little more about the men themselves, chiefly through the medium of officers' letters and memoirs. The pattern does not seem to have changed in forty years, and the bulk of the legionnaires are still unflatteringly described. They are pictured as being coarse and uneducated, the riff-raff of the cities, vagabond peasants, Corsican bandits, wanted criminals, men who had fled from family troubles, and other misfits, as well as victims of the injustices of the age, upheavals and insurrections.

There were always in the Legion ranks a number of professional soldiers who either knew, or wanted, no other trade, and they have increased in number, especially during the last forty years or so. Today the Legion contains a fairly large element of them, who are invariably of good character, and who set a high efficiency standard. Many others came to love the life in the Legion also and developed good soldierly qualities, but in the first place, especially in the old days, their reason for joining was far more compelling.

Although in the nineteenth century the bulk of the legionnaires were disparagingly described, there invariably seems to have always been a tiny number of interesting and romantic exceptions, which probably gave the idea and a grain of truth to the later imaginative writers of Legion fiction. There seems occasionally to have been some member of a noble family, or even of minor European royalty, who for some obscure reason of his own sought anonymity in the Legion ranks. For example, at the Battle of Magenta, in 1859, the last descendant of King Sobieski, who saved Vienna from the Turks, was killed whilst serving as an ordinary legionnaire. In more recent times an ordinary legionnaire died in hospital at Gerryville, and when his personal effects were searched it was found that he was a minor German prince. A German warship specially put into Oran to take off the body with full honours.

Again, there were occasionally other notable or distinguished personalities whom misfortune, disgrace or poverty forced to enlist in the Legion ranks. At the Battle of Solferino, in 1859, an ordinary legionnaire was killed who proved to have been one of 17 Austrian generals who had been involved in a revolt against Russia in 1849, and had been condemned to death. Ironically, he was killed by his own countrymen.

At least half a dozen cashiered British officers served in the Legion at one time or another. One, an ex-engineer officer, was employed to map the area around Sidi Bel Abbes and south into the Sahara, although serving as an ordinary legionnaire. It must be said that the Legion has always had the happy knack of putting the right man to work at the right job. How many other interesting characters and personalities have served and died unknown in the Legion is a matter for conjecture—but they must have been many.

At the beginning of the Second World War, both the Count of Paris, the Pretender to the French throne, and Prince Napoleon, not being allowed to serve in a French unit, enlisted in the Legion as ordinary legionnaires.

The Legion was unusual in that when a man presented himself for enlistment 'no questions' were asked, and any name he cared to give was accepted. This practice developed and as many a legionnaire deliberately sought anonymity, he was only too thankful to take advantage of such a regulation and serve under a *nom de guerre*. Inquiries were ignored, both for the sake of convenience and to avoid having to make embarrassing explanations. France did not wish to be accused of harbouring political agitators and criminals, and so she was only too happy to accept a *nom de guerre* without question, and thus officially to know nothing about such matters.

About the 1880s the maxim of *Legio patria nostra*[1] became officially adopted in practice as well as principle. Absolutely no information about serving legionnaires was given in answer to any queries. The cloak and protection of anonymity became complete. As regards foreigners serving in the Legion this had practically always been so, but there had been examples of relatives and friends (and enemies) of French legionnaires instigating inquiries and once it was found where the man was, political and other pressures were brought to bear, with the result that the man had either to be discharged or transferred to another regiment, often against his will. In either event, it caused a lot of fuss and bother, especially when the person concerned was either a notorious criminal or a political personality, which did not improve the reputation and standing of the Legion.

This attitude continued for some twenty years, but at the turn of the century there was a growing tendency on the part of a number of legionnaires to dislike the policy of a rigid barrier of silence. True, many wanted their presence and identity kept secret for obvious reasons, either criminal, political or domestic, and the majority perhaps did not care very much one way or another. However, a few wanted their presence known—or at least not kept secret, having nothing to hide, and probably having joined for purely economic reasons. But the legionnaires who deliberately sought publicity were heavily stamped upon and had a hard time. The Legion was reluctant to change its policy.

After the First World War the Legion became slightly more selective in accepting recruits, and as a precaution against enlisting well-known and well-wanted criminals, began to finger-print recruits at Marseilles and to allow the police to vet them. In 1931, the centenary year, it was

[1] The Legion is our fatherland.

237

decided that if inquiries were made about any serving legionnaire, the man's commanding officer could answer them—but only if the man himself had no objection. This seems to be the policy prevailing to-day.

The conditions of enlistment have hardly changed since the Legion was established, the main and paramount one being physical fitness. There has always been a stringent medical examination which dispels the fanciful theories that women have occasionally slipped through a lax net and served as ordinary legionnaires.[1] At first the initial term of service was three years, but this period later became changed to five, at which it has remained since. The legionnaire may extend his service for a further period of five years, or less, and qualifies for a modest pension after fifteen years' service. In time of war, enlistments for the duration of hostilities only are accepted.

The age limits were officially set at between 18 and 40 years of age, and this has never altered, but as no identification papers were de-manded, the age of the recruit had to be taken at face value, with the result that in practice there may be a wide disparity in ages, the very young serving alongside the very old.

The legionnaire may still, and does, join under any name he cares to give and need not produce any identification papers. No questions are asked but he is finger-printed and held at Marseilles until he is cleared by the police. He may continue to serve under his chosen *nom de guerre*, and be discharged under it if he wishes; certainly many have died under it. However, today, towards the end of his service, he is urged to 'rectify' himself if he is able to do so, that is to declare his true name and country of origin, and to allow the Legion to check on his criminal and political background. No pressure is asserted—he can please himself.

Once a legionnaire is 'rectified' he has certain privileges and, for instance, he may go home on leave to his own country. Yes—to

[1] There is almost an exception to this, and that is the instance of an English-woman, Miss Susan Travers, who joined the 13th Demi-Brigade, in England, in 1940, as an ambulance driver, and determinedly stuck to it throughout. Not only did she accompany the 13th Demi-Brigade on every step of its long odyssey during the Second World War, but she stayed with it, still as a driver, to serve in Indo-China.

Miss Travers's exploits during her service with the French Foreign Legion make anything novelists write pale into insignificance and to quote but one example she was the person who drove General Koenig in a jeep through the minefield on the break-out from the Bir Hakeim 'box', in 1942.

Germany or Poland, or wherever he has come from. The Legion say that this is one of their best recruiting schemes, and invariably the rectified legionnaire returns from his home leave bringing back with him three or four friends as recruits. *Sous-officiers* may marry on the strength once they have been rectified, and may wear civilian clothes in certain circumstances. A legionnaire would have to be rectified before being granted a commission in the Legion.

The pay of the Legion has always lagged behind that of the French soldier, and he was never so well treated in the matter of campaigning and other allowances. But now he has drawn level and his pay is on par with his French counterpart. When all his active service and other allowances are taken into account he is one of the better paid soldiers in the world today.

For the first twelve months of his service the legionnaire is paid very little, the French theory being that until he is a trained soldier he is a liability. Once he has completed twelve months his pay rises considerably. To give a rough idea, speaking in very round figures, a legionnaire gets about £18 a month, a *caporal-chef* £45, and a *sous-officier* up to £95. It must be appreciated that these figures depend upon a variety of circumstances.

The legionnaires have always kept very much aloof and to themselves, seldom mixing freely with French soldiers. There has always been a certain amount of reserve, not to say suspicion, tinged perhaps with jealousy, between the two. The men of the 13th Demi-Brigade had their eyes opened for the first time when they saw the comradeship between British, African and Indian troops in East Africa. It was not until the Indo-China fighting that this barrier broke down to some extent. This suspicion tends still to remain, as whilst the Legion has always been a hit with the fiction-reading British public, it has never been fully accepted by the French in quite the same light. A section of the French public, and indeed of military opinion, is of the mind that the Legion is something that one does not speak about, rather like a less reputable relation.

DISCIPLINE

The legionnaires in the nineteenth century were a tough bunch to handle, excellent in action and on the march, but restless in slacker times and during tedious garrison duty. Rigid discipline was required to keep them in order, and accordingly punishments were harsh, salutary and speedy. Commanding Officers had wide powers of punishing soldiers, as did all officers.

Field punishments of various kinds, known as *tombeau*, were awarded, such as tying a man to a gun-wheel for a period. Other forms of fancy punishment of a like nature made their appearance from time to time, depending upon the circumstances and the sadistic mind of the person in charge of it. Pack drill, *la pelote*, was frequently awarded. Usually a punishment squad was kept in each battalion, and was given all the tedious and heavy fatigues to do, both in camp and on the march. As far as can be ascertained, flogging was never resorted to in the Legion. The offender could be awarded punishment on the spot for all minor or military crimes, only the more serious ones being remanded for a formal court martial, with the attendant possibility of heavier sentence.

When foreign officers declined in number, and as at times there were insufficient French officers, it meant that the Legion on occasions was under-officered, which caused greater responsibility to pass to the *sous-officiers*, who were not always as closely supervised as they should have been. The *sous-officiers* had a position of greater importance and prestige than is customary, and were saluted by the legionnaires. They could also award minor punishment on the spot. Owing to this, and lack of supervision, abuses crept in from time to time, the incidents giving rise to the lurid rumours of sadistic practices, without which no Legion escape-book would be complete.

Sous-officiers themselves can be, and are, reduced to the ranks for a wide variety of minor military crimes, which thought perhaps moderates any tendencies towards abuse that may be in their minds. The happy relationship I saw between the *sous-officiers* and the men does not indicate that sadistic practices or abuse of authority are widespread or prevalent, and even an 'awkward squad' I came across completely unexpectedly on an obstacle course was being dealt with more in sorrow than in anger.

Generally, off parade and in barracks, the legionnaires behaved no better or no worse than before. They had little diversion in their off-duty moments, and they drank heavily whenever they could afford it. Accordingly, the authorities kept them busy fighting or working. For example, when the initial active campaigning in Indo-China was over, a Disciplinary Unit had to be formed at once, which indicated that the legionnaires, as ever, possessed a surplus of devilment and energy that peaceful garrison duty did not use up.

The number of Legion Discipline Units, or Companies, in existence at a time varied, depending upon the state of the Legion and its strength. They were usually situated in the more remote and less desirable places, such as Fort Flatters or Colomb Bechar, but they moved to wherever tough jobs had to be done. There is now one at Kanadsa. Conditions in these units were severe and the *sous-officiers* in them were specially selected for the job. Time spent in them by the legionnaire does not count towards his service.

The discipline remained harsh and strict for many years, the commanding officers having the power to send a man to a Discipline Unit, and not until 1912 was it laid down that a sort of regimental court martial had to assemble to pass judgment before this could be done.

In 1937 an unusual step was taken and a commanding officer was allowed to discharge a legionnaire if he was of a very bad character. But he had to be very bad indeed. The customary rule now is that he has to have been in detention for over 200 days a year for at least two consecutive years, before he can be sent packing under this edict. It must be really quite an effort for a legionnaire to deliberately work his discharge in this way. It rarely happens, I am told.

Sous-officiers are still saluted by the men and have the power to award minor punishment on the spot, but these awards are subject to the strict scrutiny of an officer, who may modify or increase them.

MORALE

Morale has generally been maintained at a high level in the Legion, although there have been dark periods. Little is known with any degree of accuracy of its exact state in the Old Legion, but it is suspected that in the early years it was not always too good, especially when the men were employed on constructional or other manual work. It seems to have picked up when the men were committed to battle, and by the time the Legion was shipped over to Spain, spirits and hopes had soared. Once in Spain morale sank lower as the Legion was neglected. After Barbastro it dropped almost to zero, and was at its lowest ever.

The New Legion started somewhat shakily in this respect, being a little unsure of itself, but the taking of Constantine raised its spirits, and a succession of African fights resulted in a surge of new-found confidence. Evidence of really high morale first became obvious towards the end of the Crimean Campaign, when a terrific *esprit de corps* blossomed out. After this campaign few accepted the unusual opportunity to leave the Legion and transfer to a French regiment. In Italy it was the same.

In Mexico the Legion started well but drooped when put on escort duties. The epic of Camerone revived it so much that in spite of the depressing circumstances of the latter stages of the Legion's stay in that country and its withdrawal, morale remained very high.

A special sort of psychology was adopted and developed to inspire the men. Regimental spirit and traditions have always been accentuated in all armies, the French as much as any other, but the French were faced with the difficulty of persuading men to give undying, and dying, loyalty to units that bore numbers which were frequently changed. As the name and substance of the Legion remained always basically the same, it had the advantage right from its early days of being able to develop and impart a strong regiment spirit, which was absorbed by both the officers and the men. Recruits were indoctrinated with its traditions and aspirations to a fantastic degree, to an extent seldom carried out in any other unit. The legionnaires were steeped in its past glories and persuaded that they must emulate, and even better, its former heroes, and to die for the Legion if necessary.

The doctrine of *Legion patria nostra* was exploited and the Legion became indeed a refuge and a shelter for the homeless, the stateless and the fugitives. Many of these men had no one to turn to in need or distress, and generally no one cared whether they lived or died. When countries angrily demanded the return of political or other wanted persons, the Legion denied all knowledge and refused to make any inquiries. It was a refuge in fact which most of them sought, especially in the nineteenth century, and the promise of anonymity was faithfully kept. The Legion took them under its wing and gave them protection and security.

In return it demanded, and invariably got, undivided allegiance and loyalty. Wisely, no great play was made to persuade the legionnaires to be loyal to France, as France was a country few of them knew and many disliked; instead it was insisted that their first duty was to the Legion itself. The Legion motto of *Valeur et Discipline* was emphasized, and France was only mentioned as an afterthought. This brought out all that was good in most of the legionnaires, and in return they invariably gave faithful and devoted service to the Legion.

Constant indoctrination assisted in keeping morale high, and past victories won by the Legion, as well as individual legionnaires' feats of bravery and endurance were drummed into the men. When Camerone occurred, this indoctrination was intensified, and it became the secret ambition of every legionnaire to emulate his predecessors, who fought so hard and well in that derelict Mexican farm house. We perhaps are inclined to think of 'brain-washing' as something completely modern, as is the expression itself, but it was practised successfully in the Legion a hundred years ago—and still is.

The men are persuaded that there is no regiment on earth like the Legion, none has fought so well, none will fight so well in the future, and that it is up to every single legionnaire to do his utmost to maintain the traditions and to keep the standard high. This is driven into their subconscious minds, not casually, but firmly, and fiercely nailed there. The legionnaire's greatest degradation is to let the Legion down.

The so-called suicidal tendencies, made much of by writers of fiction, do exist, and in battle, suddenly for no good reason at all, a legionnaire will get up and charge the enemy, going out to certain death in the process. Many have walked out calmly under fire to rescue wounded comrades, blow up buildings or simply shoot up the enemy —all suicide missions.

Old Legion officers have told me that they have seen incredible acts of bravery performed by quiet, mediocre men who gave little indication of possessing a fanatical streak: suddenly on the spur of the moment and without orders. These acts stem from the indoctrination given in the Legion, which leaves its permanent mark on the minds of the legionnaires, and shows that every one has a 'Camerone in his heart', and is resolved to do his utmost when the time and the opportunity come. This attitude kept morale at a fairly high level between 1860 and 1880, the period of change, when commanding officers came and went with rapidity.

Being given distasteful tasks and suicide missions, and not always getting full credit for what it did, seemed to stimulate rather than deflate the Legion, which by 1914 had developed into an efficient fighting machine, with an *esprit de corps* and traditions envied by many another so-called tough fighting regiment.

The suicide rate was always a problem in the Legion, especially in remote garrisons where there was little to occupy the mind when off duty. At times the morale of certain units dropped for this reason. Drink, coupled with long spells of monotonous duty, led to fits of melancholia, *le cafard*, which all too frequently ended in suicide.

Were men ever deliberately left to die in the desert?

This is extremely doubtful, and can hardly be accepted as the truth, as if this were so the morale of the Legion would have suffered adversely, and it did not. The legionnaires prided themselves on being tough, on being able to march long distances and on being able to carry huge packs. It was a point of honour never to fall out on the march, and any man who did so suffered more from the slights and sneers of his comrades than from authority. The desert was cruel, the sun merciless and the marches long, and the legionnaires occasionally reached the limit of their endurance, but there is no evidence available to indicate that any man has ever been deliberately abandoned to his fate in the desert alone.

During the First World War morale remained high, but after Morocco was pacified and the Legion devolved into little more than a labour corps, it sagged. Desertion and suicide increased. The Second World War brought the spirit to life again, and the Indo-China fighting fanned it into vigorous flame. Today it is fighting in Algeria, it has all the tough sectors to control, it is given more than its share of all the difficult jobs going and takes part in all the action there is. The fact that the men are all *non-electeurs*, and that the Legion gets small publicity in France for what it achieves, has not affected morale.

Today the Legion is a purely volunteer force, composed in the main of men who want to be soldiers, and who enjoy the life they are leading. Their officers are intelligent, skilled and battle-tried, and care for their men to a degree unknown in the French army. Both officers and men are thoroughly imbued with the Legion spirit, and whilst these conditions obtain morale must necessarily stay at a very high peak. There can hardly be a corps in the world today in better heart.

The other side of the coin is that the Legion tends to live in a world of its own.

CEREMONIAL

Ceremonial has always played an important part in the Legion as it is held to be closely connected with morale. In this respect Regimental

Colours are always very much in evidence on every possible occasion. The first was presented in 1832, and is still in existence. On one side of it is embroidered *Le Roi des Francais à la Légion Etrangère,* and on the other, *Honneur et Patrie.* The motto of the Legion later changed to that of *Valeur et Discipline,* which was retained until just after the First World War, when it was granted the old, traditional device of the former Royal Swiss Guards, that of *Honneur et Fidelité.*

Each regiment had a Colour, which was carried right into battle until recent times. When Napoleon became Emperor, a brass eagle was carried atop the Colour staff. Battle honours, as they accumulated, were embroidered on to the Colour.

In 1871, the new French Republican Government ordered the Legion to burn its Napoleonic flags and destroy the Napoleonic eagles. It is not known whether this order was in fact carried out, or how it was received. There are no traces of the Colours today but there is no record of them having been officially burnt, so it is nice to think that they may have been carried off by some zealous officer and hidden, and that they may yet come to light one day. The brass Napoleonic eagles, which should have been destroyed, were found in a second-hand shop in Sidi Bel Abbes some years ago.

The French developed the practice of decorating the Colour whenever a regiment distinguished itself in battle, as well as individuals, and the various Legion Colours have been awarded such decorations as the *Légion d'Honneur,* the *Croix de Guerre* and the *Médaille Militaire,* some several times. At the end of the First World War the Colour of the R.M.L.E. was the most decorated in the French army, having attached to it the *Légion d'Honneur,* the *Médaille Militaire* and the *Croix de Guerre* with nine 'palms', indicating that the regiment had won the latter decoration ten times in all.

Today all the Legion regiments have a Colour, some of which are heavily decorated. The Cavalry and the Saharienne companies have *fanions* instead, which are smaller. The Colour is the symbol of command, and when commanding officers change over there is a parade, and the Colour is formally handed over by the old commander to his successor in full sight of the men of his regiment.

Fourragères, or multiple lanyards, are worn on the shoulder as a mark of distinction by some Legion regiments: for example, the 3rd R.E.I. wears a dark red one, awarded for service in the First World War. The 13th Demi-Brigade wears a green and gold one, the colours of the ribbon of the *Médaille Militaire*, and other regiments wear lanyards of different colours, each marking some battle honour. Occasionally, corded 'knobs' of the colours of the ribbon of some decoration hang from these lanyards.

Regimental bands were an early feature with the Legion, and most regiments had one. The stirring Legion slow march *Boudin*, was composed by a Legion bandmaster, known as Wilhelm, on his return from the Crimean Campaign. The origin of the title is obscure, and the words even more so. The title means 'black pudding', or perhaps 'black sausage', and the words of the chorus are about this food. The ceremonial march of the Legion is slow, about ninety paces to the minute only, and the men march with fingers stiffly outstretched. It is very impressive and one can almost imagine the sand swirling about the ankles of the men as they slowly march along in their colourful ceremonial dress. Occasionally the men sing to order on the march.

Annually, on Camerone Day, April 30th, every legionnaire, no matter where he may be, is paraded and an officer reads out an account of the Battle of Camerone. It is made into an impressive formal ceremony. At Sidi Bel Abbes there is a huge parade, and the false hand of Captain Danjou, which was found in the debris at Camerone, is carried in front of the men. Medals are presented and then the Legion marches past, led by its bearded 'pioneers', who wear white aprons and carry axes.

The previous evening there is always a torch-light parade through Sidi Bel Abbes, when the legionnaires stage tableaux on floats and parade in period uniforms. When the Camerone Parade is over, the legionnaires have the remainder of the day off, and the next one as well—presumably to get over their merry-making. The Camerone Day ceremonies and festivities are now a well established practice, but the Legion has not always made such a fuss, as records show that the first one was not held until 1904.

Christmas is the other big occasion of the Legion year. Christmas as such is not given much prominence as a military ceremony in the French army as a whole, but has developed in the Legion, due no doubt to the German influence. The barrack rooms are decorated, carols are sung, and there is special food and gifts for the men.

The origin of the badge of the Legion, the 'seven-flamed grenade', is obscure, and there seems to be no record of precisely when it became

246

official. It simply appeared and was generally accepted—perhaps just before the Crimean War. The 'grenade' itself had always been the mark of a *corps d'élite* in the French army, and at first only the Legion *compagnies d'élite* wore it. Later all the legionnaires wore yellow grenades on their collars. It was officially adopted as the cap badge in 1882.

Curious customs grow up in most regiments, and the Legion is no exception, possessing a crop of them. One deserving of mention is the traditional cry for help, '*A moi la Legion*', 'To me the Legion'. The legionnaires were always unpopular with both French and native troops, as well as the native inhabitants, but for varying reasons, so perhaps for this reason, if no other, they clung together. Whenever a legionnaire was attacked and in danger of being beaten up, or worse, he would raise the cry of '*A moi la Legion*', which was echoed by all other legionnaires who heard it. All had to rush to their comrade's aid, and undoubtedly this prompt action saved the life of many a legionnaire, both in battle and in the more dubious quarters of some of the native towns he was allowed to frequent.

WORK

The tradition of hard work in the Legion took root early and slacking on the job, no matter what it was, was a punishable crime. In the early days, between periods of fighting and marching, the Legion was kept busy constructing roads, building houses and forts, sinking wells and draining land. Artisans were found from within the ranks for almost any sort of task that was required to be done, and put to work. The Legion has always made a practice of using a man's skill to the very best advantage. Like the Roman Legions of long ago, the legionnaires were ever ready to lay down their tools, seize their arms and march out to deal with the enemy.

Sidi Bel Abbes, the home of the Legion, was founded and developed entirely by the Legion, no other unit was ever stationed there, or did anything to help. As traders and *colons* arrived the legionnaires built a church, schools, a police station, planted trees alongside the streets and harnessed water from the river. The legionnaires' industry and ability caused a small town to spring into existence. Many discharged legionnaires, having nowhere else to go, settled in the town and helped to swell the population. Before the Legion arrived there was nothing but the solitary tomb of the marabout, Sidi Bel Abbes, whilst today there is a flourishing town of some 80,000 inhabitants. Sidi Bel Abbes is known as the cradle of the Legion.

The first permanent barrack block at Sidi Bel Abbes was completed in 1849, replacing the provisional structures—it is still in use. By 1914, the barracks at both Sidi Bel Abbes and Saida had been extended and improved, and were a source of pride to the Legion. Many a legionnaire regarded the buildings he had helped to construct with regret as he walked through the barrack gates for the last time on discharge into civilian life. The massive, and impressive, Memorial to the Dead, in the barracks at Sidi Bel Abbes, was constructed and erected by the legionnaires themselves.

Beginning in 1848, the Legion established a farm adjacent to the camp at Sidi Bel Abbes to supply fresh vegetables, fruit, poultry, eggs and pork. Legionnaires who were expert in these pursuits were produced from the ranks, like rabbits from a conjuror's hat, and in a short space of time a flourishing farm was producing extra food for the Legion. The Legion became the best-fed unit in Algeria. When the Legion was shipped off to Mexico and was in some danger of being sold to that country, and of never returning to Algeria, it handed over its farm to the town of Sidi Bel Abbes, which turned it into a public garden. It is now one of the finest in Algeria.

The first Legion farm was such a success that it started what has since amounted to a habit that whenever possible the Legion establishes farms to supplement its rations. It has been frequently said that the Legion is the best-fed corps in the French army, which is probably quite true, but this is entirely due to its own efforts and to the policy of growing its own produce whenever it can. Today, there are two large Legion farms in Algeria, one near Sidi Bel Abbes and the other at El Kreider, as well as a small one starting up in Madagascar.

The Legion built wherever it was sent, and in Indo-China, for example, when the initial fighting was over, it built barracks for itself, erected forts on the frontiers and at strategic points and constructed roads. The Legion barracks were invariably in direct contrast to many of the others, being well built, well designed, and were always kept smart and clean. The Legion left a lasting mark on Morocco, as in Algeria, in the form of roads. In addition, a legacy of forts was left behind in Morocco, of which it built a large number. These were small, square-shaped, with squat towers at each corner, and parapeted walls: in other words, the typical French Foreign Legion fort of screen and fiction. Invariably, they were perched on hill-tops for tactical reasons, and they mostly had a water supply problem.

The ten years or so preceding 1939 was a period of depression for the Legion in Algeria and Morocco. Between the World Wars detachments of the Legion were lent or hired out to local authorities to work on roads, farms or other projects as labourers. All this had a very bad effect on the men themselves, as the Legion degenerated into what was virtually a labour corps.

Even so, the standard of work remained high and the legionnaires still took a pride in what they did, and the roads made by them, for instance, were durable and of the best. In Morocco, in the Atlas Mountains, between a place called Midelt and another called Erfoud, is the *Tunnel des Légionnaires*, the 'Legionnaires' Tunnel', which was cut through sheer rock by the Pioneer and Sapper Company of the 3rd Regiment, in 1928. It had been ordered to build a road but the mountain stood in the way, so, without special tools, the legionnaires pierced a tunnel through it, which still remains as a silent memorial to the Legion, its ingenuity and its industry.

Between 1947 and 1954 a certain amount of constructional work was done by the legionnaires in Indo-China, and several units of specialists were assembled for special tasks, such as road building, drainage or building forts and defences. Since their return to Algeria, the legionnaires have been mainly busy fighting and have had little time to spare for work, but nevertheless new buildings have been completed, old ones repaired and extended, and roads improved. The Legion does not need a 'barrack maintenance service'—it does all its own repairs and servicing.

DESERTERS

Desertion has always been a vexing problem to the Legion, and in the first months, during the process of turning the rabble into a disciplined body, there was an initial heavy spate. A trickle has continued ever since, in peace and war. This was bad enough in itself, but in the early stages of the conquest of Algeria, several of them went over to the Arabs, who were then in the habit of employing European soldiers of fortune.

Kader welcomed deserters, especially from the Legion, and it is said that he had several hundreds in his army as mercenaries on a regular basis at one time or another. Precisely how many is not actually known, but there were certainly enough to cause the French an embarrassing headache. One report states, for example, that a body of 40 Spanish legionnaires, in a skirmish on one occasion, deserted and went over complete to Kader. There were other incidents of a similar nature, but concerning less numbers of men at a time. Usually it was in small handfuls they dribbled through to his lines, or as individuals, often with their arms. It will be remembered that the bloody fratricidal fight in the Pass of Tenia de Mouzaia was between a unit of Kader's Legion deserters and their former comrades.

In the latter part of the nineteenth century the desertion rate remained high, especially for recruits during their first months of service. Actual figures have never been disclosed. After recruit training, it was claimed that the desertion rate dropped off sharply as the men settled down. There was desertion in the Crimea, in Italy and in Mexico, as well as the other wars in which the Legion fought. In the Crimea, one deserter went over to the enemy taking with him a plan of the French sapping.

In the Moroccan Campaign of 1907, desertions were frequent, especially amongst the Germans, who were aided by their countrymen, many of whom were traders in Morocco. Also, in that country there was more opportunity to get on to foreign ships, especially at Casablanca. In the later fighting, a few went over to the Muslim side. It was the policy of the Moroccans to encourage desertion from the Legion, being partly influenced by the hope that the deserters would bring their arms over with them. Also, they were not unaware of another angle, that desertion, particularly in battle, has a sharply adverse effect on morale.

The majority of Legion deserters were helped by the Muslims to get home, which mostly they did as soon as they were able; a few lingered on for a while, being more or less forced to lend the Moroccans a helping hand, whilst yet a tiny minority openly took service with Abdul El Krim, and fought against the French, under whose colours they had so lately served. One of the latter group, who achieved some notoriety, was a German deserter, named Klems, who had an intense dislike for the French. Indeed, it is a strange thing that many German legionnaires do not like France as a country, but are paradoxically intensely loyal to the Legion, and whilst they do not care whether they injure France or not, they are extremely jealous of the Legion's reputation and would not allow it to be slandered in any way.

Klems, who had been in the German army in the First World War and had fought against the French, joined the Legion in 1921, in company with many of his compatriots. Rumour had it that he was a German officer, but that cannot be accurately confirmed. He was posted to the Mounted Company of the 2nd Regiment, and rapidly rose to the rank of sergeant. However, in 1922, he was reduced to the ranks; reports vary as to the precise reason, which may not have been anything of a serious nature, as *sous-officiers* could be reduced for a host of offences, trifling, technical or otherwise. This embittered him and he deserted, going openly over to the Moroccan side, volunteering to fight against the French. At one stage he was a military adviser to Krim himself and he taught Krim much about the art of war. At one time he had a say in Moroccan military counsels. Shortly after Krim's surrender, Klems was captured. He was tried by court martial and sentenced to death, but this was later commuted, owing to an appeal from the German government. Klems served seven years' imprisonment and was then released.

A few other Legion deserters who had fought against the French were caught about the same time, and most of them were given terms of imprisonment. A few—the precise number is not known—were shot, but with as little publicity as possible.

Desertion over to the enemy during both World Wars was not frequent, but was not unknown. After the Second World War, in Indo-China, the agents of the Viet Minh directed propaganda to this weak spot. Both deserters and captured legionnaires were invariably well treated, and a number were sent home by way of Red China. In an unguarded moment, the French admitted that there had been some 2,000 Legion deserters during the whole of the nine years of war there, but it is thought that perhaps double that number would be nearer the truth. In the earlier days a few lingered on with the Viet Minh, giving a hand with military training and administration before passing on, but as the Red Chinese aid increased, their services as such were not required any more.

One estimate of those who actively fought against their former masters is 300—which may be fairly accurate. One, an ex-Austrian army captain, deserted and helped them organize their defences, becoming at one stage a military adviser to Ho Chi Minh, having adopted a Viet Nam name. There were one or two instances of legionnaires deserting to give information to the enemy, but these were of little moment as the Viet Minh agents were so well informed that there was little or nothing the legionnaires could tell them that they did not already know.

Today, in Algeria, desertion continues, and 'escape routes' are organized for the legionnaires by the F.L.N. A stream persists all the time, which at one stage almost became a flood, one Legion regiment having to be hastily moved from one part of Algeria to another because of this. A few, it is thought about half as many as in Indo-China, paused to fight briefly against their former masters, the French, before returning home.

WELFARE

A final few words can be said about welfare, a subject not popularly associated with the Legion. Welfare organization plays an important part in all modern armies, and it is now accepted that men fight better if they are well looked after. The Legion has an extremely good and efficient one, at Sidi Bel Abbes, known as the *Service du Moral et des Oeuvres de la Légion Etrangère*, S.M.O.L.E. for short. This is a combined welfare and rehabilitation section, which has taken on a multitude of responsibilities of this sort. It earns the cash for the Legion funds, controlling the farms, the Legion shops and the other Legion cottage industries. The farm produce either goes to the men by way of extra rations, or is sold, as are the other Legion products, such as pottery, carvings and souvenirs. The money provides small comforts for the men, especially at Christmas time.

As regards food, with its gift for putting the right man in the right job, as may be guessed, the Legion has the best cooks available, who produce excellent food under all sorts of conditions. The food is good, well cooked and ample, and the best army stew I have ever tasted in my life (and that is saying something) was in a Legion cookhouse. The legionnaires have coffee and a sandwich in the early morning, and then a substantial meal about noon, with a litre of wine thrown in as well. Those who wish can have beer instead. The other main meal is the evening one about 6 p.m. The spread that is put on during the Camerone festivities has to be seen to be believed.

S.M.O.L.E. also deals with pensions, family allowances, and disabled soldiers, as well as running four rest camps, where legionnaires can spend their leaves in Algeria. It also deals with matters pertaining to 'rectification'.

The Legion has become a wealthy corps, being a landowner and having a healthy bank balance, but this has happened entirely through its own efforts, and its wealth is used for the benefit of the serving legionnaires primarily, of course, but by no means forgotten are the disabled. A rehabilitation and convalescent centre for the Legion, known as the 'Home of Captain Danjou', is maintained in the south of France, where wounded men can be sent. This is entirely privately maintained. Those who have lost limbs are fitted with and taught to use artificial ones there, and all disabled legionnaires go there to learn a trade.

The legionnaires' 'off duty' time has always been completely his own and has never been organized for him, as is the tendency in our army. Organized sport and recreation are hardly known in the Legion, although there are signs that they are beginning to make their appearance. It has always been a strong criticism in the past that off-parade the Legion neglects the man and allows him to drink, revel or mope as he wishes in his own time, and to go to the devil in his own sweet way. This may be still largely true, even today, and the Legion authorities are loth to interfere with a legionnaire's leisure. However, as a start, S.M.O.L.E. has stepped in and now everywhere there are Legion cinemas, which show modern, up-to-the-minute films every night, at all the posts, even the remotest.

Appendix 'A'

After I had completed the MS. of this book the Historical Section of the Legion, at Sidi Bel Abbes, sent me a brief summary of what it considers to be the principal battles in which the Legion has fought, and this is reproduced below, without any alteration or amendment. This represents the Legion's view and forms an interesting comparison, as it contains names I have not mentioned, and also I have included engagements not regarded of primary importance by the Legion.

It will be seen that the spelling of place names differs sometimes, but that is a small detail, and that in two or three cases the precise date varies by a day or so. As regards the latter, there are differing reports as to the dates on which certain battles and engagements were fought, and in writing I selected the one I think probably may be the most accurate. Complete war diaries or detailed records of some actions do not exist, or were written long after the event, so even though this can be regarded somewhat in the light of an 'official' Legion list, I have not made any alterations to my original estimates.

The List is not always in strict chronological sequence, but that is how I received it.

PRINCIPAUX FAITS D'ARMES DE LA LEGION ETRANGERE DEPUIS SA CREATION JUSQU'A NOS JOURS

Ancienne Légion Etrangère 1831–35

Combat de Maison-Carrée	27 Avril 1832	Btn. Suisse-Allemand
Combat de Sidi-Chabal	11 Novembre 1832	Btn. Espagnol
Combat de Mouley-Ishmael	26 Juin 1835	4° et 5° Btns.
Combat de la Macta	28 Juin 1835	

Campagne d'Espagne 1835–39

Combat contre les lignes d'Arlaban	17 Janvier 1836
Combat de Tirapegui	26 Avril 1836
Combat de Zubiri	1° Août 1836
Combat de Huerca	24 Mars 1837
Combat de Barbastro	2 Juin 1837

255

Nouvelle Légion Etrangère 1836–40

Attaque de Constantine	13 Octobre 1837	1° Btn.
Combats de Djidjelli	Mai 1839	1° et 3° Btns.
Combat du Col de Tizi	12 Mai 1839	
Combat du Djebel Dreuth	28 Mai 1837	

Campagne d'Algérie 1840–82

Combats du Col de Mouzaia	12 Mai et 14 Juin 1840	1° et 4° Btns.
Opérations dans l'Oasis de Zaatcha	18 Mai au 26 Novembre 1849	
Combat de M'Chounech	15 Mars 1844	2° R.E.
Combat de Ischeriden	24 Juin 1857	2° R.E.
Combat de Chott Tigri	26 Avril 1882	Cie Montée du 1° Etr.

Campagne de Crimée 1854–56

Bataille de l'Alma	20 Septembre 1854	Btn. d'Elite
Bataille d'Inkermann	5 Novembre 1854	1° Etranger
Attaque des tranchées de la Quarantaine défendues par le 2° Btn. du 2° Etranger	19 au 20 Janvier 1855	2° Etranger 2° Btn.
Attaque des Ouvrages Blancs	1° au 2 Mai 1855	1° Etranger
Combat de Malakoff	8 Septembre 1855	1° Etranger

Campagne d'Italie 1859

Bataille de Magenta	4 Juin 1859	1° et 2° R.E.
Bataille de Solferino	24 Juin 1859	2° R.E.

Campagne du Mexique 1863–67

Combat de Jalapa	30 Avril 1863
Combat de Camerone	**30 Avril 1863**
Combat de Cotastla	12 Septembre 1863
Combat sur la ligne de chemin de fer Vera-Cruz – Tejeria	20 Octobre 1863
Siège d'Oajacca	du 16 Janvier au 8 Février 1865
Défense d'El Chamal	11 Janvier 1866
Combat de Santa Isabel	28 Février 1866

Campagne de France 1870–71

Combat devant Orléans	10 Octobre 1870	5° Btn.
Bataille de Coulmiers	9 Novembre 1870	R.E.
Combat de Montchevis	19 Janvier 1871	2° et 5° Btns.
Siège de Neuilly	Avril à Mai 1871	

Campagne d'Indochine et du Tonkin 1883–1945

Prise de Son-Tay	11 au 17 Décembre 1883	1° Btn.
Prise de Bac-Ninh	12 Mars 1884	
Siège de Tuyen-Quang	du 23 Janvier au 3 Mars 1885	1° Etranger
Prise de Lang-Son	13 Février 1885	
Retraite de Chine	Mars–Avril 1945	5° Etranger
Combat de Ban-Na-Ngha	20 Mars 1945	5° Etranger

Campagne du Dahomey et du Soudan 1892–94

Combat de Dogba	19 Septembre 1892
Combat de Poguessa	4 Octobre 1892
Combat de l'Ouakon	3 Novembre 1892
Prise d'Abomey	17 Novembre 1892
Combat d'Ackpa	13 Octobre 1892

Campagne de Madagascar 1895–1904

Combat de Maratanano	9 Juin 1895	3° Compagnie
Prise de Andriba	22 Août 1895	
Combat de Mahatsara	22 Novembre 1896	
Prise de Maroakoha	20 Décembre 1896	2° Compagnie
Combat de Soaserena	11 Mars 1898	1° Compagnie

Campagne de France 1914–18

Combat du Bois de Bolante	26 Décembre 1914	4° de Marche du 1° R.E.
Combat de la Ferme de Navarin	28 Septembre 1915	2° de Marche du 1° R.E.
Combat des Ouvrages Blancs	9 Mai 1915	2° de Marche du 1° R.E.
Combat de Belloy en Santerre	4 Juillet 1916	R.M.L.E.
Combat de Cumières	20 Août 1917	R.M.L.E.
Combat de Hangard en Santerre	25 Avril 1918	R.M.L.E.

Campagne d'Orient 1915–18

Combat du Ravin de Kereves Dere	4 Juin 1915	1° R.M.A.
Combat du mamelon 'La Dent de Scie'	16 Décembre 1915	1° R.M.A.
Retraite de Serbie	9 au 13 Décembre 1915	
Bataille de Monastir	19 Novembre 1916	1° R.M.A.
Bataille de la Trana Stena	26 Mars 1917	1° R.M.A.

S

Conquête du Sud-Oranais et du Maroc 1903-34

Combat d'El Moungar	2 Septembre 1903	
Combat de Menabha	16 Avril 1908	24° Cie Montée du 1°
Combat d'Alouana	15 Mai 1911	22 Cie /1°
Combat de Gaouz	9 Août 1918	Cie Montée du 1°
Combat de Scourra	6 Mai 1922	3° Btn. du 3° Etranger
Combat du Djebel Sagho	28 Février 1933	Cie Montée du 2° Etr.

Campagne de Syrie 1925

Combat de Messifre	17 Septembre 1925	5 /4° R.E.I. et 4 /1° R.E.C.
Combat de Kafer	22 Juillet 1925	4° R.E.I.
Combat de Rachaya	24 Novembre 1925	4 /1° R.E.C.

2me Guerre Mondiale 1939-40 et 1943-45

Combats du Bois d'Inor	Juin 1940	11° R.E.I.
Combat du Djebel Mansour	Janvier 1943	3° R.E.I.M.
Combat d'Osenbach	4 Février 1945	1° R.E.C.
Prise de Stuttgart	21 Avril 1945	2 /R.M.L.E.
Combat du Col d'Arlberg	7 Mai 1945	1 /R.M.L.E.

Campagne de la 13me D.B.L.E. 1940-45

Combats de Narvik	du 28 Mai au 2 Juin 1940
Prise de Massaouah	8 Avril 1941
Bataille de Bir-Hackeim	27 Mai au 11 Juin 1942
Combat d'El Himeimat	24 Octobre 1942
Combat d'Illhaeusern	23 Janvier 1945

Campagne d'Extrême-Orient 1946-54

Combat de Phu-Tong-Hoa	25 /26 Juillet 1948	2° Cie du 3° R.E.I.
Combat d'An-Hoa	26 Janvier 1951	1 /13° D.B.L.E.
Combat de Dong-Khe	du 16 au 18 Septembre 1950	3° R.E.I.
Repli de la R.C.4.	Octobre 1950	3° R.E.I. et 1° B.E.P.
Ninh-Phuoc	1° Juillet 1949	2° R.E.I.
Dien-Bien-Phu	8 Mai 1954	1° B.E.P., 13° D.B.L.E., 3° R.E.I., 2° R.E.I., C.M.R.L.E.

Opérations de Maintien de l'Ordre en Algérie 1955-60

Bataille d'Alger	Janvier 1957	1° R.E.P.

Opérations dans chaque département, accomplies par toutes les Unités de la Légion Etrangère.

Appendix 'B'

Madagascar 1947 and Suez 1956

There are just two more Legion actions worthy of note which I have not been able to conveniently fit into any of the chapters, so they can be mentioned in this brief Appendix to ensure that the record is as complete as possible, especially in view of the fact that neither is mentioned in Appendix 'A'.

First, in 1947, the Legion was called to intervene on an old stamping ground—Madagascar—when revolt flared up on that island. One battalion of the 4th R.E.I., a squadron of the 2nd R.E.C. and a company of Legion sappers were dispatched to assist in quelling it. One battalion still remains, and is known as the *Bataillon de la Légion Etrangère de Madagascar*.

Secondly, the Legion participated in the joint British–French attack on Egypt, in 1956—'Suez'—sending one paratroop battalion and an armoured squadron, totalling in all about 1,500 men. The legionnaires took part in the fighting at Port Said and distinguished themselves in the street battles there.

Index

The following words are not included in this Index as they appear on most pages, or on most pages in the relevant chapters: Africa, Arab(s), France, French, Foreign Legion, Foreign Regiment, Legion and legionnaire(s).

Aage (Prince), 229
Abd El Aziz (Sultan), 120, 128
Abeokuta, 106, 109
Abomey, 106, 109, 111, 112, 113
Afloa, 116
Ahmadu (Sultan), 114, 115
Ain Sefra, 53, 116, 208
Ait Maklouf, 175
Algeciras (Conference of), 119
Algiers, 25, 27, 28, 29, 32, 42, 43, 45, 48, 56, 120, 204, 206
Ali Kari, 115
Allemany, 156
Allie(s)(d), 62, 63, 64, 149, 154, 157, 160, 161, 164, 165, 167, 170, 186, 216, 233
Alma, 59, 62, 65
Alsace, 99
Alsatians, 232
Amazons, 107, 108, 109, 110, 111, 112
America(n), 83, 84, 166, 167, 168, 192, 219, 223
Amiens, 154
Amilakavari (Colonel), 165, 166
Amnahimazina, 143
Andriba, 134, 138, 139
Annam(ese), 95, 186, 187, 189, 190
Aoulai, 176
Arab League, 206
Aragao (Major), 71
Aragon, 39
Archangel, 158
Archinard (Colonel), 114
Ardennes, 161
Argonne, 149
Arlberg, 171

Army List (French), 217
Arras, 150
Arctic Circle, 160, 170
Artois, 150, 156
Arzew, 32, 208, 210
Astar, 175
Atlantic, 120, 128, 130
Atlas (Mountains), 27, 53, 116, 120, 174, 249
Auberville, 153
Aures (Mountains), 208, 211
Austria(n), 65, 66, 67, 68, 69, 145, 157, 171, 172, 231, 232, 234, 235, 236, 251
Avignon, 146

Bac Kan, 191
Bac-Ninh, 87, 89, 90
Balkan(s), 17, 157
Bamako, 115
Bang-Bo, 96
Bannier, 71
Bao Dai, 187
Barbastro, 39, 40, 234, 241
Barbary Coast, 27
Barbary Pirates, 28
Basse, 115
Bastille Day, 153
Bataillon(s) de Marche, 52, 53, 62, 71, 72, 96, 105, 134, 137, 139, 142, 143, 144, 157, 214, 215
Bavarian, 18
Bazaine (Sergeant, later Marshal), 64, 84, 85, 229
'Beatrice', 197, 199
Bedeau (Major), 42, 43, 45

Behazin (King), 110, 112, 113
Bel-Air-Les-Aides, 71
Belfort, 169, 170
Belgian(ium), 23, 25, 148, 223, 231
Belloy-en-Santoy, 152
Beni Ouzien, 128
Beni Snassen, 55, 126, 127
Berg (Corporal, later Lieutenant), 81, 82
Berguent, 118
Bernelle (Colonel), 32, 36, 37, 38, 233
Berthonval, 150, 151
Bertram (Colonel), 115, 116
Besançon, 72
Betsiboka (River), 135
Bey (Beylik), 28, 29, 52
Bibane, 176
Bible, 16
Bir Hakeim, 165, 166, 170, 238
Biskra, 52, 53, 208
Black Flags, 87, 88, 89, 90, 91, 92, 93, 94, 95, 96, 97
Black Forest, 170
Black (River), 195
Blida, 29, 31
Boer War, 123, 229
Bolante, 149
Bone, 25, 28, 29, 31, 32, 33, 42, 43, 45, 46, 47, 48, 59
Bou Denib, 128
Boudin, 151, 246
Bou Hamara, 120
Bougie, 28, 47, 59, 208
Bou Khamoudja, 174
Bou Ziane, 54
Brayer (Colonel), 67
Brest, 161
Brian (Major), 84
Britain(ish), 17, 19, 33, 61, 62, 64, 104, 116, 119, 120, 132, 138, 140, 148, 151, 154, 164, 166, 167, 186, 210, 213, 232, 236, 239
Bulgaria(n), 61, 62, 157
Bugeard (General), 47, 49, 50
Butet (Colonel), 59, 76
Buttes-Chaumont, 73

Cabbage Column, 65
Cafard (le), 244
Cambodia, 187, 192
Camerone, 78, 79, 81, 82, 84, 85, 86, 117, 174, 180, 194, 201, 210, 226, 229, 242, 243, 246, 252
Cameroons (French), 164
Canrobert (General), 55, 62, 63, 229
Cape of Good Hope, 164
Caporal-chef, 239
Caprel (Colonel), 63
Carlist, 34, 37, 38, 39, 40, 42
Cartouchière de Negrier, 223
Casablanca, 121, 122, 123, 124, 126, 167, 172, 250
Catalonia, 37
Cavalaire, 169
Central Europe, 26, 232
Cercottes, 72
Chabrière (Colonel), 57, 67, 68
Challe (General), 207
Channel Ports, 162
Charles VII, 16
Chellala, 100
Cheren (see Keren), 170
Chevilly, 72
Chiers (River), 161
China(ese), 87, 88, 90, 91, 92, 93, 94, 95, 96, 97, 183, 184, 186, 190, 193, 232
China(ese) Nationalist(s), 183, 186, 187, 188, 193
China (Red), 192, 202, 251
Chinese Communists, 193
Chott Tigri, 101, 103
Christian, 27, 28
Christinos, 37, 38
Chu (River), 90
Claire (River), 88, 90, 91, 97
'Claudine', 197
Cochin-China, 186, 187, 188, 189, 190, 192
Coleah, 59
Colmar, 169, 170
Colomb Bechar, 117, 118, 163, 167, 241

Colon(s), 56, 211, 247
Colonial Forces (French), 114
Combe (Colonel), 32, 44, 45
Communes, 19, 72
Communist, 194
Compagnie(s) d'Elite, 52, 53, 55, 62, 214, 215, 221, 247
Conrad (Colonel), 38, 39, 40, 63
Constantine, 28, 29, 33, 42, 43, 45, 46, 48, 51, 52, 56, 59, 211, 214, 229, 241
Constantinople, 28
Consul (French), 29
Corsica(n)(s), 66, 99, 235
Cossacks, 147
Cot (Colonel), 152
Cotonou, 105, 106
Coulmiers, 72
Courbevoie, 73
Courtes-Chausses, 149
Crimea(n), 56, 57, 61, 62, 65, 66, 76, 77, 215, 222, 224, 233, 234, 242, 246, 250
Croix de Guerre, 151, 245
Cumiers, 154
Czech(s), 230, 234

Dahomey(ian), 98, 104, 105, 106, 107, 108, 110, 111, 112, 113, 114, 215, 223, 225
Dakar, 184
d'Amade (General), 123, 124, 125, 126
Damas, 164
Damascus, 164, 165, 178
Danjou (Captain), 77, 78, 79, 81, 246, 253
Danube (River), 171
Danubian Principalities, 61
Dap Cau, 183
Dardanelles, 157
de Gaulle, 162, 164, 211
Delta (Tonkin), 96, 189, 190, 195, 196, 198, 201
de Mallaret (Colonel), 60, 99, 100
Demi-brigades, 216
Denmark, 229
Dent de Scie (La), 157

Dey (Deylik), 28, 29
Diaz (General), 74, 83
Dien Bien Phu, 196, 197, 198, 199, 200, 201, 202, 233
Diego Suarez, 132
Disciplinary Unit(s), 240, 241
Djidjelli, 47, 48, 59
Djebel Garci, 168, 170
Djebel Iskritten, 177
Dodd (Colonel), 104, 111
Dogba, 110
Dommiers (Plateau of), 155
Dong Khe, 193, 194
Douala, 170
Doui-Menai, 117
Drude (General), 121, 122, 123
Druse, 178, 179, 180, 181
Duchesme (General), 134, 136, 139, 141
Dunant (Henri), 70
Dutch, 17, 25, 232

East (Army of), 72
East Africa, 170, 239
Eastern Europe, 232
Ebro (River), 37
Egypt, 204, 206
Elba, 18
El Chems, 181
El Goleah, 116
El Himeimat, 166
El Kreider, 248
El Mers, 174
Empress (of China), 87, 91, 95
Empress Eugénie, 71
Empire (French), 21
England(ish), 16, 17, 104, 164, 238
Erfoud, 249
Espinasse (General), 66, 68
Estella, 37
Eritrea(n), 164
Eupatoria, 62
Europe(an), 16, 26, 28, 33, 43, 46, 61, 70, 103, 105, 107, 108, 109, 114, 120, 121, 128, 130, 132, 134, 143, 145, 168, 171, 172, 173, 174, 175,

Europe(an), *contd.*
177, 202, 203, 216, 219, 222, 235, 236, 249

Far East, 87, 187, 215
Fashoda Incident, 116
Faurex (Colonel), 105, 110
Ferhat Abbas, 205, 211
Fez, 50, 120, 121, 128, 129, 130, 131, 172, 174
Figuig, 116, 117, 118
Finland, 160
F.L.N. (Algerian National Liberation Front), 204, 205, 206, 207, 208, 209, 211, 212, 252
Fondouk, 47
Forges, 154
Formosa, 94, 95
Fort Chaamba, 118
Forthassa, 118
Fort Flatters, 241
Fort Tessala, 50
Fort Vincennes, 221
Foum El Gouafel, 167
Frederick Charles (Prince), 229
Free Algerian Provisional Government, 211
Free French, 164, 165, 216
Friedrichshafen, 171

'Gabrielle', 199
Gallieni (General), 143
Gallipoli, 61, 157
Gamsheim, 170
Gaouz, 173
Garibaldi, 148, 149
Gare du Nord, 73
Garden of Allah, 52
Genoa, 66
George V, 151, 229
Georgian, 165
German(y), 17, 25, 30, 37, 71, 72, 77, 98, 99, 119, 128, 131, 145, 146, 147, 149, 150, 151, 152, 153, 154, 155, 158, 159, 160, 161, 162, 163, 166, 168, 169, 172, 184, 229, 231, 232,

233, 234, 236, 239, 246, 250, 251
Gerryville, 101, 116, 127, 208, 236
Gezo (King), 106, 107, 108, 109
Ghana, 104, 113
Ghardaia, 116
Giap (General), 189, 191, 192, 193, 195, 196, 198, 199, 200, 202
Gold Coast, 113
Goumiers, 101
Grand Army, 18
Grand Companies, 16
Grandes Capotes, 58
Grand Popo, 107
Great Western Erg, 116
Greece(Greeks), 18, 157, 232, 234
Grenadier(s), 214, 215, 224, 227
Guelma, 208
Guercif, 130
Guinea, 114

Hague (Convention), 234
Haipong, 87, 189, 190
Hall of Honour, 81
Hangard Wood, 154
Hanoi, 87, 88, 186, 189, 190
Haute Alsace, 169
Hill '140', 150, 151
Hindenburg Line, 155, 156
Hoa Moc, 94
Ho Chi Minh, 186, 187, 189, 193, 251
Hohenlohe, 18, 21, 24
Honneur et Fidélité, 17, 245
Honneur et Patrie, 245
Hova(s), 132, 134, 135, 136, 137, 138, 139, 140, 141, 142
'Huguette', 197
Huichapan, 85
Hundred Days, 18
Hungarian(y), 46, 157
Hung Hoa, 90

Igly, 116
Indian, 239
Indian Ocean, 132
Indo-China(ese), 19, 74, 86, 87, 89, 94, 95, 97, 104, 143, 163, 183, 184,

186, 187, 188, 189, 190, 192, 196,
199, 202, 205, 208, 215, 216, 217,
219, 220, 223, 225, 226, 233, 238,
239, 240, 244, 248, 249, 251, 252
Inkerman, 62, 65
Inor Wood, 166
In Salah, 115
Isabella II, 36
'Isabelle', 197, 199, 201
Ischeriden, 57, 58, 59
Isly (River), 50, 52
Isser (Valley), 43
Irish, 17
Italian(y), 17, 25, 26, 31, 32, 33, 34,
37, 59, 61, 65, 66, 76, 77, 99, 148,
149, 150, 164, 166, 168, 170, 215,
216, 222, 224, 231, 233, 234, 242, 250
Ivory Coast, 113

Japan(ese), 183, 184, 186
Jeanningros (Colonel), 76, 81, 83
Jebel Mansour, 167
Jews, 18
Juarez, 74, 84

Kabylia(ies), 42, 43, 44, 45, 46, 47, 52,
53, 54, 55, 56, 57, 58, 59, 98, 99, 208
Kader (Abdul El), 31, 32, 33, 34, 36,
42, 43, 46, 47, 48, 49, 50, 51, 52, 53,
98, 249, 250
Kafer, 178
Kana, 112
Kanadsa, 117, 241
Kankan, 115
Kao Bang, 190, 191, 192, 193, 194
Karo, 115
Kassala, 164
Kasserine Pass, 167
Kayes, 114
Képi Blanc, 226, 227
Keren (*see* Cheren), 164
Kenifra, 131, 172
Kerouane, 115
Klems, 250, 251
Koenig (General), 238
Kola, 31

Koto, 111, 112
Krim (Abdul El), 173, 174, 175, 176,
177, 250, 251
Ksar d'Alouana, 129

Laghout, 116
Lake Garda, 69
'Lalaine', 198, 199, 200, 201
Lalco Ita, 129
Lambas Blancs, 136
Langres, 22, 23
Lang-Son, 96, 97, 194
Laos, 187, 196, 198
Lattre de Tassigny (Marshal), 195
Lauterbourg, 170
Lebeau (Major), 38
Légion d'Honneur, 97, 118, 245
Légionnaire de première classe, 215
Legio Patria Nostra, 237, 242
Liberia, 114
Libya, 167
Loire (Army of), 71, 72
Lombardy, 66
Lorraine, 99, 154, 232
Louis XVI, 17
Louis II (Prince), 230
Louis-Philippe, 18, 21
Lyautey (Colonel, later Marshal), 117,
127, 130
Lyons, 57, 146, 160, 169, 170

MacMahon (Colonel, later Marshal),
49, 52, 55, 58, 59, 66, 229
Macta, 34, 36, 42, 43
Madagascar, 98, 131, 132, 136, 142,
144, 221, 225, 248
Madrid, 37
Magenta, 66, 67, 68, 70, 77, 236
Magrin-Vernerey (Colonel), 162
Maine (Corporal, later Lieutenant),
81, 82
Maison Carrée, 30, 31
Majunga, 132, 134, 137, 141, 142
Mali, 113
Maltese, 99
Manandrave (River), 144

Marche ou Crève, 140
Mareth Line, 168
Marcollo, 67
Marseilles, 221, 237, 238
Martinez (Major later Colonel), 59, 60, 65, 67, 68, 228
Mascara, 28, 31, 33
Massaoua, 170
Massawa, 164
Massu (General), 206, 211
Maudet (Second Lieutenant), 77, 80, 81, 229
Maximilian, 74, 76, 85
M'Chounech, 52
Medea, 28, 33, 46
Médaille Militaire, 154, 156, 170, 245, 246
Mediaeval Europe, 16
Mediouna, 122, 123, 176
Mediterranean, 27, 99, 113, 165
Mekera (River), 49
Mekong (River), 196
Mellah (River), 125
Menabha, 127
Messadi, 181
Met (Major), 131
Metropolitan France, 217
Metzinger (General), 134, 135, 140, 141, 142
Meuse (River), 161
Mevatanana, 135
Mexico(an), 60, 74, 76, 77, 78, 79, 80, 81, 82, 83, 84, 85, 86, 215, 217, 219, 222, 224, 226, 227, 229, 233, 234, 242, 243, 248, 250
Mexico City, 74, 76, 83
Mghala, 176
M'Karto, 126
Midelt, 249
Milan, 66, 68
Milan (Colonel), 77, 78, 79, 81
Miliana, 28, 33, 46, 47
Milson von Bolt, 229
Mina (*see* Martinez), 65
Mohammedanism, 27, 178
Moiner (General), 128

Monaco, 230
Monastir, 157
Mountain of Paris, 155
Montbeliard, 169
Monterey, 84
Monts Verdun (Les), 156
Moors(ish), 50, 51, 52, 113, 119
Moroccan(o), 27, 29, 48, 50, 51, 52, 55, 60, 98, 99, 101, 103, 116, 118, 119, 120, 121, 122, 123, 126, 127, 128, 129, 130, 131, 145, 153, 163, 172, 173, 174, 175, 177, 181, 182, 206, 207, 208, 209, 210, 215, 216, 217, 219, 220, 221, 222, 225, 229, 234, 244, 248, 249, 250, 251
Morocco (Spanish), 173
Moscow, 23
Mostagenem, 32, 59
Moulay Hafid (Sultan), 128, 130
Moulay Ishmael, 34, 36, 42, 76
Moulay Youssef (Sultan), 130
Moulinier (Captain), 84
Mounted Companies(y), 101, 102, 103, 114, 116, 117, 118, 121, 127, 128, 129, 172, 173, 178, 179, 181, 219, 251
Mouret (Colonel), 49
Mousiefre, 178
Mozambique Channel, 132

Naked Heights, 135, 136
Nantere, 73
Napoleon, 18, 23, 214
Napoleon III, 57, 59, 69, 70, 71, 76, 84, 98, 228, 245
Napoleon (Prince), 236
Narvic, 160, 170
National Assembly, 72
NATO, 206
Navrin Farm, 151
Navy (French), 29
Nazi(s), 158, 159, 163, 167
Near East, 156
Negrier (Colonel, later General), 87, 88, 89, 90, 94, 95, 96, 100, 102, 103, 218, 222, 229

Neuilly, 73
New World, 106
Nglia Lo, 195
Niger (River), 113, 114
Nigeria, 104, 106
Noi Thon, 195
Nom(s) de Guerre, 22, 237, 238
Norway, 160, 161, 162
Norwegian, 160

Oboserskaia, 158
Ochenbein (Colonel), 57
Oran, 25, 28, 29, 31, 32, 33, 43, 48, 49,
    56, 60, 98, 99, 100, 101, 103, 116,
    118, 166, 182, 208, 210, 221, 236
Orleans, 71, 72
Ottoman Empire, 28, 120
Ouargla, 55
Oueme (River), 111
Ouida, 213
Ouidah, 106, 107
Oujda, 50, 121, 126, 130, 131, 172
Ouled Sidi Cheikh, 98, 99, 100, 101

Palestine, 164
Pamplona, 37, 38, 40
Papame, 112
Paris, 17, 19, 21, 59, 70, 71, 72, 145,
    153, 171, 205, 217, 221, 226
Paris (Count of), 236
Parras, 84, 85
Pau, 45
Pelote (la), 240
Perral, 85
Pétain (Marshal), 176
Peter (King), 229
Petrograd, 158
Philippeville, 57, 59, 98, 99, 209
Phu Tong Hoa, 191
Picardie-Soissonais, 156
Plessier (General), 55
Po (River), 66
Poland, 239
Poles(ish), 17, 18, 25, 33, 34, 37, 38,
    47, 77, 81, 230, 231, 232, 234
Pont du Fahs, 168

Porguessa, 110, 111
Port Lyautey, 128, 129
Porto Novo, 106
Port Sudan, 164
Portugal(ese), 18, 120, 232
Potsdam Conference, 186
Praetorian Guard, 28
Provence, 169
Prudhon (Captain), 50
Prunay, 147
Puebla, 76, 83
Pyrenean(ees), 37, 38, 40, 159

Quarantine, 63, 64
Queen Regent (Spain), 36, 37

Rabat, 128, 129, 130, 131, 172
Rachaya, 180
Radicorfani, 169, 170
Red (River), 193, 194, 195
Red Army, 158
Red Cross, 18, 70
Régiment(s) de Marche, 122, 130, 145,
    146, 147, 148, 150, 151, 159, 160,
    167, 172, 173, 214
Rennes, 162
Republic(an) (Government), 21, 245
Revolutionary Government, 17
Rheims, 147, 150, 153
Rhine (River), 169, 170
Riff (Mountains), 120, 173
Roberts (Lord), 123
Rollet (Colonel, later General), 153,
    230, 231
Roman Army, 16
Roman, 50, 247
Rome, 168, 170
Rommel, 167, 168
Rouen, 146
Royal Household Troops, 16
Rumania, 61, 157
Russia(ian)(s), 23, 56, 57, 61, 62, 63,
    64, 65, 147, 148, 157, 158, 222, 231,
    232, 234, 236

Sahara, 27, 52, 53, 55, 56, 98, 99, 100,

Sahara, *contd.*
   101, 103, 115, 209, 218, 220, 227, 236
Sahariennes, 227
Saharienne companies(y), 209, 211, 221, 245
Saida, 60, 73, 103, 145, 146, 172, 180, 181, 248
Saigon, 188, 190, 192
Sakalava(s), 132, 135, 140
Samory, 114, 115
Sangre (River), 37
San Martino, 66
Santa Isabella, 84, 85
Santerre, 148
Sardinia(n)(s), 25, 65, 69, 99
Sassandra (River), 115
Scots, 16, 17, 141
Scoura, 174
Sebastopol, 59, 62, 63, 64, 65
Segu, 114, 115
Senegal(ese), 113, 114, 163, 165, 167
Serbia(n), 157, 158, 229
Setif, 48, 56, 59, 61, 98
Settat, 124, 125
Shawiya, 121, 126
Sicco (Major), 22
Sidi Brahim, 122
Sidi Bel Abbes, 15, 49, 50, 53, 56, 59, 60, 61, 71, 74, 81, 82, 83, 89, 99, 103, 125, 143, 145, 146, 160, 163, 166, 172, 181, 182, 188, 196, 208, 220, 221, 223, 226, 231, 232, 234, 236, 245, 246, 247, 248, 252
Sidi Chabal, 31
Sidi Moumen, 122
Silistria, 61
Sippe (River), 153
Slave Coast, 104, 106
Sobieski (King), 236
Sofas, 115
Soissons, 153, 161, 162
Solferino, 69, 70, 236
Somme, 148, 152
Sontay, 87, 88, 89, 90, 93
Soueida, 178, 180
Soult (Marshal), 22

Sous-officiers, 24, 25, 77, 99, 148, 157, 159, 192, 226, 232, 239, 240, 241, 251
South Africa, 124
South-East Asia, 94
Spahis, 117
Spain, 17, 18, 25, 26, 29, 31, 32, 33, 34, 36, 37, 38, 39, 40, 42, 45, 76, 77, 81, 99, 119, 120, 121, 130, 159, 174, 176, 222, 224, 231, 232, 233, 234, 241, 250
St. Arnaud (Captain, later Marshal), 45, 51, 55, 61, 229
St. Cyr, 230
Stoffel (Colonel), 23, 24, 32
Stuttgart, 170
Suberbieville, 136, 137
Sudan, 98, 113, 114, 115
Swedes(en), 17
Swiss, 17, 18, 23, 25, 27, 37, 66, 68, 70, 72, 169, 170, 231
Swiss (Royal) Guards, 17, 18, 25, 30, 245
Switzerland, 169
Syria, 82, 159, 164, 165, 170, 172, 178, 180, 181, 217, 219, 225

Tache de Taza, 130, 131
Taddert, 122
Tafilalet, 173
Tafna (Treaty of), 43
Taforalt, 127
Taghit, 117
Tamatave, 134, 143
Tananarive, 134, 136, 139, 140, 141, 142
Taounat, 175
Tarragona, 36, 37
Targuist, 177
Taza, 120, 131, 172, 173, 174, 175, 176
Tebessa, 209
Temouchent, 51
Tenia de Mouzaia, 46, 59, 250
Terny-Sorny, 155
Tichoukt, 174
Ticino (River), 66

Timbuktu, 113, 115
Timimoun, 116
Tirapegui, 38
Titteri, 28, 33
Tombeau, 240
Tonkin, 87, 90, 95, 96, 183, 186, 187, 189, 190, 192, 193, 196
Toulon, 169, 170
Toulouse, 146, 147
Trans-Jordan, 164
Transvaal, 229
Travers (Susan), 238
Tra-Vinh, 190
Tripoli, 120
Tlemcen, 28, 33, 103, 120, 208
Tsarasoatra, 137
Tseghouchen, 174
Tsientsin (Treaty of), 95
Tsinaindry, 140, 141
Tuileries, 17
Tunis, 120
Tunisia(n), 27, 59, 99, 100, 166, 167, 168, 170, 204, 206, 207, 208, 209, 210, 211
Tunnel des Légionnaires, 249
Turenne, 182
Turbigo, 66, 67
Turkey(ish), 28, 157, 178, 235, 236
Tuyen-Quang, 90, 91, 93, 94, 183, 192

Under Two Flags, 104, 213
United States, 83, 84
U.S. Marine Corps, 217

Valeur et Discipline, 242, 245
Varna, 61
Vaudesincourt, 153
Vauyaillon, 155, 156
Ventri, 183
Vera Cruz, 74, 76, 85
Verona, 69
Vichy, 162, 163, 164, 165, 166, 167, 183, 233
Victor Emmanuel II, 65
Vienna, 236
Vienot (Colonel), 63

Viet Minh, 186, 187, 188, 189, 190, 191, 192, 194, 195, 198, 199, 200, 201, 202, 251, 252
Viet Nam(ese), 186, 193, 252
Vietri, 192
Vilain (Lieutenant), 77, 80, 229
Vilette, 73
Villebois-Mareuil (Colonel), 229
Villiers-Cotterets, 155
Vittoria, 38
Vohingezo, 144
Voirol (General), 33
Volta, 114
Voltigeurs, 214, 215, 224

Wales (Prince of), 151
War Lords, 91
Waterloo, 18
West Africa(n), 109, 113, 114, 115, 116, 170
Western Desert, 165, 170
White Russia(ans), 158, 165, 219, 229, 232
White Works, 64, 154
Wilhelm, 246
World War(s), 145, 172, 181, 183, 216, 231, 249, 251
World War (First), 132, 145, 156, 158, 159, 172, 215, 216, 223, 225, 229, 231, 232, 237, 244, 245, 251
World War (Second), 145, 158, 170, 183, 203, 216, 217, 219, 220, 223, 225, 226, 230, 233, 234, 235, 236, 238, 244, 251

Yorubas, 106
Yunnan(ese), 87, 91, 96, 97, 184, 186

Zaatcha, 53, 54, 59, 229
Zaghouan, 168
Zanaga, 117
Zeralda, 209
Zouaves, 53, 54, 76
Zouave Wood, 147
Zousfana (Valley), 116
Zubiri, 38

Formations, regiments and units.

Algerian Regiment, 134
5th Army, 168
8th Army, 165, 166
Bataillons d'Afrique, 104, 217
1e *Bataillon Etrangère Parachutiste*
(1st B.E.P.), 192, 194, 195, 196, 197,
198, 202, 209
2me *Bataillon Etrangère Parachutiste*
(2nd B.E.P.), 192, 195, 197, 200,
202, 204
Brigade Etrangère, 57, 61, 63, 64, 65
Bavarian Regiment, 17
Chasseurs d'Afrique, 100, 101
Compagnie des Transports Marocains,
221
1e *Compagnie Saharienne Port de la
Légion* (1st C.S.P.L.), 220
2me *Compagnie Saharienne Port de la
Légion* (2nd C.S.P.L.), 220
3me *Compagnie Saharienne Port de la
Légion* (3rd C.S.P.L.), 211, 220
4me *Compagnie Saharienne Port de la
Légion* (4th C.S.P.L.), 220
Dauphin Etrangère (2nd R.E.C.), 211
4th Demi-Brigade, 163, 167, 208, 216
13th Demi-Brigade, 160, 161, 162,
163, 164, 165, 166, 167, 168, 169,
170, 171, 188, 190, 195, 197, 199,
202, 208, 216, 225, 238, 239, 245
14th Demi-Brigade, 162
Depot Commun de Régiments Etrangères,
182
Garibaldi Brigade, 148, 149, 150
Groupe '97', 160, 161
Groupe Autonome, 167
Groupement de la Légion Etrangère
(G.A.L.E.), 217
Inspection de la Légion, 217
*Inspection Technique de la Légion
Etrangère*, 217, 221
Légion Etrangère, 21, 22, 60, 103
90th Light Division, 168
Moroccan Division, 147, 150, 151, 152
5th Moroccan Division, 169

24th Mounted Company, 220
Régiment Etrangère, 59, 99
1e *Régiment Etrangère*, 57, 103, 146, 147
2me *Régiment Etrangère*, 57, 103, 146
1e *Régiment Etrangère de Cavalerie*
(1st R.E.C.), 163, 168, 169, 170,
173, 190, 192, 193, 202, 208, 209,
219, 220
2me *Régiment Etrangère de Cavalerie*
(2nd R.E.C.), 163, 209, 211, 220
1e *Régiment Etrangère d'Infanterie*
(1st R.E.I.), 163, 188, 208
2me *Régiment Etrangère d'Infanterie*
(2nd R.E.I.), 187, 188, 197, 201,
202, 208, 210
3me *Régiment Etrangère d'Infanterie*
(3rd R.E.I.), 163, 173, 188, 190,
191, 192, 193, 194, 197, 199, 200,
201, 202, 208, 210, 245
4me *Régiment Etrangère d'Infanterie*
(4th R.E.I.), 163, 173, 178, 208, 210
5me *Régiment Etrangère d'Infanterie*
(5th R.E.I.), 182, 184, 186, 193, 195,
200, 201, 202, 208, 210
6me *Régiment Etrangère d'Infanterie*
(6th R.E.I.), 164, 165, 181, 225
11me *Régiment Etrangère d'Infanterie*,
160, 161
12me *Régiment Etrangère d'Infanterie*,
160, 161
1e *Régiment Etrangère d'Infanterie de
Marche* (1st R.E.I.M.), 167, 168
3me *Régiment Etrangère d'Infanterie de
Marche* (3rd R.E.I.M.), 167
*Régiment de Marche d'Afrique au
Tonkin*, 95, 97
Régiment de Marche d'Algérie, 157
*Régiment de Marche de la Legion
Etrangère* (R.M.L.E.), 151, 152,
153, 154, 155, 156, 168, 169, 170,
171, 173, 188, 230, 245
2me *Régiment de Marche* of the 1e
Régiment Etrangère, 146, 147, 150,
151

3*me Régiment de Marche* of the 1e *Régiment Etrangère*, 148

4*me Régiment de Marche* of the 1e *Régiment Etrangère*, 148, 149

2*me Régiment de Marche* of the 2*me Régiment Etrangère*, 146, 147, 150, 151

Régiment de Marche de Volontaires Etrangères (R.M.V.E.), 159, 161, 162

21re *Régiment de Marche de Volontaires Etrangères* (21st R.M.V.E.), 159, 161

22*me Régiment de Marche de Volontaires Etrangères* (22nd R.M.V.E.), 159, 162

23*me Régiment de Marche de Volontaires Etrangères* (23rd R.M.V.E.), 159, 162

1e *Régiment Etrangère Parachutiste* (1st R.E.P.), 209, 210

2*me Régiment Etrangère Parachutiste* (2nd R.E.P.), 209, 211, 212

Service du Moral et des Oeuvres de la Légion Etrangère (S.M.O.L.E.), 252, 253

Stewart Regiment, 17

Swiss Legion, 57, 59, 222, 225

Swiss Regiment, 57, 66